Reconceptualizing Education for Newcomer Students

Reconceptualizing Education for Newcomer Students

Valuing Learning Experiences Inside and Outside of School

Jordan Corson

TEACHERS COLLEGE PRESS
TEACHERS COLLEGE | COLUMBIA UNIVERSITY
NEW YORK AND LONDON

Published by Teachers College Press,® 1234 Amsterdam Avenue, New York, NY 10027

Copyright © 2023 by Teachers College, Columbia University

Front cover images (top to bottom): Susan Jane Golding via Flickr creative commons, Kyo Azuma via Unsplash

All rights reserved. No part of this publication may be reproduced or transmitted in any form or by any means, electronic or mechanical, including photocopy, or any information storage and retrieval system, without permission from the publisher. For reprint permission and other subsidiary rights requests, please contact Teachers College Press, Rights Dept.: tcpressrights@tc.columbia.edu

Library of Congress Cataloging-in-Publication Data

Names: Corson, Jordan, author.
Title: Reconceptualizing education for newcomer students : valuing learning experiences inside and outside of school / Jordan Corson.
Description: New York : Teachers College Press, [2023] | Includes bibliographical references and index. | Summary: "Based on research in a newcomer school, the author examines undocumented educations-practices that fall outside of schools-to spark different ways for researchers, educators, and activists to think and study with recently immigrated youth"— Provided by publisher.
Identifiers: LCCN 2023011714 (print) | LCCN 2023011715 (ebook) | ISBN 9780807768488 (paper : acid-free paper) | ISBN 9780807768495 (hardcover : acid-free paper) | ISBN 9780807781791 (ebook)
Subjects: LCSH: Place-based education—United States. | Community and school—United States. | Children of immigrants—Education—Social aspects—United States. | Inclusive education—United States. | Multilingual education—United States. | Multicultural education—United States. | Identity (Psychology) in youth. | Culturally relevant pedagogy—United States.
Classification: LCC LC239 .C67 2023 (print) | LCC LC239 (ebook) | DDC 371.826/912—dc23/eng/20230418
LC record available at https://lccn.loc.gov/2023011714
LC ebook record available at https://lccn.loc.gov/2023011715

ISBN 978-0-8077-6848-8 (paper)
ISBN 978-0-8077-6849-5 (hardcover)
ISBN 978-0-8077-8179-1 (ebook)

Printed on acid-free paper
Manufactured in the United States of America

Contents

Acknowledgments	ix
Prologue: Scenes of Education	xi
Introduction	**1**
This Book's Questions, Themes, and Terms	2
Guiding Theories: Unconditional, Uncategorizable, and Imaginative Educations	10
Participants in This Book	12
Notes on Entangled Methodologies and Positionality	15
Organization of the Book	18
Conclusion	20
1. Questioning Marginalization and Schooling	**21**
A Very Brief Overview of Margins and Schooling Immigrant-Origin Youth	23
Marginalization and an Ethnographic Present	25
Conclusion	28
2. A History of Immigrant-Origin Students in the U.S. Education System	**31**
Early History of "Americanization" for Immigrant Youth	34
Systems in the Gap	37
The Rise of Bilingual Education and the History of Newcomer Schools	39

	Looking Toward Other Educational Worlds	48
	Conclusion: Challenging the One Best System	50
3.	**The Birth of the Newcomer as an Educable Subject**	**53**
	Schools Reckon With and Respond to "New" Immigration	56
	Discourses of Newcomer Educability	59
	Educating Desirable Newcomers	60
	Conclusion	67
4.	**Surviving, Succeeding, and Making Do at WISH Academy for Newcomer Youth**	**71**
	Tracing the History of WISH in New York City's 21st-Century Neoliberal Context	72
	Making WISH	74
	WISH's Curriculum	75
	Survive and Advance: The Evolutions of WISH	76
	WISH vs. Everybody	84
	The Cost of Public School	87
	Conclusion	90
5.	**Educations in Place and on the Move**	**93**
	Newcomer Youth Participants	96
	Education and Space/Place	101
	Entangled and Moving Educational Practices	115
	Borderless Constellations of Learning	122
	Conclusion	126
6.	**Undocumented Educations**	**129**
	A Reflection on Authoring and Documenting	131
	Legitimate Education Is Something to Access	132
	The Supplement of Out-of-School Time	135
	Education, Equality, and Opportunity	137

	Subjugated vs. Undocumented Education	142
	Culturally Relevant Teaching to Demands of Schooling	143
	Conclusion	144
7.	**New Possibilities and Conceptions of Education**	**147**
	Wildness and Education	149
	Potential of Everyday Educational Practices	152
	Daydreams of Newcomer Students	158
	Daydreams as Educational Acts for Newcomer Youth	160
	Daydreaming Impractical Educations	162
	Conclusion	164

Epilogue	**167**
Introducing a School of Otherwise	168
The School of Otherwise: A School Made for Being and Thinking Otherwise	168
Conclusion	172

Endnotes	**175**
References	**177**
Index	**193**
About the Author	**199**

Acknowledgments

This book was conceived and written amid conversations with the youth and educators of a newcomer school in New York City. First and foremost, I thank the people of this school. Many teachers at this school invited me into their classrooms. The principal allowed me to roam the hallways. It was in this school that I met the nine youth participants whose ideas and work shape this book. I am eternally indebted to these youth for their care, intellectual generosity, and relentless exuberance as we traveled New York City together. The community into which they and everyone at this school welcomed me is what makes this book possible.

I thank so many people at Teachers College, Columbia University, CUNY, and Stockton University. Students, colleagues, and teachers have accompanied me in the adventure of book writing and contributed to this book in countless ways. In particular, María Paula Ghiso, Elsie Rockwell, Ansley Erickson, and Thomas Hatch all provided thoughtful and supportive comments on the dissertation from which this book emerges. My dear friend, collaborator, and mentor Daniel Friedrich has supported this project (and me in general) from a disastrous dissertation proposal toward its current form. Many people at Teachers College Press, especially Caritza Berlioz, offered insightful feedback and patience throughout the writing process.

My small family has been a guiding force. I send love to my biological and chosen family, particularly my parents, Michael Corson and Diana Corson. Almost everything I am is because of you (so, it's your fault). In your endless care and pride, enjoy displaying this book.

This book is dedicated to Laran Kaplan. From Philadelphia to Worcester to Chicago to New Jersey to New York City to Mexico City to New York City to Philadelphia. With cats and foster kids. Across discovery, illness, struggle, and joy. As teenagers and people who are kind of older now. For over 20 years, in every way, I love you.

Prologue
Scenes of Education

If Matias had arrived in New York City from the Dominican Republic 100 years earlier, around the beginning of the 20th century, he would have had to teach himself many things. A new and rapidly changing city, a language, skills for work, for interests, maybe the curriculum of a school—these facets of everyday life presented countless, dynamic educational possibilities. Perhaps, as did so many people during this time, arriving by boat, as the city broke across the horizon, he would have felt joy, a bubbling sensation of possibility at arrival. Migration officials would assess and question Matias, teaching him about whether he "belonged" in this new place. He would have had to figure out where to stay, perhaps with the small but growing community of Dominicans living around West 15th Street (Torres-Saillant, 2014). Similar to present day, an education would have been born of Matias living, studying, and learning with the people in his community. Once settled, he might have wandered, learning the city's geography by riding cable cars. Bearing with a winter's cold slicing through the car, Matias would have learned by watching the city unfold before him. Maybe his love of music would have fueled an education in saloons playing ragtime. Matias's autodidactic vibrancy would have flourished there—his darting yet pensive eyes studying the slide pianos and their syncopated rhythms. No matter the similarities to the educational pathways he would eventually take, the city, its settings, his variegated desires, and relentless questions—these things would all drive Matias's education.

What if Matias found his way through the rapidly increasing school enrollment numbers, the hundreds of children being turned away from schools for lack of space (Tyack, 1974), and the vast segregation of immigrant populations in which schools almost universally organized around siloed cultures and languages, something that would have likely pushed Matias from the school doors (Berrol, 1969)? He would have been categorized and named (for one of many times in

U.S. history) as a "new immigrant." Schools likely would not have known what to do with him. It is not that he would have evaded the classism, racism, and xenophobia that spilled through the school and city. Rather, his dark skin and flowing Spanish would have marked him for exclusions different from those facing students from Italy or Eastern Europe. He would be made both invisible and unequal (Torres-Saillant & Hernández, 1998). In some ways, youth like Matias—those migrating to the United States from the Dominican Republic—would not become educable figures for decades, at least according to the institution of school.

The "new immigrant" youth of this time entered the middle of a national discourse that veered toward assimilation and away from any forms of difference (Perlmann, 1990). Matias might have participated in a "steamer" or "naturalization" class, receiving English-only language and cultural instruction before entering "normal" schools. During the school day, instruction subjugated him to a draconian form of teaching (Tyack, 1974). There would have been an implicit but far-from-subtle curriculum, too, one that instructed on the "opportunity" of being American and the hierarchical distinction between "Americans" and "foreigners." Matias would have faced narratives of immigrants' inherent wildness, dirtiness, and deviance (Olneck, 1989). English-language instruction and history textbooks stressed cleanliness, punctuality, shaming cultural difference, and thus promoting "Anglo-conformity and middle-class standards" (Tyack, 1974, p. 236). Throughout, the goal would have remained the same: assimilate, belong, and Americanize. To succeed, or at the very least remain in the school, his identity, knowledge, so much of what makes Matias Matias, would have had to mold to the school's vision of Americanness.

And yet, even as high schools rapidly expanded, 15-year-old Matias would have arrived at a time when most people in the United States did not finish secondary school. He might never have enrolled in school. His educations would then have fallen to work and a curriculum of earning a wage. Educational trajectories could alternatively have flared through friendships, interests, and explorations across the city. Matias may have joined the somewhat "invisible" (Miyares, 2004; Torres-Saillant & Hernández, 1998) population of Dominicans in New York City. Perhaps, like the writer Pedro Henríquez Ureña, who arrived, at 17 years old, with his brothers in 1901, he would have discovered or forged an artistic community born of the metropolis, learning a craft on his own (Nuñez, 2011; Torres-Saillant, 2014). He

Prologue xiii

could have found a job with the Spanish-language publication *Las Novedades*.

A communal and cultural education might have taken shape at work or at home as he encountered other Latin American communities in the city. Educations could have emerged in conversations with growing Cuban and Puerto Rican populations. Yet, were it like 2016, Matias would not have arrived with the class privilege with which Dominicans like Henríquez Ureña came to the city. He might instead have joined study groups in the labor movement. He could have crossed paths with Arturo Schomburg, learning through debates and struggles for Cuban and Puerto Rican independence. Educations, for Matias and as framed throughout this book, were thus practices not bound to school but the learnings, formations, cultural navigations, and intellectual work moving through his everyday life.

* * *

Had he arrived in the 1960s, things would have looked quite different for Matias. Joining thousands of people coming to New York from the Dominican Republic after the assassination of dictator Rafael Trujillo (and subsequent U.S. military intervention and occupation), many from the Global South who migrated after the abolition of the national origins quota system in 1965, and arriving amid a juridical push toward more affirmative school policies, Matias's nationality, (perceived) language needs, and much else would have become matters of concern for the New York City Board of Education. Unlike the "sink or swim" approach of previous decades, Matias may have found himself in a slightly more affirmative school space. The educational goal would still be, in a way, assimilation, but Matias would have been welcome to hear and speak Spanish as he learned school subjects. Rather than invisible, Matias would have become part of a group known, analyzed, and educated within the New York City system.

Coinciding with legibility, Matias would have become a "problem" for the Board of Education. With a burgeoning concern for identities, schools suddenly had to move beyond homogeneous pedagogies to address what they understood as the educational needs of specific populations. His schooling would have proceeded through a battery of interventions, as labels like "ELL," "LEP," or "LESA" stuck to Matias. Matias may have been mistaken for or treated as if he were Puerto Rican. Even within a bilingual program that promoted speaking Spanish, Matias's Dominican Spanish would not have been the "right type" of Spanish (Pessar, 2001; Zentella, 2010). Ultimately, the very framing of Matias's schooling would have been rooted in remediation, with assumptions of deficit poking through each contour of the curriculum.

Entering New York City schools in the 1960s, as Sonia Nieto (2015) describes her own experiences in 1950s and 1960s New York City, there would have been a dual curriculum. Learning English and school subjects would have entangled with "learning school." The codes and rhythms of schooling in New York City would have presented layered educational demands that Matias would have had to navigate. There would also have been a political education of the role and uses of schools. From teacher strikes to community organizing, he would have come to school during a particularly tumultuous time in the history of New York City schools (Ravitch, 1974). This education would have exposed Matias to ongoing struggles as communities fought for control of their schools. He might have learned alongside growing cultural organizations in Washington Heights. Alternatively, an education may have emerged within the growing conservative spaces of Dominican Pentecostal churches in the city (Cremin, 1988).

A new education would have emerged around learning and legality. The legality of his presence would have relied on a piece of paper. Most visas were reserved for the white, conservative, and middle-class Dominicans who were cautious of post-Trujillo political shifts. It is possible that his stepfather or mother, who both arrived before Matias, might have secured him a visa. But visas were difficult to acquire (Krohn-Hansen, 2012). He might have arrived as a tourist and stayed in the city, participating in the "new phenomenon" of "migrant illegality" (Hendricks, 1975). School might have charged him a fee. He would have been impacted by a pervasive sense that Dominicans in 1960s New York City had little concern with citizenship or political participation (Pessar, 2001). As he would eventually ask me, Matias would have explored questions of how one learns, navigates, and survives in a place when they are marked in such precarious ways.

Matias might have left school early and jumped into wage labor. Unlike earlier decades, Matias could have relied on a broad network of community support in finding a job. He could have found work in a factory or in the community and learned from someone like Jose Delio Marte, who opened small businesses in Washington Heights and merged this work with activism (Krohn-Hansen, 2012).

Visibility would have been a messy thing. When asked to sign in for English classes at a church, he might have worried about who would see his name and how it would be used (Hendricks, 1975). Any job, particularly if it meant working outside of his direct community, would risk exposure. Yet, Matias's educational life would not have been defined by fear and precarity. He might have spent nights playing dominoes or dancing. Increasing Dominican presence throughout the 1960s would have offered care and community in which Matias learned. Simultaneously, it would have brought a dangerous form of visibility as U.S. institutions aimed to make sense of Matias and fit him into the order of things.

* * *

New York City in the 1980s would have welcomed Matias to a fracturing educational landscape, as competing discourses of how to school immigrant-origin youth intensified. In one camp, he could have arrived amid a push for English-only instruction. The harsh, racist assimilationism of the early 20th century found renewed force. Here, his schooling might have been the old face of exclusionism or welcoming him by suppressing himself. At the same time, culturally affirmative policies and pedagogies shaped the 1980s. The 1982 *Plyler v. Doe* Supreme Court decision, which granted students a legal right to schools regardless of documentation status, offered the possibility of a school becoming a sanctuary space. Matias may have joined one of the experimental schools where Spanish was taught as the main language and English was introduced as a foreign language (Hendricks, 1973). He might have found his way to these emerging affirmative spaces and graduated from high school.

As with the 1900s or 1960s, there would also have been work, community, and vast educational endeavors sprawling before Matias. By the 1980s, Dominican communities had established stronger institutional roots in a number of neighborhoods. Maybe Matias would have joined the Alianza Dominicana Cultural Center or some other organization (Duany, 2008). He could have supported political campaigns. Education may have simply been part of conversations in the bodega or encounters in the neighborhood. It is not that the 1980s would have shown defined progress. Entrenched resources and legibility expanded but so did increased risks. Across time, his educations would have shifted and transformed, moving across places as he negotiated his identities, interests, politics, forms of study, and much else.

* * *

These moments reveal expansive educational possibilities, ones that move within and beyond school as educational practices shifted across time and space. A question remains, however, of how these moments shape Matias's educational story. If, as I will discuss, a goal of this book is to challenge when and where education happens, what gets to count as education, and what possibilities emerge from specific educational practices, why focus on these times and places so commonly explored? Why not start, for instance, with Juan Rodrigues, a Dominican man who came to New York City in 1613 and is often considered one of the city's first immigrants (and first non-indigenous residents)? Why not focus on an underexplored time in immigration or schooling history with Dominican youth?

No matter where I begin or what kinds of education I explore, the answer is ultimately that there have always been immigrant youth in schools and engaged in education in their everyday lives. So, too, have there always been exclusions. And racism. Or community organizing. Ultimately, these different historical moments show that Matias would have learned and practiced in dynamic ways. While bound to history, his educational life moved beyond the school doors and traveled with him in everyday life.

And maybe there is more.

* * *

What if Matias's educational life served other purposes, occurred in different places, or happened in other ways? What if he studied, learned, and lived in ways not commonly seen as part of education? That is, what if he lived a life that institutions, policies, and much else simply read as uneducated when in fact Matias was doing things brimming with intellectualism and curiosity? What if the archives—breathing with histories of schooling, community, political, and cultural life of immigrants in New York City—did not include the kinds of education Matias took up? What if inclusion was never the goal?

In many ways, the educational lives of immigrant-origin youth appear in histories. Their names register on class lists for students in need of language support in schools. Their achievements or struggles become visible in statistics reported by school boards. Outside of school, they might be included in company payrolls. Images of faces register in archives with vague captions. Of course, youth live beyond institutional landscapes, persisting in family stories, myths of people who lived in the neighborhood, or names etched into a sidewalk.

Within established orders—the school, the anthropological study, the policy—stories are limited. There are always things the scholars and policymakers miss, do not write down, do not recognize, refuse to see. Educations are left undocumented. And yet, immigrant youth are there, not waiting for inclusion in institutions or recording in official reports but calling out for expression, craning toward something else. A "something else" sits at the core of this book. It is a look toward small practices, everyday events, and seemingly simple things. It is something other than the educational purposes that researchers and dominant educational discourses have defined. Perhaps, it is a teenager learning how to use an app on their phone or two friends tinkering with multilingual rap lyrics. Or something else could be sitting in the back of a classroom playing with makeup. The point is that there are educational practices flowing through everyday life that demand something beyond inclusion or success in schools, moving toward a horizon not yet understood but one that nonetheless calls for a rethinking of education itself. Such practices are part of already-present everyday enactments rooted in equality and against hierarchical categories.

Such educational practices challenge established ways of speaking about and understanding students. They disrupt the policies documenting a group's educational needs. They invite educators to think otherwise, to see, to study and struggle with youth in new ways. They push beyond the school doors, spill into neighborhoods, into everyday life, not to understand and reform, but to pursue some very basic questions: Who and what counts in education? How might thinking and speculating with already-present educational practices invite a realization of other worlds?

* * *

As he describes it, Matias arrived cold and scared. He came to New York City on a plane shortly before Christmas of 2016. His mother, little brother, and stepfather had already settled in Washington Heights. Trepidation dominated those first days. He roamed the unfamiliar landscape of upper Manhattan, tried to acclimate to the cold and to learn the subway system. Shortly after New Year's, at the recommendation of a family friend, Matias and his stepfather entered a Department of Education (DOE) placement center, looking for a school for Matias. He spoke only a few phrases of English. He valued his Dominican heritage. From age 6, he attended school in the Dominican Republic, but he did not feel like he learned much in school.

Matias quickly enrolled at WISH (Welcome Immigrants, Succeed Here Academy), a high school in New York City specifically designed for students who had recently immigrated to the United States, often called a newcomer school. The person who helped Matias at the placement center hinted that Matias would likely have failed in another school. As a newcomer school, WISH would include Matias and welcome him through culturally and linguistically affirmative forms of schooling. At WISH, Matias almost instantly found success. He formed bonds with teachers, began learning English, and cultivated a passion for music. School became a place of care and safety. In school and beyond, he felt labels stick to him: Immigrant and language learner among others. His mom and stepfather often fought. They eventually separated. Matias cared for his little brother. He became desperate for a job. These issues crept into his school life. He came to wrestle with a label that has had many names but finds its way into schools all over—"at-risk."

Matias moved into a specific English as a Second Language (ESL) class that offered extra support within WISH. Teachers met with him after class. He spoke to a counselor. Yet, after a year, a label of "at-risk" began to congeal around his identities in school. When I met Matias at the start of the 2018–2019 school year, he had been in New York City for over 18 months. He still felt like school was a struggle. He wanted to be ahead of where he was with English. He also felt a pull toward playing basketball and making music, something he saw as directly competing with school success. Sometimes, Matias would head up to the 8th-floor gym rather than attending afternoon classes.

Outside of school, he felt similar struggles. His mom had kicked him out of the house on multiple occasions. He felt like people on the subway or in the neighborhood didn't see him as a person but as a threat. And yet, Matias continued learning, creating, playing, and daydreaming. He imagined a life playing in the NBA, supporting his brother, and returning to the Dominican Republic. Sometimes, dreams were their own educational acts. Other times, tangible skills shaped learning. Friends taught him how to improve his free throws. He studied rap with precision and dedication.

WISH never discounted these ideas but they never quite fit into the curriculum. Occasionally, his test scores improved. But the way Matias rambled down a street in Spanglish revealed an ethics of care and goofiness that never seemed to fit in a school, even one like WISH. There were no teachers suppressing his ideas, no school policies refusing his linguistic expressions. His educational worlds sometimes found their way into lessons but they mostly teetered on the edge of WISH's curriculum. In some ways, his educations moved against the school; not WISH specifically but the broader making and doing of school, particularly as it concerns immigrant-origin students. And yet his educational life continued and thrived, challenging labels of "at-risk" and showing what joys, struggles, care, and new possibilities everyday education life forges.

Introduction

Leaders, educators, and researchers search desperately for a new innovation, a different policy, a game-changing reform, something that will improve schools and move toward perfecting education systems. For immigrant-origin youth, beyond the racist and exclusionary policies that dominate the United States, schools seek out ways to further include youth and ensure their academic success. Meanwhile, others imagine more radical possibilities, seeing schooling and education not as something to improve but as a place to challenge the very roots of social structures. Such possibilities of education move toward abolitionist dreams of another world. Part of these radical possibilities can be found in listening to youth, not just in school or in community organizations, but also in their everyday lives. What might initially appear to be disengagement, meaningless play, or simply exhaustion are often joyous, playful, and rebellious educational practices. Far from waiting around for better inclusion mechanisms, in moments of pleasure and inquiry, youth are already enacting other worlds, using education to build spaces and moments of equality and communal engagement.

As I will describe throughout this book, Matias and the eight other youth who shape this project are radical thinkers. Each in their own ways, they overflow with creativity and care. How is it, then, that an intellectual like Matias could appear in history or modern life just in passing, at least within research or schooling frames? Throughout New York City's educational history, there are countless names visible only as educational problems. It is not that Matias's life is interchangeable with others, though I will argue that his story is interconnected with a complex history of immigration and education. Rather, as part of ongoing struggles and emerging bodies of critical writing on immigration and education, there are direct responses to these issues, ones that push toward possibilities more radical than further inclusion or improved academic success in schools.

THIS BOOK'S QUESTIONS, THEMES, AND TERMS

As the youth who participated in this book verify, people routinely take up educational practices that slip from common understandings of what counts as education. Through ethnographic and historical study, I hope to ignite different ways for researchers, educators, and activists to think and study with recently immigrated youth and to listen toward new educational worlds. I resist trying to make sense of or analyze such educational practices as a researcher, instead I levy a challenge to the structures that marginalize such educations. Rather than joining a chorus of reform efforts, I listen to the rigorous, wild, and ethereal educational practices already present in youth's lives. These practices unveil the way different forms of education are already at work, making do, opening new trajectories, and finding routes to different places.

This book emerges from engagements with two research questions. First, I asked how WISH emerged as a thinkable and practical intervention for recently immigrated youth. Here, I did not want to just evaluate the school's efficacy in educating recently immigrated students. I instead sought to understand how it became possible, specifically within New York City's educational landscape, to see a school like WISH as a desirable space to educate newcomer youth. How did understandings of the category of "newcomer" and discourses around language and culture solidify into educational structures like WISH? Second, I asked what possibilities for those studying education emerged from encountering everyday educational practices in youth's everyday lives. This question led to work in many places, seeing different kinds of education forming, and exploring the relationships between curriculums and pedagogies across time and space. Bringing together these questions and ideas, I now turn to the three themes organizing this book: new considerations of immigration and education, education beyond schools, and the unmaking of worlds.

Immigration and Education

In recent decades, the United States has seen school taking up more and more space. From after-school activities to the importance of credentials for future opportunities, time spent in school and the discursive space it occupies has crept into everyday life. This makes sense, as school has come to signify all kinds of pathways—prosperity, stability, self-discovery, and much else. For immigrant-origin youth, school is framed as a particularly important place. "American education matters more than ever. While a hundred years ago immigrant youth could (and routinely did) drop out of school without hampering their futures, today the costs of doing so are substantial" (Suárez-Orozco et al., 2010, p. 88). Graduation rates in New York City have, in recent years, climbed to over 80%. Yet only 60% of emergent bilingual youth who have been labeled as English language learners (ELLs) in New York City graduate[1] (New York City Department of Education, 2022; see also Zimmerman & Disare, 2017). With this group "having the highest dropout rate of any population in the city," the New York Immigration Coalition, an advocacy group for immigrant rights, dubs this problem the "ELL Dropout Crisis" or a "crisis among newcomer immigrants" (New York City Immigration Coalition, 2020). To combat these problems, schools', policies', and research's central focus is how to improve academic outcomes for immigrant-origin youth.

The long struggle of many coalitions to create programs such as bilingual education (Santiago, 1986) or the right of undocumented youth to attend school has altered the educational trajectories of many. But improving access and outcomes are not the only educational considerations. During one of our first conversations, Sofia, one of the nine youth who are part of this ethnographic research, described some of her educational desires: "I already know English and I already know Spanish," she said. "So, like, I want to see what else is out there. I want to learn something else." She wandered through acting, tennis, French, and history, not as classes to master but as interests without specific results in mind. They were simply areas of inquiry, fields to study and to engage.

An overwhelming emphasis on access and outcomes strangely narrows education. School may act as a gateway of opportunity, but the dynamic and emergent forms education takes—both the means and the ends educations serve—all conform to these goals. Questions might include: How to improve? Where to expand? What to tweak? But, the broader structure remains. It is in this vein that Patel (2013) describes how research and practice have become "very fond of models and examples of 'best practices'" (p. 5). While the pursuit of more equitable public schools is a complex and noble task, it is not the only one, specifically in the field of immigration and education. If the only thing left to do were to continue incrementally expanding opportunities, the focus of this book would be, after Foucault (1972), to espouse the role of an educational bureaucracy that makes sure all of inclusion's papers are in order.

When researchers and policymakers ask what can be done to ensure better outcomes for immigrant-origin students, questions emerge of "Whose outcomes?" and "To what ends?" Strengthening lines of work in education and immigration look to critically engage issues of racialization and equality (Rodriguez & Conchas, 2022), the politics of belonging in liberal multicultural frames (Abu El-Haj, 2015), or the disruption of established narratives (Abrego & Negrón-Gonzales, 2020). This book similarly centers immigrant-origin youth attending a newcomer school in New York City and attends to the politics of immigration and education.

The first theme of this book asks about and studies with immigrant-origin youth's educations beyond the confines of a twin binary of inclusion/exclusion or success/failure. What educational practices operate beyond the horizon of these educational logics? What do such educational practices do? Where? With and for whom? How do these kinds of practices inform the work of moving toward this "something else"? Focusing so heavily on success and inclusion risks what is already present with immigrant-origin youth. These binaries are attuned to the frequency of rigid institutions. Rather than chart, categorize, and understand educational practices, I ask what new understandings and educational possibilities they provoke. Thinking with these practices looks to challenge dominant understandings of education and speaks back to the making and doing of educational research and practice. In such an inquiry, it is not just the researchers and policymakers who ask the questions or dictate the terms of education. Furthermore, while this book is not intended to be one of testimonio or educational biography, new questions and routes of study depict different kinds of immigrant stories. Youth participants in this book shared stories and ideas that deviate from notions of "overcoming" or "grit" that too often frame immigrant stories and end in definite outcomes of success or failure. Instead, the ethnographic moments explored here are ongoing and unqualified, revealing practices often unconcerned with success or inclusion.

Exploring Education Beyond School Doors

When someone says they "are educated" or "have an education," they almost always refer to schooling. Varenne (2009) details how school has overwhelmed education to such an extent that the terms have become nearly synonymous. Of course, though, education is happening all the time. In grand moments of learning and mundane activities, education is present. I would even argue that there is no outside to education. Regardless of any programmatic intervention, education is at work. As Harney and Moten (2013) describe, the kind of thought, questioning, and inquiry taking place in schools (when schools are at their best) is something that also occurs on porches, in kitchens and basements, at parties, in factories, and all over. "To do these things," they write, "is to be involved in a kind of common intellectual practice" (p. 110). The second theme of this book is thus to move beyond the school doors, looking to see education at work in immigrant-origin youth's everyday lives.

Many scholars of immigration and education look outside of school. But, quite often, the largeness of schooling takes over, pushing out culturally sustaining work to reinforce schooling's supremacy. Moll et al. (1992) famously suggest that teachers look to students' "funds of knowledge." Their work suggests that "by capitalizing on household and other community resources, we can organize classroom instruction that far exceeds in quality the rote-like instruction these children commonly encounter in schools" (p. 132). The cultural life of youth, particularly immigrant youth, may not be a deficit for teachers to overcome but an active asset in building curriculum. In this context, drawing on cultural and linguistic identities serves the twin binaries of inclusion/exclusion and success/failure that dominate educational discourse. Home and community life are useful tools in the logics of schooling.

Researchers and activists certainly recognize the possibilities of education in other places operating autonomously from school. Nonformal education programs can, Gutiérrez (2016a) suggests, generate "radical shifts in our views of learning and in our perceptions of youth from non-dominant communities" (p. 187). Language and literacy thrive in community spaces without maintaining school as a central reference point. In "community spaces such as the Laundromat," Ghiso (2016) shows how "children participated in literacies that displayed an ethics of care, were attentive to social inequality, and situated transnational experiences as an epistemic resource" (p. 3). In a similar vein, Pacheco (2012) turns to home and community spaces as places generating (and generated by) "everyday resistance," seeing these practices as potentially serving "as thinking and analytic tools for learning in school contexts" (p. 121). As this kind of work depicts, there are educations present and thriving in nonformal and everyday spaces that do not rely on the space or logics of schooling.

Moving from inclusion in schools toward everyday education, from the outcome of success toward the process of practice, sees education spilling from the cracks between institutions and programs. It passes beyond the boundaries of organized learning. From this perspective, education work acts as a networked interconnected practice, similar to how Escobar (2016) frames "relational ontology." Escobar writes that such worlds are "enacted minute by minute, day by day, through an infinite set of practices carried out by all kinds of beings and life forms, involving a complex organic and inorganic materiality (p. 18).

Looking beyond the twin binaries of inclusion/exclusion and success/failure, therefore, entails looking to new places, both physically and intellectually, and looking at how educational life moves and evolves across spaces. That is, this book examines the generative possibilities of seeking out new forms of education in a multitude of places. Among other questions, I asked: How do language practices form and move as they go from school to the subway? How does learning a skill change as it is learned in school versus at a job? What pedagogical relationships form in neighborhoods? Do teachers and other school-like positions take shape in everyday life? What new possibilities and ways of being emerge from such practices? Looking across the places of education sees how certain kinds of education are governed and made possible.

Moving beyond the school doors, or even moving beyond nonformal venues of education, brings up an over-asked and under-defined question. What even is education? If it is all over the place and it is always happening, what gives it shape? In other words, if a central concern of this book is disentangling education from schooling, how do I avoid it simply becoming synonymous with a different thing, the living of everyday life? I offer a broad framing that aims to listen to divergent educational practices of this book's participants and builds on Cremin's (1990) definition of education as "the deliberate, systematic, and sustained effort to transmit, evoke, or acquire knowledge, values, attitudes, skills, and sensibilities, as well as any learning that results from that effort, direct or indirect, intended or unintended" (p. viii). Beyond this definition, this book sees the following five qualities of education.

First, education includes processes and outcomes of *learning*. Learning is a complex mixture of developing skills and knowledge. Learning English or the way around a neighborhood is an educative process. Second, education entails *formation*. It is the becoming or making of things, a coalescing that never quite solidifies. This facet of education might include subject-making, as participants negotiate the production of categories of types of people. Third, education is *pursuit*. Much like radical study, education is an engagement with knowledge or ideas themselves rather than seeking some kind of specific outcome. Fourth, education works as *resistance*. Resistance pushes against the adaptive qualities of education, creating counter-truths told against an educational truth like "a dropout crisis." Fifth, education is centrally a *creative* thing. The creativity of education brings something forward that had not previously existed. Taken together, education is movement, toward the new, the unknown, the obscured, and the uncertain. Educations in different places may carry some elements of each or only fragments of one aspect, but these fluid understandings help frame a view of education that moves through different settings and ideas. Exploring what education is and where it happens leads to the third theme of this book, asking what these inquiries make possible.

Unmaking Worlds

Reporting on a student returning to school after an 18-month absence during COVID-19, Joffe-Walt and Glass (2022) suggest that "school is a machine that is designed to move forward. Kids move class to class, grade to grade. A machine does not stop. It's not designed to go back in time, to meet [students] where [they're] at right now . . . you can feel the conveyor belt of schools moving forward." As schools trudge toward a liberal capitalist notion of utopia, their march is incessant, reminiscent of Walter Benjamin's (2020) "angel of history." Where Benjamin's angel sees the past as a series of catastrophes—an endless pile of rubble—looking through the history of education in the U.S. finds reforms and policies piling a wreckage of exclusion and marginalization of youth's lives. The winds that sweep this angel, "what we call progress," as Benjamin says, create circumstances for schools to accept marginalizing youth. This is not a critique of failed policies or directly exclusionary schooling. It is, rather, a critique of successes, of the treadmill of "continuous improvement," and what these successes leave in their wake. Along the road of progress, incremental changes make students who do not benefit from the innovative model and who resist the new policy into victims of progress. In celebrating the successes of increased attendance, graduation, diversity, knowledge, skills, critical thinking, socio-emotional awareness, participation, test scores . . . marginalized youth become accepted statistics that cannot be included until new reforms are discovered, or new routes are carved.

An answer should not be to march with more vigor, pushing linear progress even further. It is not, to use Tyack's (1974) refrain, that "old reforms need to be reformed anew" (p. 291). I argue that schools cannot simply expand into infinity. The third theme of this book seeks to deeply contest progressive narratives that "things are getting better" in favor of a more radical understanding of the role of education. It is possible to refuse both the march of progress and the stasis of marginalization. Yes, schools operate within and often reinforce a bordered settler-colonial state. And yes, including students in schools in meaningful ways can alter their intellectual journeys and material conditions. Other questions about education, though, and other places of education, see things otherwise. These questions return to the radical consideration of something else, of the possibility of education moving to challenge social orders.

The majority of youth who participated in this book were labeled "at risk" of dropping out of school. This third theme does not seek out a better intervention or blame any teacher but critically engages the structures that produce youth into categories like "at risk" or, in terms of people on the move, "undocumented." In doing so, I ask why research and schooling as broad institutions so often obscure the beautiful, wild intellectual practices seen throughout this book (though, of course, many individuals and communities regularly resist). This critical engagement seeks a disruption of the flow and attempts to unmake the machines of schooling rather than calling in the repair people.

There are other worlds out there, ones forming, shifting, pushing against established educational orders. They can be found in the other places of education, flickering alive as "a ceaseless experiment with the futurial presence of the forms of life that make such activities possible" (Harney & Moten, 2013, p. 74). For researchers and educators, these worlds reveal possibilities beyond conditional inclusion or establishing better systems. These kinds of educations imagine what else is possible. As the youth participating in this project and I explored, these educational practices are rooted in speculation and play. Contesting dominant educational worlds and moving toward others, I recognize that other worlds are not only possible but have already been made and continue to be made. Graeber and Wengrow (2021) provoke something similar in their rethinking of questions of equality. "What if we treat people, from the beginning, as imaginative, intelligent, playful creatures who deserve to be understood as such? What if . . . we ask how we came to be trapped in such tight conceptual shackles that we can no longer even imagine the possibility of reinventing ourselves" (p. 9)? The imaginative play of speculation moves toward other educational worlds, listening to and thinking with people in the way Graeber and Wengrow describe and simultaneously posing their question of how dominant systems of education have become such sprawling, all-encompassing things that are also mired in their forward march.

Other worlds do not rest on empty terrain. The other worlds bubbling and bursting throughout this book do not abandon the publicness of public schools. They embrace the deep labor of study. They are also collective rather than competitive, leisurely and fulfilling instead of draining. They affirm the sentiments of WISH that "no one is illegal/ nadie es illegal" and that cultural life should be celebrated. And they move beyond any authoritarian voice speaking these sentiments. In doing so, they move toward worlds not defined by "deservingness" or "good immigrants," but by Leo's, another of the nine participants, questioning of opportunities and learning experiences. "Why is school so competitive? I should get these things because I'm a human." Unmaking of educational worlds while seeking an educational otherwise is something antihierarchical, antiracist, anticolonial, against borders. It is for the productive, creative, liberatory potential of abolitionist educations as part of a different kind of educational commons.

Challenging Dominant Educational Structures

This project's timeline almost perfectly coincides with the years of the Trump presidency. With that in mind, there is an untimeliness to this book's themes. As I took fieldnotes and transcribed Matias's unfinished freestyles, families were torn apart, children were locked in cages, and racist border policies thrived. This project stands fiercely against borders and in solidarity with youth on the move. Yet, this book offers no policy recommendations to protect immigrant rights or ways to positively impact curriculum or life at WISH. I offer no proposals to scale a school like WISH. These concerns expand when I think about how far outside of school the project moves. In this book, I critique systems of thought and institutions of education while holding space for the possibility of public schools as a commons to verify equality. Even still, that does not offer actionable takeaways for teachers or direct reforms for policymakers.

There is, I hope, also something timely in this critique. I hope that researchers and educators can take away different understandings of the possibilities of education with people on the move. As images of violence swarm, the stories of this book are filled with joys and wonders, educations exploding with possibility. It leaves behind hierarchical frameworks to study with youth. This book directly engages youth participants as education workers, offering a lesson that we educators have nothing to teach but unconditional welcoming and that youth are always already equal. Educators of all kinds constantly enact these forms of care. Through such work that is both timely and untimely, I hope that educators reading the book might take away different ideas of what challenging dominant structures might look like and find renewed moments to stop the machinery of school and look at what youth are already enacting.

GUIDING THEORIES: UNCONDITIONAL, UNCATEGORIZABLE, AND IMAGINATIVE EDUCATIONS

Just as three themes move through this book, three interwoven theories guide it. Within the scope of research, theories simultaneously operate as a way of seeing and understanding and as ongoing activities in which participants engage. These theories loosely organize around keywords of equality, speculation, and ungovernance. First, taking lessons from philosopher Jacques Rancière, I theorize everyday educational practices as things infused with the possibility of verifying already-present equality. School is so often framed as the place where people become equal, not in the democratic space of people participating in a shared community but as an upward movement within a hierarchical social order. Once someone "gets" an education, this status, these credentials, creates the possibility of becoming equal. Yet, education is not a commodity or a process that works toward an equality yet to come. Rancière (1991) provokes an idea that equality is not an endpoint or goal but rather a beginning assumption. Material conditions may have been made unequal, but verifying equality is something possible for any person in any moment.

Rancière further challenges the way the world has been divided up, with one form of democracy being a passive, distributed thing "Go vote for people to speak for you!". In worlds of education, schooling's supremacy turns education into a thing that must be conditional and handed out. Students must wait for the knower to guide them. They need the grade to certify their knowing. This, in turn, confines schools and teachers within limited and unimaginative roles. Of course, people in schools (particularly teachers and students) challenge this kind of order every day. Everyday educational practices reveal another way in which "these mechanisms [passive equality and the social order] are stopped in their tracks by the effect of a presupposition . . . the equality of anyone and everyone" (Rancière, as cited in May, 2008, p. 40). This "stopping in their tracks" happens in moments when people act to verify their equality. After momentary ruptures, the social order re-forms. But the verification of equality changes something, makes possible something in a moment that ripples outward. It cannot be put back in the box. A thing is learned that the system had not authorized. An expression of intelligence moves beyond the grid of intelligibility. People that institutions see as unknowing enact knowledge across everyday life.

For researchers and educators, equality as a fundamental principle and starting point uproots the foundations and grounding assumptions of education work as they come to see that "I must teach . . . that I have nothing to teach" (Rancière, 1991, p. 15). This form of equality also takes away the conditions of inclusion where marginalized youth must be "deserving" of education. School can be a site to verify equality, but youth are not simply waiting around for schools to make them equal. Attending to these practices reveals "that the incessant and irreversible intellectuality of these activities is already present" (Harney & Moten, 2013, p. 110).

Second, theories of other worlding and speculation guide this book. Again, even as conditions are made unequal, people dream and imagine different possibilities regardless of authorization to do so. Speculation is intellectual work that attends to the ever-present life of educations of the past, of other places, and of what might yet become. Rather than developing knowledge and skills along linear paths, speculation moves rhizomatically; entangling time, space, knowledge, and being to explore education's possibilities. What was learned in social studies at WISH can play a role in what is practiced on a street corner in Washington Heights. Moreover, these different educations might all influence speculations of different and future lives, bringing forth new individual and collective educational worlds.

Speculation is something more than a schooling question of "What do you want to be when you grow up?" The thinking–feeling–wondering of participants as we walked about the city or chatted between classes meandered toward all kinds of ideas and dreams. Though not a form of "critical fabulation," speculating echoes Saidiya Hartman's (2008) counter-history work, as a "strategy for disordering and transgressing the protocols of the archive and its statements"

(p. 9). Beyond moving marginalized voices to the center, to some reconcilable legibility, the speculative "dares us to dream of radical ontological and epistemological possibilities outside of normative structures (Mirra & Garcia, 2020, p. 301). In joy and play, speculation contests the marginalizing effects of categorization. Matias, labeled "at-risk" and "ELL" in school, dreamed of worlds beyond these categories, both his "passing" out of them but also of their entire abolition, "just being in school, learning my things. And like a person who speaks different languages," as he described. Here, Foucauldian ideas influence a critical examination of the forces that produce and use these categories to govern people.

Beyond such governance, a third assemblage of theories emerges—the practice of becoming ungovernable. Resisting governance is about living and studying freely, against confining, hierarchical, and marginalizing structures. Where governance seeks to perfect and sustain desirable types of people and a stable order of things, ungovernance is an "unrestrained, uncivilized, disorderly, and ferocious, anti-colonial relationship to thought and being" (Halberstam, 2014). Building on wide-ranging writing (Halberstam, 2020; Harney & Moten, 2013; Hartman, 2019), ungovernance is a resistance to the codifying practices that march toward institutional utopia. Against simply fitting into the system, higher achievement, becoming the "right" kind of person, ungovernance embraces the euphoric practices of everyday life that defy who people are supposed to be and resist what they are supposed to do. Ungovernance is an ongoing affirmation of equal, unfixed identities that are collectively self-determined and always in motion, part of "a fluid articulation of the self that is never fixed or linear because it is constantly developing" (Ramirez, 2020, p. 163). Troublemaking in classrooms or boisterousness as youth spill from school onto subway platforms are not moments to correct or tamp down. Instead, educators might come to see the liberatory potential in these moments and how, within such ungoverned expressions, education thrives. With these frameworks in mind, I now turn to the people, places, and things at the core of this research.

PARTICIPANTS IN THIS BOOK

Nine youth's generosity and intellectual discourses shaped much of this book (see Table 1.1). They are participants who joined the long haul of research and interlocutors who conversed about the big ideas central

Introduction

Table 1.1. Youth Participants

Youth Participant	Description
Miguel	Serious person. Wants to enlist in the army. Loves photography.
Mateo	Works long hours at McDonald's. Wants to become a doctor or lawyer. Loves learning languages and playing basketball.
Sofia	Shy person, occasionally assertive. Wants to be an actor.
Leo	Academically ambitious, focused on social justice. Balances many academic and work commitments. Wants to pursue psychology.
Matias	Caring, respectful. Loves music. Wants to be able to take care of his family.
Ximena	Social, peacemaker. Spends lots of time with friends. Loves art. Wants to be an artist.
Felipe	Quiet, thoughtful. Loves playing video games and baseball. Unsure about his future.
Luna	Fabulous, helpful, fearless. Leads the school's Gender and Sexuality Alliance (GSA). Wants to stay in New York City.
Pablo	Loves hanging out with friends. Spends lots of free time with his son. Wants to be a fashion designer and to make rap music.

to this book. Descriptions of participants have, sometimes to their chagrin, been slightly altered to protect identities. These co-constructed descriptions offer deeply limited overviews of who participated in this project, though I further introduce participants in Chapter 5. All participants attended WISH. All but one came to New York City from the Dominican Republic. They ranged in age from 15 to 19. All identified as Latinx youth. Three identified as Afro Caribbean. Six identified as male, and three as female. I do not list or describe youth's documentation status, even when it was disclosed.

Beyond these participants, the school, the city, and their histories and politics all played a role in this project.

Location of Ethnographic Research

Youth in this project did not speak in empty space; they did not learn in decontextualized environments or write their educational lives upon blank slates. New York City courses through the book. The George Washington Bridge and Central Park framed the view of walks. Squealing brakes on the D train interrupted intimate conversation.

Bodegas offered brief refuge as we escaped the summer heat. And the structured nonformal educations youth took up occurred in underfunded libraries, stalwart cultural institutions, and high-rise buildings overlooking Union Square. The city was alternatively soft background music, focal point, and quiet maker of research and educational practice.

New York City itself is no blank slate. Its schools anchor the city's architecture and everyday flows. Despite unparalleled diversity of schools (from schools on boats to schools for incarcerated youth, New York City seems to be a place of infinite permutations of schooling), there is a persistent grammar to the New York City school building. Once inside schools, whether a small charter school or the well-known magnet, Stuyvesant, I've always found an eerie similarity amongst hallways or classrooms. There is also another kind of uniformity in New York City schools. The vibrancy of teachers, students, and many other people, all engaged in the messy struggle of creating a place of and for a public. Some of my favorite moments during research emerged from the twilit moments after school when students milled about in front of the building and teachers stopped to chat on their way to the subway. They reconnected, decompressed, shared moments about the day, and then moved on.

My time at WISH occurred amid a decades-long assault on public schooling in New York City, something discussed in Chapter 4. Outside of schools, where much of the research for this book occurred, New York City also faced ongoing crises of gentrification and police violence (these things are also part of the everyday life of schools). Most directly, ICE raids or frequent dehumanizing stares from subway passengers loomed over moments of research. I always approached my role in the city, and my position with participants, as that of guest. These issues intensified my attention to mutual care, to listening to how youth used the city to find and make places of refuge, and to a need to intentionally limit research. It also deepened the role of WISH, both in participants' lives and its place in this project.

WISH Academy. Even as research sprawls across the city and wanders into students' intellectual daydreams, school remains an important character in this book. It was at WISH Academy that I met the youth who participated in the project. WISH is a small public high school serving recently immigrated youth in New York City—a newcomer school. Over 90% of the students are Latinx immigrants. The vast majority of students arrive from the Dominican Republic. The school also includes students who arrived from West African nations and countries in the Middle East. More than 90% of students qualify for free or reduced-price lunches.

At WISH, support for undocumented students or pride for immigrant identities are visible through informational flyers shared with students, posters of encouragement hung throughout the school, and school events such as Cultural Heritage Day. It would be easy to say that WISH is simply an iteration of a newcomer school such as Gregorio Luperón—the school at the center of Bartlett and Garcla's (2011) study—a place that many at WISH see as a template or sibling school. Yet WISH is a unique place of caring and struggle that has transformed itself over the years.

NOTES ON ENTANGLED METHODOLOGIES AND POSITIONALITY

I started hanging out at WISH at the start of the 2018–2019 school year after working there as a student teacher supervisor the previous year. From the start of the school year, hallway chats, recruitment scripts read in three classrooms, snowball sampling, and other ethnographic tools contributed to nine WISH students joining the project. Given the school's size, all participants knew each other. All participants identified at least one friend in the project. The nine youth in the project were not unified by a specific club or educational activity. Sometimes, I attended an after-school program with Luna and Ximena. Other times, I spent a lunch period chatting with Felipe, Matias, and Pablo. Ethnographic work entailed looking at educational practices in these different configurations and places. I sought to spend time in three settings: school, nonformal educational programs, and unstructured time. Within these spaces, I spent hundreds of hours over 13 months. Additionally, I conducted three semi-structured interviews with each participant and held three whole-group charlas/chats with all participants.

Participants and I worked together through talk, sense, feel, and movement. This approach to ethnographic work owes much to affect theories (e.g., Anderson, 2006; Stewart, 2007). Indescribable, incomprehensible, and lingering educational events occurred. We sensed things affecting and being affected, even when we could not name them. Intense feelings, wandering daydreams, sensations of uncertainty—these things found their way into ethnographic work. Intensities or forces of potentiality (words used to describe *affect*) swam through spaces and things of research. The background of the city, the utility of a chair, so much began vibrating when looking beyond a rationalistic approach to studying educational practices.

Working affectively opened new routes to attend to often obscured parts of education research. I never wanted to "get to the bottom" of things (Rutherford, 2016). Affect looks "not to the demystification and well-known picture of the world, but rather to speculation, curiosity" (Stewart, 2007, p. 3). Ethnographic work thus moved from cataloguing and making sense of toward living amid messy wonder. In walks and group discussions, participants and I "gaze[d], imagine[d], sense[d], [took] on, perform[ed], and assert[ed] not a flat and finished truth but some possibilities (and threats)" that arose in ethnographic work (Stewart, 2007, p. 5).

Affect does so in a way that responds to a major risk and concern of this book. It creates opportunities for new legibility but does so against submitting participants' educational lives to new controls (Corson, 2022a). It provokes a manner of study that encounters different ways of being, ones not simply then consumed by established systems of thought. The rhizomatic pathways of affect opened space to the unknown and unresolved, allowing unexpected, unbounded things to creep into research. Miguel spent an hour toying with a camera battery. Sofia played on her phone. Rather than the in-between or the outside, these moments were integral to the project. Why did some moments catch our eyes? Which things "mattered" as educational practices in everyday life? Where did these things flair, connect, flow, emerge, and trail off? Participants and I invited contested definitions of education and focused on educational practices where interlocutors felt joy, usefulness, relevance, or interest. Even these terms indexed broad things. I/we never drew a line, making room for meaning making but recognizing the un-bordered, porous work of affect that lives in all kinds of speculative, wonderous educations that surge and spill from stuck places.

Throughout our time together, an ethics of care, safety, and support guided the work. Centrally, those participating in the project *are not research subjects to be studied and understood*. I came to this project with a particular awareness of my role as a white U.S. citizen and researcher. Adding extra care and flexibility, I negotiated the ways that my presence, questions, and much else shifted the terrain of everyday educational life. When I started the project, I thought it would act as a kind of educational testimonio—a personal and political narration of educational life, one in which participants would speak back to the truths told about their lives as "risky," "deviant," or "marginalized" (Stephen, 2013). As we worked together, I came to see testimonio as being beyond the scope of this project.

Ethnographic moments and direct aspects of participants' lives remain hidden throughout this book. I wanted to, as Duarte (2022) suggests, "invert and subvert the powers that demand [undocumented] invisibility" (or the marginalization of other immigrant-origin groups with documentation). I do not want to narrate someone else's educational life but rather to show how research and policy, even in affirmative and inclusive impulses, maintains structures—and how listening to hints of and encounters with educational life, education might be thought of differently. I ultimately arrived at a focus on educational practices. Practices offer something not possessable but expressed. Practice is, furthermore, the work not of mastering a skill but of joy and engagement. Educational practices slip from a cohesive, categorizable totality to show what is done, verified, what emerges in flashes, and what occurs in the flows of everyday life.

Even when focusing on these practices, though, I aimed for what Jackson (2013) describes as "thin description," "a response to a certain kind of overconfidence" in ethnographic research (p. 13) and a different way of doing ethnographic work that brings ethnographers into dialogue with people. "Thin description values that dialogue, acknowledging as a way of knowing that privileges continued non-knowing" (p. 153). Thin description indexes, first, a critique of ethnographic impulses to catalogue and share everything and, second, an affirmation of participants' autonomy.

Entangling with ethnography, historical work engages "the 'complex dialectic' between central educational movements, such as hegemonic forms of schooling, and the diverse educational and cultural traditions that cross through and confront them on multiple space/time scales" (Rockwell, 2011, p. 66). Everyday educational practices operate relationally with dominant understandings of education, ones that carry persistent histories. I looked at different archival sources from specific historical moments to uncover the ways governments, schools, and other institutions have understood the populational category of "immigrant" in educational terms. Attending to these factors, as may already be obvious, I have used a number of terms to refer to immigrant-origin youth. While I primarily use "immigrant-origin," I use other terms based on the context and sources. For instance, when writing about immigrant-origin youth in relation to or from the perspective of WISH, I mostly use the term "newcomer," since WISH is commonly known as a newcomer school or a school serving newcomer youth.

This approach to history is not the connecting of a straight line drawn from European immigrants attending late 19th century schools in the Lower East Side directly to WISH in the 2010s. Oppressive educations did not progressively march toward affirmative educations. I instead took up a "history of the present" (Foucault, 1988/1979), exploring the forces that made certain understandings and discourses possible. Through analyzing these discourses, I sought to understand how a category like "newcomer" emerged and schools like "newcomers schools" have come to flourish. A history of the present seeks to destabilize dominant truths that have been produced and make alternative histories and understandings possible.

Similar to ethnographic work, I encountered history with care and caution. Something like a policy document is not a lifeless paper to play with but a political marking with direct impacts on youth's lives. Talking about Walter Benjamin, Lather and Kitchens (2017) describe a need "to safeguard against how such alternative histories, if recognized at all, can too easily become the tools of the oppressor" (p. 4). As history blends with ethnographic work, I once more affirm culturally sustaining practices while resisting showing these practices as a next step in the march toward utopia.

ORGANIZATION OF THE BOOK

The chapters in this book start historically and move toward ethnographic engagements present in everyday educational life. The book crawls outward from the classroom, to hallways, beyond the school doors, and finally beyond the very logics of schooling. In the first chapter, I explore the making and maintenance of marginalization. Referencing the twin binaries, the chapter looks to how exclusion and failure emerge and persist, not as the struggles of individual immigrant-origin youth but as structures crucial to schools. The second chapter spans decades of history, "thinking like schools" to look at the different ways, schools have educated immigrant-origin students. The chapter centrally addresses moments in which schools attempted to "solve," through different forms of institutional inclusion, the "problem" of immigrant-origin students. The chapter also looks beyond institutional perspectives to see the organizing work happening as communities struggled to forge different educational conditions.

Introduction

Chapter 3 takes a genealogical approach to understanding the term *newcomer* as an emergent educable category. Where this term has appeared throughout schooling history in the United States and elsewhere, I argue that the emergence of comprehensive and culturally affirmative newcomer schools in the 1980s birthed a political subject known as "newcomer." Where schools previously understood immigrant students as needing only to fit into the broader grammar of schooling, the "newcomer" as an educable subject came about as institutions understood immigrant youth needing particular educational interventions beyond supplemental programs or suppressive measures like English-only instruction. With the birth of the newcomer as an educable subject, Chapter 4 explores how WISH Academy emerged as a desirable educational intervention for newcomers. From interviews with teachers and administrators, and an analysis of school policies, proposals, and curricular documents, the chapter explores how the desire to create an affirmative environment has frequently come into conflict with the broader political demands of schooling in New York City.

The fifth chapter shifts to ethnographic work, looking at how educational practices emerge, move, and interact across time and place. I explore the knowledge, curriculum, and ways of being operating and valued in dynamic time-places. Throughout this chapter, theories of public pedagogy inform how school, nonformal education, and other educational spaces all influence each other and move. Chapter 6 interrogates what happens to some educational practices that do not conform to the demands of schooling, even in culturally and linguistically affirmative spaces. In this chapter, I suggest that there are always knowledges and ways of being that slip from the rigid structuring of schooling. Informed by the way a number of interlocutors framed these educational practices, I consider them as "undocumented educations," educational practices falling outside of legitimated educational institutions or appearing only in marginalized, liminal ways. These educations do not disappear or remain precarious simply because they do not fit into school and other spaces.

Asking what "undocumented educations" do and make possible, Chapter 7 shares vignettes of participants daydreaming and engaging in acts of experimentation and play. The chapter presents possibilities for educations rooted in radical alterity. It is here that I most directly turn to the theme of education beyond twin binaries of success/failure and inclusion/exclusion. Against the measurable, centrally defined ideas of education as a school-based activity concerned with outcomes, examples of education as a wild daydream reveal educational life as something pleasurable, joyful, impractical, and indeterminate.

The book concludes with a short, playful experiment. Having pushed geographical and intellectual boundaries of education, I return to school. This epilogue conjures the possibility of a coming school, one not built around codifying knowledge, where welcoming is unconditional and untethered from normative expectations, a school founded on ungovernance and practices of collective autonomy. The epilogue is a provocation informed by my time with participants and draws on global examples of radical forms of schooling.

CONCLUSION

The goal of this book is to stare into and critique the violent social orders that exclude immigrant-origin youth or include them along institutional, conditional, and reformist lines. From this critique, the book wanders amid the wonderous possibilities of conspiring with youth as they take up educations across time and space. For educators and researchers, the book aims to show educational life beyond schooling logics and against the hierarchical categories that too often define immigrant-origin youth's educational lives. Bursting from these moments are possibilities to challenge the way things are and rethink the everyday work and purpose of teaching and research. The work enacted throughout this book pushes toward a reconceptualization of the very meaning and logics of education. Beyond the horizon of inclusion and success, educational communities can construct places of breathing, hospitable boundaries, offering particular potentialities and trajectories for those who participate. Ultimately, this book works toward an emergent educational otherwise. Before moving toward this otherwise, I begin with an interrogation of how marginalization emerges and operates in the schooling of immigrant-origin youth.

CHAPTER 1

Questioning Marginalization and Schooling

> The best way to appreciate how heroic was this construction of vision is to notice what fell outside its field of vision
>
> —James Scott, *Seeing Like a State*

Margins are quite central to education. What knowledge sits where within curriculums? How can other ways of knowing move toward a center? Why are some people pushed aside? What can be done to better include those who fall to the edges? These are questions with which curriculum theorists and philosophers of education routinely grapple. Likewise, schools ask themselves questions about their students: Who is doing well? Which students are "at risk" of failing and dropping out? Concerns with margins extend to the very roots of the U.S. school history. Horace Mann and others dreamed in the 19th century, conjuring the common school as an achievement of universal education. Within their framework of who counted as everyone, they imagined schools becoming places of complete inclusion, welcoming students regardless of race, class, gender, or national origin for a free public education. In favor of the common good of U.S. society, "universal education is centre and circumference," a totality capable of washing away any margins (Mann, 1868, p. 638). The history of schooling in the United States has, in many ways, been an ongoing search for margins in pursuit of this dream. Schools, research, and policy interrogate over and over why marginalization happens, how it is made, and what can be done to "solve" it. Of course, the dream of educational structures free from exclusion, risk, and all that marginalization entails, resides in a time yet to come. Marginalization in schools and elsewhere persists, predominantly impacting queer, working-class and racially and linguistically minoritized students.

Thinking of margins is inherently bound up in thinking about borders. Schools fundamentally concern themselves with finding the people who belong within their borders. Who, they ask, are the subjects of our place? Who are the people of our community? International discussions about "out-of-school" youth, the right of undocumented youth to attend free public schooling in the United States, or issues of truancy, questions of inclusion, access, and belonging fill discourses about the many borders that assemble around and within schools. Pablo learned English as he listened to folks talking on the subway. He made music in his free time. He found himself at the center of these educations. Yet, within school, he became marginalized. His educational work fell outside of the desirable borders of education. Pablo was considered "at-risk," placed in a "low" ESL classroom.

At the same time, the borders that help produce margins are not merely used to keep these things out. Harsha Walia (2021) builds on Angela Davis to suggest that borders also keep in. The same security guards who routinely rechecked Pablo on his way into school also stood between Pablo and the weighty exit doors, keeping him inside the school building. Mechanisms that rendered labels of risk onto Pablo also locked him into this category. Marginalization traveled with him, a difficult status to escape. All of this is to say that certain ways of knowing and being move through the school doors. New people and new knowledges are regularly included. But bordering regimes construct space and curriculum that marginalize or push out much else. In the liberal, multicultural capitalist system that defines U.S. education, the impulses of universal education carry marginalizing effects.

To these issues, I add questions of why lines have been drawn in this way and how they might be unmade. The terms *at risk, troublemaker,* and *dropout,* and many others, are categories that are made and deployed as a way to pursue the dream of universal education while strangely relying on and producing stable notions of the margins. Yet margins are not so simple as the kids who struggle in school or the kinds of knowledges not fully included in a curriculum. One might also consider margins as relational. They appear, move, vanish, or thin out depending on the context. Seeing margins in this way shifts the terrain to ask whose margins, which margins, and when margins exist. For instance, according to almost any administrator working in New York City, immigrant-origin youth in the 2020s would be considered marginalized if they do not finish high school. Yet a century earlier, it was common for any student to not finish high school. Or knowledge that is marginalized in one place—with youth succeeding in schools "despite" their knowledge and identity (e.g., Chang, 2016)—might be affirmed in other places such as with family and community.

While I devote much space in this book to challenging marginalizing labels like "at risk," these things carry very real effects. Miguel fought against the labels that sought to marginalize him, but he also worked to better succeed in school. Marginalization is not exclusive to immigrant-origin students and is not synonymous with exclusion or oppression. Yet there are distinct ways that immigrant-origin students have been actively pushed to the margins in schools. Stromquist (2012) points to ways that schools in the United States, even in their efforts to include, marginalize and limit the formal educational opportunities of immigrant (specifically Latinx) youth. These borders are, furthermore, made and maintained by white supremacy (Cabrera & Corces-Zimmerman, 2019; Rosa & Flores, 2017). Linguistic and cultural hierarchies bolster the scaffolding, pushing multilingual, racialized kids toward one kind of margin.

A VERY BRIEF OVERVIEW OF MARGINS AND SCHOOLING IMMIGRANT-ORIGIN YOUTH

Marginalization in schools can be linked to the dominant structures of schooling. Tyack (1976) points to the rise of compulsory education, in the early 20th century for primary school and mid-20th century for secondary school, as times when attending and completing school became a statistical and discursive norm for young people. Consequently, those struggling in schools or "dropping out" were pushed to school's margins. From an institutional perspective, marking students on the educational margins became a question of including and successfully moving students through school. With this shift, many groups' educations (including knowledges and values) moved toward (or further toward) precarious, subjugated places.

For immigrant-origin youth, marginalization has defined much of the history of their relationship to schooling. The very start of compulsory education emerged from perceived delinquency and "uneducatedness" of immigrant youth. Tyack (1976) writes that "immigrant children in crowded cities, reformers complained, were leading disorderly lives, schooled by the street and their peers" (p. 363). Students' very inclusion emerged from marginalization. The pursuit of universal education included finding groups like immigrant children and including them in the moral and intellectual norms of schooling. In this way, the production of margins is something quite violent. Suggesting that immigrant youth are marginalized affirms linguistic, racial, and civic norms (Rodríguez, 2018). Students are marginalized when schools perceive them as lacking linguistic competency. Their marginalization assumes a deficit of knowledge and way of being that runs against the normative grain of schooling. The issue here is thus not that of any individual or school but of how schools exist within and are tasked with the maintenance of a social order bound to whiteness and citizenship.

Even moments of inclusion and success include marginalization. For instance, since the 1982 *Plyler v. Doe* decision, public schools in the United States have been for, at least legally speaking, the youth who arrive at their doors regardless of immigration status. Schools may not ask about or use knowledge of immigration status to alter a student's access to public schooling. And yet, as Mangual Figueroa (2012) notes, immigrant-origin families labeled as undocumented still face resistance in enrolling in schools. Once enrolled in schools, many youth face persistent forms of marginalization, manifesting through challenges such as low attendance or high attrition (Gibson & Bejínez, 2002). In positive and negative ways, schools take up a battery of interventions to respond to perceived needs of recently immigrated youth. Language programs, acculturation, and other inclusion mechanisms gently coat the shared histories of immigration and marginalization in U.S. schools.

Issues of marginalization may also be inverted. Researchers and educators may ask not how to "solve" marginalization but may ask why something like linguistic diversity becomes read as a "lack" of English and thus becomes marginalized in schools (relatedly, Flores & Rosa, 2015). In a similar vein, Varenne and McDermott (1998) show how structures of success are built on failure. They point out that "it is not by accident that the fundamental question in educational research is phrased negatively: Why can't Johnny read?" (p. 4). Asking why a group or individual has become marked on the margins leads to a question of how the norms of schools and criteria for inclusion/success have been constructed. In this vein, why do curricular material like textbooks so rarely include Latinx narratives (Noboa, 2021) and dominantly describe immigration in ways that reinforce marginalization or deeply conditional inclusion?

Education beyond marginalization is further explored in later chapters, but it is also important to note that immigrant communities have regularly contested these structures. Striving for different kinds of inclusion in schools, working against the material effects of marginalization, and building alternative educational spaces have all been regular parts of the work of immigrant-origin communities. "These counter-spaces," Conchas (2016) describes, "begin to fill the cracks in the schoolyard that create disparity, failure, and marginalization" (p. 4). Even as communities resist and respond to marginalization, its effects deeply impact immigrant-origin youth.

MARGINALIZATION AND AN ETHNOGRAPHIC PRESENT

In her frequently cited book, *Subtractive Schooling*, Angela Valenzuela (1999) examined issues of marginalization with Mexican American youth. She explored what she calls the "subtractive" schooling experiences of youth who "oppose a schooling process that disrespects them; they oppose not education but schooling" (Valenzuela, 1999, p. 5). Beyond the statistics or terms like *dropout crisis* mentioned in Chapter 1, in New York City in the 2010s, subtractive schooling remained a marginalizing reality for immigrant-origin youth. Following Valenzuela's study, Bartlett and García (2011) undertook an examination of a newcomer school that is "additive." They looked at the learning trajectories of students in a school that "builds on and extends the social, cultural, and linguistic assets brought by multilingual, diverse student populations, and aims to prepare bicultural and bilingual students to negotiate their complex worlds" (pp. 21–22). Where a long history of schooling combats marginalization with assimilationist means, newcomer schools offer a curriculum lined with cultural and linguistic affirmation.

Without discounting the generative, supportive work of these schools, and while championing the new educational trajectories born of the possibilities of public schooling, it is important to note that students still struggle and fall to the margins in these affirmative settings. If students would be marginalized in other, "subtractive" settings, and they do not find schooling success in spaces like newcomer schools, what is to be done? What about those youth who fall to the margins of margins? Such questions arose sharply during a conversation with a prominent newcomer school administrator at the beginning of this project. As I asked about how they understand categories like "risk" and posed questions about how they respond to students who struggle in school, the administrator abruptly stopped me. "We're trying to help every student," they explained, "but nobody's ever going to get to 100% of these things." In other words, the grand success of a newcomer school with over 90% graduation rate will still have students who struggle, become "at risk," and drop out. Even in the dream of universal education, and even in an affirmative space meant to welcome and uphold, margins remain.

Conversations like this one, and a deep concern about how educators and researchers might respond to this issue of "the margins of margins," ignited the first parts of this research project. I wondered both about the making and maintenance of structures that marginalized difference and about schools as social institutions that are both tasked with welcoming immigrant-origin youth and continuing the social order. I also wondered about youth whose educational lives and identities exceeded and oozed from the ways dominant conceptions of schooling defined them. Within schools that intentionally centered cultural life as part of the school curriculum, it seemed as though education ultimately contorted and reformed until it could fit into the container called "school." Education, much like language, was ultimately not something that one does, a regular practice of everyday life. Even within the newcomer school, it was still seen as something obtained and possessed, centrally defined. Still something relying on margins.

On the last day of school in his junior year, Leo shared a poem during the final assembly. "I am mixed," he said as he described complex feelings and racial identities, a series of fractures and splits among place, history, and politics. As he finished reading, students and teachers clapped with uneven hesitation. The moment stood in stark contrast to the more rigidly defined procedures of cultural celebration and end-of-year activities. It also stood in contrast to the way those in the school typically responded to Leo. Leo was often seen as something of an academic superstar. Racial and linguistic social forces marginalized Leo in New York City, but his grades and overall academic success had not marked him as marginalized within WISH. And yet, here was an example of his knowledge and manner of expression marginally fitting into the school. The long educational journey of Leo exploring his identity was pushed aside, received with apprehension and uncertainty. In some of our chats, Leo discussed how these facets of himself were not part of the school curriculum. Of course, the poem did ultimately appear within the school, albeit in an unsettling way for many in the school. But, in the course of more than a year of working with the youth involved in this project, and in spending hundreds of hours at WISH, there were countless instances when creative acts, ideas, and identities lingered or fell to the margins. Tensions arose as cultural and linguistic practices moved away from the demands of academic outcomes and the ways in which school sites have defined these terms. The margins are thus not only the marking of bodies within an institutional space. Ways of being and educational pursuits that veer from or challenge dominant discourse also become marginalized.

Understanding the obstinance of margins—and recognizing that schools ultimately reside within larger social structures—the story might stop here. This book does not propose a totalizing solution to the problem of margins, because none exist. There is also productive strategy and resistance found in margins. There is hope in expanding models such as newcomer schools, resisting the violence of English-only programs, and centering additive educational approaches. Perhaps the goal for those who want to conspire with and support immigrant-origin youth is simply to keep pushing for better funding, continually improving impactful interventions, and finding routes that can positively alter the educational trajectories of immigrant youth. Even as the margins appear, the goal of education work might be nothing more than making them smaller and smaller, "solving" them each time they inevitably appear, and simply "tinkering toward utopia," as Tyack and Cuban (1995) famously described.

This utopian dream lives within the liberal multicultural capitalist imaginary of a fair, just system that only needs to keep reforming toward perfection. It imagines a world with no margins and disguises the fact that margins remain central to these structures. Within this structure, the cultural and linguistic assets immigrant youth bring to school are a matter of diversity, but a diversity "treated as fundamentally individual and private—flavoring but making no political demands on the public sphere" (Abu El-Haj, 2015, p. 115). An increasingly diverse school system, one that includes additive school, may not yet be perfect. Adjustments might be necessary. The real task of education, though, is to include more immigrant youth in this "nation of immigrants." In doing so, this system, of whiteness, of bordering regimes, relying on the complex mechanism called school, violently maintains the order of things.

As mentioned in the Introduction, the story of immigration and education in the United States is dominantly framed by twin binaries of success/failure and inclusion/exclusion. In research and media, stories appear as schooling success (commonly, success through or despite) or the failure of various structures to support immigrant-origin youth. Schools frame individual educational life through academic outcomes, sticking to school goals and identities that fit within a success/failure binary. Questions of inclusion and exclusion within schools and society entangle with all moments of U.S. educational history. As Patel (2013) suggests, "the struggle for inclusion is the bedrock of individual, social, and national identity." And, "newcomer immigrant youth fully embody this struggle" (p. 1). Of course, the twin binaries are not the only concerns when considering the purposes of schooling. Policymakers, educators, activists, and researchers have explored school as a place of self-discovery, political practice, and much else. But the twin binaries remain driving forces of schooling. It is within these binaries that schools make sense of and respond to marginalized youth. The twin binaries dictate the conditions of schooling for marginalized youth. They act to prove conditions of equity or oppression. Despite this dominance and the seeming trap of utopia, there are other ways of considering educational life and other ways of studying with immigrant youth. As Leo's poem reveals, there are educational practices that resist the utopian dream of universal education and wander toward educational worlds beyond and against the constructs of liberal multiculturalism.

CONCLUSION

Across time and place, educational margins appear and remain. Dominant anti-immigrant policy demands inclusion along assimilationist lines. Even within the thin sliver of culturally and linguistically affirmative schools, marginalization persists. Policymakers and researchers are not ignorant of this fact, but most approaches tweak and revise, hoping to improve educational outcomes without disrupting the very systems that create marginalization.

The complex histories of youth's lives and the intellectual, unrelenting, ecstatic educations of this book's participants contest these systems at their very roots. I suggest that if we can peel back the "partition of the sensible" (Rancière, 2001)—that policing border that maintains the social order, says who can do what, who knows what, and who is authorized to be on margins or in the center—educational research may come to listen to, respect, and care for educational lives lived against the order of things. In doing so, perhaps educators, researchers, and activists can disrupt the notion that those on the margins only need better reforms. Perhaps, we might even find a way to prolong such a disruption, creating radical understandings of education that resist social order reshaping. Before further exploring such disruptions, I now turn from seeing how marginalization produces forms of exclusion toward a history of the different mechanisms of inclusion schools have used for immigrant-origin students.

CHAPTER 2

A History of Immigrant-Origin Students in the U.S. Education System

> When a newcomer arrives in America,
> He will surely be seized and put in the wooden building
>
> —from poems of detained Chinese newcomers, read by Eddie Wong

In *The One Best System*, David Tyack (1974) explores the gradual centralization and urbanization of the U.S. school system. He traces a shift and an ongoing push toward a singular systemic model for schools. This system provides an alleged response to questions of how to best educate students and create schools that reflect and maintain U.S. society. The one best system emerged and took shape in the late 19th and the early 20th century as bureaucratization, urbanization, and educational leaders drove an isomorphic shift toward schools across the country sharing values, structures, and curriculum. Of course, the borders of the school system, much like any system, crack and rupture as students, teachers, and communities negotiate and challenge the system. Even at a broad scale, the one best system is constantly, as Tyack suggested nearly 50 years ago, "under fire." Depending on one's reading of the history of schools in the United States, it may never have taken hold. Yet a one best system, an imagining of a singular and unifying answer to forming and doing schooling, creeps through U.S. history (Howell, 2020).

Immigrant-origin students have gone to school in and been part of this one best system. Noguera (2003) points out that immigrant youth are "at the mercy of 'the one best system'" (p. 80). They attend school within a U.S. system that often rejects their identities. But systems within, beyond, and against the one best system have also emerged to consider how to educate immigrant-origin students.

Unlike the unification Tyack tracks, schooling immigrant-origin youth in the United States has rarely, if ever, been so singular. Moreover, particularly since the 1960s, the policy elites Tyack identifies as driving the formation of a one best system have not shared a vision for schooling immigrant-origin youth (Salomone, 2008). What has taken shape beyond a system of exclusion has been a variety of systems that have sought "best answers."

Best answers have long and complex histories,[1] ones that seep into and heavily influence the educational lives of students like the youth who participated in this project. Ways of educating immigrant-origin youth have taken different forms—at times aligning or coexisting and sometimes competing—and shifted, swaying back and forth through school's rotations like Foucault's pendulum. They express often-contrasting politics and values and offer varied pedagogical beliefs. School systems have not come together to shape a unified system for educating immigrant students in the United States. Policy elites driving and sustaining a one best system accept and promote multiple answers. Where the one best system conjures a singular, universalizable figure of students, the way schools and broader U.S. society have racialized, classed, and generally made sense of immigrant groups has historically been—and remains—varied and competitive. As a report from the Obama administration suggests, "there's no one approach" to educating immigrant students. Instead, a variety of "factors such as state law . . ." or students' "age, formal education background or [first language] literacy" contribute to producing different answers (Faulkner-Bond et al., 2012, p. xxii). Schools view immigrant-origin students as requiring different models or answers that depend on perceived educational needs of different groups and contingent on political forces.

These various answers have formed their own winding histories, ones that morphed, coalesced, and crisscrossed other systems. They have competed for oxygen in educational ecosystems, operated as isolated answers, and faded away and emerged again at different points in time. They have spilled outside the one best system and operated within it. Depending on the time, the population, politics, perceived needs, and community demands, different systems have formed and evolved. These students require assimilation. A school here should focus on cultural identities. Where the one best system acts as a kind of Standard Model governing the laws of schooling for all those who participate, the history of schooling for immigrant-origin students may, potentially, be read as a pluriverse of best answers. That is not to say that these answers came to constitute unique worlds untethered from the one best system. Different understandings of assimilation, for instance, have stood in direct conflict with one another. Rather, throughout this chapter, I pose a question of how schools as institutions grappled with questions of inclusion and how these different models relate to and depart from a one best system.

I use the term *pluriverse* in two ways. First, pluriverse is a response to the one best system, seeing the instructional models, policies, and general approaches to schooling immigrant-origin youth. These educational approaches show different governing rules than those of the broader system but exist within it. Consider, for example, a basketball game in a park. While it resides and operates within the park, the rules on the basketball court take on their own life. Likewise, the answers explored in this chapter largely take place within the one best system but constitute their own, subordinate worlds. ESL classrooms have, for instance, formed and operated as places with their own kinds of rules and rhythms—loosely constituting a distinct world within the one best system. These worlds have been both affirmative practices to welcome immigrant-origin students on their own educational terms and exclusionary interventions that intentionally segregated them from opportunities offered in the one best system. It is here that I "think like a school," examining these worlds from an institutional perspective. Who, I ask, were the assumed subjects of these systems? What kinds of people did they aim to produce?

Second, pluriverse is not just a word for different educational interventions. It is, rather, a way of exploring the different forms of what is "real" to open up new understandings of what is possible (Escobar, 2020). The pluriverse here is a matter of collective, liberatory worldmaking. This chapter mostly emphasizes the first use of this term. I trace brief histories of how educational interventions emerged and congealed into practiced educational models. But throughout this chapter and in subsequent chapters, I explore collectively made educational worlds that often emerge and operate in opposition to (rather than within) the "one best system."

The worlds explored in this chapter move with some form of chronology. I start by touching on the English-only and directly assimilationist approaches of the late 19th and the early 20th century before looking at the educational worlds formed within the Americanization movement. These sections only hint at schools seeing immigrant-origin students as needing specific interventions. I then focus on the educational worlds born of the mid-1960s through the mid-1980s. There are many worlds I leave un(der)explored. Yet I argue that bilingual education in the 1960s marked a time in which the United States remade immigration as part of a liberal multicultural imaginary occurring within educational spaces. Racism and xenophobic exclusion remained, but within this shift, more affirmative systems for educating immigrant-origin students took hold. The chapter concludes with the emergence of newcomer schools as a new universe, a more distinct world that birthed new educational understandings of immigrant youth.

A few caveats here. These worlds are not the progressive march to finding the "right" educational models for immigrant-origin students. Many of these worlds connect, but the point is to show how this long history of inclusion bears weight on WISH and the youth participants. Additionally, I dominantly focus on New York City and Latinx youth but include examples from different groups and places throughout the chapter. Finally, in "thinking like a school," these histories largely work from the perspective of institutions and institutional actors (Tyack, 1974, uses the term *schoolmen*) shaping the pluriverse, though I attend to the complex interplay of actors ranging from national policies to coalitional community work that has contributed to the formations of these universes.

EARLY HISTORY OF "AMERICANIZATION" FOR IMMIGRANT YOUTH

In the late 19th and the early 20th century, with the influx of millions of immigrant families, students with diverse language and cultural needs became an increasing concern for educational policymakers. In places like New York City, immigrant-origin students faced segregated schools, poverty, and overcrowding. Schools sought to address these issues in some ways, but the main focus remained assimilating students into U.S. society. Writing about the early 20th century, Tyack (1974) describes how

> School people did make adjustments in the system to fit immigrants' children in certain ways: steamer classes for older children who did not speak English, a new stress on hygiene and civics, new opportunities for after-school recreation and continuation schooling, for example. But by and large they believed that the child had to fit the system. (p. 254)

Reese (2005) recounts the effects of this approach, quoting a minister's words from the common school era. "'Children go into the schools,' he said, 'English, Scottish, Irish, German, Danish, Norwegian, French—and all come out American'" (p. 51). Schools in the 19th and the start of the 20th century were concerned with expediently Americanizing students. Policy and practice actively "eradicate[ed] the foreign background of the children" (Berrol, 1969, p. 223). Some accommodations could be made, but overall, immigrant youth would be included in schools insofar as they adapted to schools as they already existed.

The system did not universally require students to Americanize through language. Bybee et al. (2014) describe that until the 20th century, a national language of instruction had not been established. The authors point out that, though linguistic practices were far from democratic (indigenous languages never received the same legibility as German, for example), using multiple languages to communicate in schools was common practice (see also, August & Kaestle, 1997). Americanization, while an early and persistent goal, remained amorphous until the 1910s.

Beneath the veneer of the emerging one best system, a different universe bubbled to life. After World War I, an increasing sentiment that "immigrants needed to learn English [so] that they could learn the U.S. Constitution, understand the government of their new country, and become assimilated into American culture" helped frame an "Americanization movement" (Cavanaugh, 1996, p. 42). Americanization responded to concerns about immigrants challenging the foundations of U.S. society. As its name suggests, the movement aimed to "Americanize" "thousands [of immigrants] who live together in 'colonies' in the congested sections of great cities, still holding to the language, customs, and manners they brought with them" (Thorngate, as cited in NeCamp, 2014, p. 2). Where previous models offered little to no variation, seeking only to extinguish immigrant identity in the pursuit of assimilation, the Americanization movement began asking specific questions about the types of schooling experiences needed to Americanize immigrant students. "The teaching of English to foreigners" became "a topic requiring unique knowledge" (Mahoney, as cited in Ray, 2013, p. 22). Adjacent to "regular" school life, new mechanisms took shape to include immigrant students in the one best system.

In many states, new compulsory schooling laws were often bundled with English-only laws (Lleras-Muney & Shertzer, 2012).

English-only, beyond a strict policy for schools in the United States, generated models of curriculum and instruction seen as necessary for immigrant students' assimilation. Dayton-Wood (2008) points out that this period "marks an important moment when language pedagogy began to emerge, aided by a proliferation of textbooks" directed at immigrant students (p. 398). Yet, many policymakers felt that "the strain immigrants placed on existing social structures . . . would stretch the existing educational system to a point at which few students would receive adequate education" (NeCamp, 2014, pp. 2–3).

Schooling immigrant students would require something else—specific times, spaces, and ways of teaching—to match perceived needs and ensure the stability of the one best system. A battery of teacher training courses, textbooks, and teaching manuals emerged after World War I and forged a different, if not-quite-distinct world, for schooling immigrant students. Ray (2013) outlines a multitude of training and instructional materials, including scripted lessons on vocabulary or exercises about letter writing (see also, Mirel, 2010). Within the segregated neighborhoods of immigrant communities, these manners of teaching entwined with literacy instruction, civic education, and teaching about presidents and American holidays.

Yet progressive notions of inclusion and anti-immigrant desires to "fully Americanize" generated neither full belonging nor a benevolent, welcoming one best system. Americanization presents a possibility that schooling could include (a certain assumed educable) all, that anyone could become an American "by declaring a desire to do so and committing oneself to a set of liberal political principles, which include democracy, liberty, equality, and individual achievement" (Pavlenko, 2002, p. 165). In those first decades of the 20th century, immigrant groups primarily arriving from southern and eastern Europe were not fully racialized as white. Additionally, despite schools surfacing as sites of Americanization, the federal government viewed immigrants through hierarchical lenses, ranking groups based on "assimilability" (Schmid, 2001). Assimilationist instructional models masked persistent forms of schooling and societal exclusion. Different instructional models used to include these new groups rested on the assumption that "the difference between a member of the American nationality and one of some foreign nationality was essentially a matter of knowledge, and that therefore could be corrected by education" (Fairchild, 1926, p. 166). Yet preparation and acculturation for a unifying one best system becomes impossible when the United States sticks in place hierarchical cultural and racial structures. Moreover, this notion of

Americanization belies the racist, anti-immigrant structures embedded in U.S. schools and the nation in general.

Understanding these tensions, researchers pose ongoing questions about the success of the Americanization movement in schools. Olneck (1989) points out, though, that the "movement is significant as an effort to secure cultural and ideological hegemony through configuration of the symbolic order" (Olneck, 1989, p. 399). That is, the Americanization movement further entrenched a normative imagining of who and what counted as belonging in the United States. In schools, the movement also solidified the idea that different educational models might be needed to achieve this form of assimilation. Americanization approaches in schools formed perhaps not a distinct world but something jutting out, protruding. Perhaps a proto-world.

The symbolic order found in the Americanization movement echoes across the history of schooling, butting up against present worlds of immigrant-origin youth. California's Proposition 227, a bill that lasted from 1998 to 2016, moved instruction almost entirely toward an English-only approach. It is a notorious example of enacting specific mechanisms to segregate and restrict the cultural and linguistic practices of students. Malakoff and Hakuta (1990) directly link ongoing English-only movements to the Americanization movement. Today, though Arizona remains the only state with such English-only laws, reverberations of ideas and approaches from the Americanization movement continue, bearing weight on the schooling worlds of immigrant-origin youth. So, too, do the worlds that arose after the Americanization movement.

SYSTEMS IN THE GAP

Passing the Johnson-Reed Immigration Act in 1924 severely limited the number of people who could enter the United States. Legally, the period of 1924 through 1965 marked a shift from "regulation to restriction." With this lull, Ngai (2004) identifies the period after Americanization as a historiographic "gap" for research on immigration, something that extends to schooling. As a matter of a practice gap (rather than historical research), Malakoff and Hakuta (1990) point out that "from the 1920s until the 1960s, little attention was given to the language needs of non-English speaking students" (p. 30). This period also marks the beginning of immigration becoming more directly a question of legality. Understanding the shift and gap, how did these new configurations play out in schools? What kind of educational worlds took hold in an age of restriction? An unspooling of different educational worlds would not explode until the early 1960s, but throughout this period educating immigrant students required different answers and systems that never sat quite right within the entirety of the one best system.

With immigration ebbing, the one best system could more easily assert itself. In the 1930s and 1940s, classrooms occasionally became more diverse, at least in terms of immigrant-origin communities (Montalto, 1977). This period also saw rumblings of culturally affirmative teaching. Selig notes that "restriction of immigration in the 1920s redirected debate from political to cultural terms, which paradoxically allowed a pluralistic approach to culture to begin to take hold." At this time, "progressive educators and activists could offer a more positive but romanticized vision of ethnic cultures" (cited in Johnson & Pak, 2019, p. 5). Increasingly, approaches that resisted total assimilation led scholars to frame this work as part of an "intercultural education movement" (Montalto, 1977). Likewise, the 1920s through the 1950s saw restriction on English-only laws. In Nebraska, Hawaii, and elsewhere courts affirmed a right of students to learn in languages other than English (Nieto, 2009). Such work still functioned to generate a one best system/melting pot image of U.S. school systems.

As with the Americanization movement, these images did not suggest an equal system or inclusive world. Despite legal changes to English-only laws, Bybee et al. (2014) point out that schools heavily favored sink-or-swim models. "Few or no remedial services were provided and students generally remained in the same grade level until enough English was mastered to advance in subject matter understanding" (p. 139). Multilingual students were still viewed as lacking intelligence and ability. Schmid (2001) further describes how "the majority of studies by psychologists consistently reported evidence that bilingual children suffered from a language handicap . . . bilingual youth were found to be inferior in intelligence test scores" (p. 66). Even with the 1947 *Mendez v. Westminster*[2] Supreme Court decision that ended segregation of Mexican American students, exclusion and segregation still characterized schooling worlds of linguistically and racially minoritized students (Gándara & Aldana, 2014).

As legalized migration and deportation "came of age" during this period (Ngai, 2004), the United States routinely deported children. Schools directly participated in this emergent carceral practice, setting a tone for the kinds of education immigrant-origin students would encounter for decades to come. Goodman (2020) points out that in the 1930s through 1950s deportation was enforced along moral and social lines. Political radicals, those engaged in sex work, or anyone else deemed "undesirable" often became targets of deportation, along with their children. Inclusion in this system demanded certain kinds of conformity and legibility. There is a direct link here to intercultural education. Even non-restrictionist and culturally affirmative approaches to educating immigrant students centered on notions of societal contributions and economic productivity. Intercultural education generated a system of celebrating not simply immigrants' cultural lives but also how their culture contributed to the broader American system (Fleegler, 2005). This period drew exclusionary boundaries around schools, shifting the responsibility of assimilation onto students and families.

While no distinct worlds took hold in this "gap," questions of who belonged, why, and how cultural identities might be used leave lingering impacts on the different educational universes immigrant students encounter today. Notably, schooling approaches bound to notions of "deservingness" reverberate, linking belonging and legitimacy in schools and other sites to how immigrants contribute to the project of making and maintaining the United States (Patel, 2015). Challenges to English-only laws and ideas of attending to immigrant students' cultural identities also seeped into the 1950s and 1960s, as the rumblings of Americanization or intercultural education exploded into new, distinct educational worlds.

THE RISE OF BILINGUAL EDUCATION AND THE HISTORY OF NEWCOMER SCHOOLS

In 1965, the United States passed the Hart-Celler Act, ending the national origins quota system put in place by the Johnson-Reed Act. At this point, the number of people immigrating to the United States rose drastically. The majority of people immigrating to New York City came from East Asia, the Caribbean, and Latin America (Foner, 2000). This shift in numbers and population coincided with schools codifying decades of community work from immigrant-origin and linguistically minoritized groups pushing for greater educational rights. The Bilingual Education Act of 1968 and the *Lau v. Nichols* Supreme Court decision helped shift the terrain. In New York City, the Aspira Consent Decree of 1974 also established a right to bilingual education

(Santiago, 1986). These laws determined that students had a right to linguistically affirmative instruction, instruction that did not have to occur within the confines of school's traditional structure. The Bilingual Education Act, for instance, asserts that *"equal education* was not the same as *identical education"* (Malakoff & Hakuta, 1990, p. 32, emphasis in original). Of course, these laws were not totalizing. And, educational worlds continued exceeding and slipping from the confines of legal, institutional makings. Yet, this confluence of increasing immigration and changing policy contributed to an explosion of educational worlds in New York City and elsewhere. Bilingual education classes, ESL teacher certification, and much else took shape.

Familiar teaching models such as submersion/"sink or swim" continued in many schools. Others identified divergent paths to English language acquisition as well as strategies for attending to students' linguistic and cultural identities. In this section, I highlight three worlds that took shape during this time, looking at how they emerged, how they relate to the one best system, the rules and logics driving them, and how they have influenced educational experiences for the people participating in this ethnographic project.

The educational worlds that emerged and congealed in the 1960s and 1970s generated different classrooms, new pedagogies, and unique instructional materials. It is important to note, however, that these worlds still operated within the spaces and structures of a system that all too often saw these worlds, and the students within them, as inferior. Deficit language streaks across the institutionalization of these worlds. These new worlds worked, schools suggested, to help students "catch up" or correct their "Limited English Proficiency" (Santiago, 1986; Schmid, 2001). Moreover, detractors often attacked programs as being ineffective or inappropriate (August & Kaestle, 1997; Padilla, 1990).

Where schools have legitimated these worlds, they do so insofar as linguistic or cultural affirmation supports the twin pillars of inclusion and success. New programs created throughout the 1960s and 1970s, while creating separate programs and structures, directly targeted stronger enrollment for immigrant-origin students. In fact, major legal rulings like *Lau* offered little in terms of necessary programs, focusing instead on a need to better include students within school districts (Gándara & Aldana, 2014). These programs also directly aimed to bolster student achievement and increase graduation rates (Carrasquillo et al., 2014). It is within these twin binaries that schools have shaped different educational worlds for immigrant-origin and plurilingual students.

Examining the English as a Second Language (ESL) Classroom

A first world comes into perspective around targeted, separate language instruction. With roots as deep as the common school as well as the 1940s (Fries, 1945), this approach expanded throughout the 1960s and 1970s. One of the most common approaches here is an ESL classroom. ESL classes involve pulling students out from classrooms to intensely focus on learning English. Teachers during these brief periods may be certified as ESL teachers. After their ESL class, students return to the "sink-or-swim" model. The structure of ESL classes varies widely, but the focus is on immersing students in learning English. Students could also/alternatively learn in "sheltered instruction," where students identified as ELLs receive instruction in a specific subject in English. These approaches emphasize impermanence and assimilation.

From one reading, the use of ESL classrooms is a way of fitting students into schools with minimal changes to their structuring. In fact, Moran (2010) describes structured English immersion as a way of legislating the one best system for students studying English. Yet, much like the Americanization movement, while operating within a larger bureaucratic framework, ESL classrooms reveal different rules and logics. For the 30 to 60 minutes in which students enter these spaces, a blip of a wormhole opens, taking emergent bilingual students to another place, one of both exclusion and possibility. Spatial separation is notable here. Attacked for being a segregationist practice, ESL and related programs occur in distinct spaces, ones marked as different from "traditional" schooling (Valdez & Gregoire, 1990). In later chapters, I describe the productive, subversive potential of these spaces, but ESL classrooms provide a clear message—some students do not yet fit within the one best system. Of course, ESL students are not the only ones spatially removed from the rest of the school day. This also says little about the disproportionate classification of immigrant-origin students and language learners in special education classrooms (Fernandez & Inserra, 2013).

This world is not simply spatially separate. ESL classrooms have also generated distinct pedagogical models. What was largely trial and error in the 1940s and 1950s (Valdez & Gregoire, 1990) became specific practices demanding certifications. ESL methods vary and constantly shift (Barrot, 2014), but since the expansion and professionalization of ESL teaching in the 1960s (for instance, the Teachers of English to Speakers of Other Languages Association formed in the mid-1960s), pedagogical practices have been grounded in a scientific methodology.

Students might practice vocabulary, undertake composition exercises, or engage in structured conversation. Teachers and students may infuse critical understandings and cultural identities into daily classroom life (Duff & Uchida, 1997). Detailed materials created for these classrooms differ from those found during the rest of the day (McGrath, 2013). But ESL instruction dominantly shares an understanding that this space is a technical one. Far from the dream of Brazilian educator and philosopher Paulo Freire, whose idea that literacy means reading both "the word and the world," workbooks and other curricular materials of this time emphasized memorization and recitation in pursuit of mastery of language. Classroom practices led to achieving the goal of language acquisition and, eventually, leaving the impermanent space of an ESL classroom. Understandings of language acquisition as a technical process within a temporary world can be traced back to the formations of teaching English as a formal discipline (Fries, 1945). While such theories of ESL have been heavily criticized, they remain a common understanding and approach to teaching immigrant-origin and multilingual students. Divorced from the learner, the teaching of English leaves behind identities and cultures, creating a world outside of the rest of school, a temporary vacuum to make up for what is missing.

The world of ESL that came to be in the 1960s and 1970s, and the one that continues today, thus rests on foundations of deficit. Referring to the fight for more affirmative classrooms, Santiago (1986) points out how students were relegated to "ESL classes until they gained superficial proficiency in the English language" (p. 158). Teaching in English and without profound recognition of students' home languages (García, 2010), ESL classes dominantly follow the subtractive bilingualism model (Lambert, 1975). Where a student speaking English as their first language might add a second or third language through elective courses, ESL students are assumed to speak their first language only as needed until they can master English.

> The idea of labelling a student an ELL is that he or she is to be seen as a clearly defined non-native speaker of English from a particular ethnolinguistic group, a constructed 'other' who will learn English (specifically standardised American English), and by implication acculturate towards Anglo-American lifestyle (and perhaps values) over time. (Nero, 2005, p. 196)

What is needed, the thinking goes, is an approach to fix what is missing, to bring students into the fold of the one best system.

Schools also dominantly view ESL as the most efficient system for educating emergent bilingual students. García (2010) points out that ESL classes have become more prominent in recent years in New York City, where "more than two-thirds of all eligible children" were "in ESL classes that increasingly 'shelter' English and make no use of students' home language practices" (García, 2010, p. 27). While families and educators have pushed for educational worlds that reflect plurilingualism and diverse cultural identities, schools have reinforced this technocratic system on the grounds that it is more effective (Dillon, 1994). Importantly, it is this general approach, a separate classroom for specific ESL instruction, that WISH has used since its inception. The perceived technical effectiveness of ESL instruction has led to the imposition of ESL for WISH's students, even as teachers and administrators push for bilingual education.

The Many Worlds of Bilingual Education

Bilingual education is at once a sibling world and one set in opposition to ESL. The emergence of bilingual education as a national concern coincided with Chicanx student walkouts/blowouts in East L.A., the rise of the Young Lords, and communities across the country pushing for stronger educational rights (Rebell & Block, 1983). As more and more Latinx families immigrated to New York City, they joined ongoing organizing with predominantly Puerto Rican communities. Fighting for the educational rights of Limited English Proficiency (LEP) children (as Santiago, 1986, puts it) ultimately led the organization Aspira to sue the Board of Education of the City of New York. Representing over 80,000 immigrant and linguistically minoritized children in New York City, Santiago suggests that *Aspira v. Board of Education of the City of New York* in 1974 initiated shifts in affirmatively welcoming children learning English in New York City schools. The fight for bilingual education marks a distinct moment when schools acquiesced, in some ways, forming new educational worlds born of community action.

The Aspira Consent Decree was also built on the expanding precedents of the Bilingual Education Act, which had already piloted bilingual education programs in the 1960s and early 1970s. Arguing that the temporary spaces of ESL classrooms were not enough to support students' needs, *Aspira* helped push toward another kind of educational world. Bilingual education proponents framed it as an inclusive, affirmative space. And yet, the New York City Board of Education fought bilingual programs in the name of integration. Conflating assimilation and integration, they suggested that bilingual education would maintain an already-segregated city (Clark & Batista, 1977). Even still, the number of bilingual teachers doubled between 1975 and 1976 (Santiago, 1986). Though gradual and uneven, bilingual education did take shape in New York City and elsewhere.

Bilingual education takes many forms. It might be "transitional," with students taking classes predominantly in their home languages. Such approaches can blend with ESL, finding other parts of a students' day in sheltered English language instruction. Transitional programs gradually phase out home languages as students learn English. Alternatively, bilingual education might take the form of developmental bilingual education. Similar in structure to transitional bilingual education, developmental bilingual education also seeks to actively maintain students' home languages. Students might also enroll in a two-way or dual-language program. Where transitional programs might be seen as a more attentive version of ESL, something still framed through deficit, dual-language takes an affirmative approach (de Jong, 2011). In other words, many of these programs begin from a "subtractive" perspective, seeking only to work toward language proficiency and readiness for the one best system. Dual language, meanwhile, takes an "additive" approach, forging multilingual and multicultural skills in the process of learning a language (Lambert & Tucker, 1972).

Bilingual education programs have often formed within existing schools, serving either students identified as ELLs or a mix of students identified as "LEP" and "non-LEP." As with ESL, bilingual education includes distinct pedagogies and materials. A report on the Chapter 720 bilingual program (Cochran & Cotayo, 1983), which began at the Louis D. Brandeis High School in New York City in the late 1970s, offers an intriguing example of the array of services, materials, and structures used to create a bilingual program. The report details hiring bilingual secretaries, a bilingual curriculum coordinator, forming a bilingual advisory committee, and developing specific evaluations and assessment instruments for the program. The practices, the people, and the understandings of language and culture all come together to form a different kind of educational world; not subservient to or preparatory for the one best system, but semi-autonomous from its logics and structures.

From their inception, bilingual education programs sought to shift control and funding back to communities and away from the one best system (García et al., 2018). The idea of bilingual education, particularly dual-language programs, is to affirm language and push toward developing "cultural awareness" (Stewner-Manzanares, 1988). Setting the stage for bilingual education, the New York City Board of Education released a policy statement in 1965, asserting that "bilingualism and biculturalism will be encouraged for all pupils, particularly Spanish-speaking ones" (as cited in Jenkins, 1971, p. 14). This sentiment then played out in classrooms. Writing about a school's bilingual program, which started in the 1970s, the school's principal (Morison, 1990) describes how Spanish "is used socially without censure and officially in all school-home communications" (p. 161). The school expanded from a transitional bilingual to a dual-language program, identifying needs to build classrooms around welcoming and affirming students as they are. Where the one best system is white and English-speaking (and listening), bilingual education strives toward plurilingual, culturally affirmative spaces that challenge the whiteness of the broader system. When bilingual education succeeds, students do not need to adapt to the system. Different systems pop up and adapt to students and families.

Against the supremacy of a one best system, bilingual education has faced persistent challenges. They have operated while situated within a system set against aims of valuing students' identities (Flores & García, 2017). Bilingual education programs in the 1980s consequently became "educational ghettos." In many cases, they have been physically relegated to school basements (García et al., 2018). They often became plural but dispossessed worlds. Criticism of bilingual education is often couched in narratives of its alleged "ineffectiveness," an understanding that relies on a narrow scope of academic outcomes and maintains the one best system as a singular reference point (Mujica, 1995). In the 1980s, these attacks helped lay the groundwork for a reemerging English-only movement. William Bennett, Reagan's Secretary of Education, notably critiqued a lack of evidence that students benefited from bilingual education programs. Padilla (1990) suggests that "the mission of U.S. education continues to be the homogenization and assimilation of diverse ethnic, racial, and cultural background children," which stands in contrast to the pluralism of bilingual education (p. 20). García et al. (2018) present the fight for classrooms that reflect students' translanguaging and plural identities as ongoing, but remind that the possibilities embedded in dual-language programs remains "a potential unfulfilled." For some, this potential has been realized in creating whole school models built around immigrant-origin youth.

Newcomer Schools

Immigration numbers grew steadily after 1965, but they intensified in the 1980s and 1990s. The number of people immigrating from the Dominican Republic to New York City rose 165% between 1980 and 1990 (Hernández et al., 1995). Shifts in immigration and student enrollment led to new questions about how to best respond to immigrant-origin students. Friedlander (1991) suggests that "given the recent demographic changes that have altered the face of America's classrooms, school districts have an unprecedented responsibility . . . to reach out to these youngsters and make them full active members of our world" (p. 4). Schools also frequently came to see recently immigrated students as a "strain on resources" (McDonnell & Hill, 1993). Bilingual education, ESL, and other interventions continued, but schools increasingly recognized a need—and families renewed fights—for something else. These shifting issues mix with long histories of exclusion, segregation, and subjugation to which racially and linguistically minoritized students have been routinely submitted (Vélez, 2008). These and other factors set the stage for a new intervention, a more permanent, less transitory world: the newcomer school.

Schools set apart from traditional public schools, sometimes called newcomer schools, have existed since the 19th century. Newcomer schools of the past were partial, scattered scaffolds of English-only acculturation, perhaps a few months of English class to "catch up." The newcomer schools that came to be in the 1980s were something else entirely. Some of these programs did remain temporary, offering one to two intensive and affirmative years in a "family-like environment" (Feinberg, 2000). Other schools pursued something more permanent. Addressing concerns about enrollment, graduation, and college preparedness and centering affirmative approaches in best serving this evolving population of students, the New York City Board of Education partnered with the City University of New York to create a new model for schooling students labeled as ELLs (Fine et al., 2005). When the International High School at LaGuardia Community College opened its doors in 1985, it welcomed 60 students into a new kind of educational world. Beyond dual-language classrooms, the school emphasized a holistic approach, creating transcultural experiences that supported students' home languages while targeting increased graduation rates and college enrollment. In some ways, it reflected the structures and motions of the one best system. But the people, the attitudes, and much else revealed a different answer, one that, in some ways, formed its own kind of world.

Unlike previous newcomer schools, International High was created with the direct purpose of making sure that students graduated from the school. It was not an impermanent space but a school where "differences among students and faculty are cherished, and students are continually encouraged to celebrate their cultural and linguistic individuality while embracing their new home" (Internationals Network for Public Schools, 2019). The success of International High led its founders to help expand the model into a network of schools. New York City, and states like California and Minnesota, now have dozens of schools from the Internationals Network for Public Schools (INPS), as well as stand-alone newcomer schools like WISH.

Curriculum, pedagogy, and criteria for enrollment vary from school to school, even within INPS. Commonly, schools welcome secondary students identified as both recently immigrated students and as ELLs. Such criteria mean that many of these schools include a large population of undocumented students and students from different countries. Approaches to language vary. Schools like WISH use ESL classes, while other schools focus on dual-language programs. INPS frames their approach this way: "every teacher is a language teacher as well as a teacher of academic content and skills" (INPS, 2019). Regardless of the approach, newcomer schools share a focus on infusing cultural and linguistic affirmation, meeting students where they are in order to create a sense of belonging and to improve academic outcomes.

In many ways, these schools are unique. Bartlett and García (2011) recall a teacher who compares her newcomer school to other educational programming for immigrant and emergent bilingual students, saying, "ours doesn't fit" (p. 116). This way of doing schooling sticks out, particularly when placed against the subtractive forms of schooling that immigrant students so often encounter in the one best system. Newcomer schools stand as what Fine et al. (2007) refer to as "sites of possibility." The making of a different way of doing schooling offers a possibility for a world of schooling immigrant and emergent bilingual students.

In this way, newcomer schools come to be seen as a kind of adjacent and distinct one best system. Other answers of schooling might fit for certain immigrant-origin and emergent bilingual students. Some may prefer models more directly integrated into the broader system. But looking across metrics from graduation rates to supports for students, newcomer schools have forged a comprehensive system, one around which other types of educational approaches might be able to coalesce (Fine et al., 2005; Lee, 2012; Sylvan, 2008). Certainly, for students whose educational lives are so often framed through deficit and whose schooling experiences are dominated by exclusion, newcomer schools sit on the edge of the educational horizon as a means for equitable education for immigrant-origin and emergent bilingual students.

At the same time, tensions with the one best system and other approaches persist. There are millions of immigrant and emergent bilingual students in U.S. schools, far too many for newcomer schools to form some kind of comprehensive system. Additionally, newcomer schools are intentionally places apart. As physical spaces with entire populations of immigrant-origin students and curriculum and pedagogy grounded in serving immigrant-origin students, newcomer schools are not sites of segregation but of affinity. They may not break the grammar of schooling, but newcomer schools offer educational worlds far from dominant subtractive schooling models. This construction allows them to function both outside the broader system and as a kind of niche within it as "islands of opportunity" (Suárez-Orozco & Suárez-Orozco, 2014). They are, furthermore, still held to the demands of the one best system. Funding, recognition, and their very existence still depend on thriving in confines dictated by the one best system. Yet, the one best system does not dictate the making and life of all educational worlds.

LOOKING TOWARD OTHER EDUCATIONAL WORLDS

Later chapters in this book move from the institutional perspective of thinking like a school toward thinking-sensing with the everyday intellectualism of the youth who participated in this ethnographic study. Therefore, it is crucial to reinforce the active, persistent role of communities and individuals fighting not just for their educational rights but also shaping their own educational worlds. These worlds form a pluriverse in the collective and autonomous sense in which Escobar (2020) uses it. Even the different classrooms, pedagogies, and curricula that make up these different educational worlds are often simply the system at work finding different answers to "solve" educating immigrant-origin students. And yet, a pluriverse has thrived within and against the one best system. Students and communities have never been passive occupants. Community struggles have influenced and constructed countless educational worlds. Some of these have taken shape within schools, such as communities pushing for German-language instruction during the common school era (Reese, 2005). Others, such as the East Los Angeles Walkouts/Blowouts of 1968, have occurred both within/against school and in study groups in homes and in the educational life of community organizing.

During the Americanization movement, immigrant communities "taught English and civics in ways that were directly relevant to students' lives, and they encouraged immigrants to maintain their linguistic and cultural heritage" (Dayton-Wood, 2008, p. 398). In 1960s New York City, Latinx communities constructed educational worlds within churches in Washington Heights, the South Bronx, and elsewhere (Cremin, 1988; Hendricks, 1975; Rios, 2005). Within predominantly Pentecostal churches, communities built English-language classes, drug education programs, and functioned as general educational centers. Considering the goals of English-language classes, the work shared much with the educational worlds of schooling. Control, structure, and space, driven by local communities, veered from school worlds.

Studying with immigrant communities in the present day, Gutiérrez (2016a) explores different kinds of educational third spaces. She calls for "new systems" and "radical shifts in our views of learning and in our perceptions of youth from non-dominant communities" (p. 187). One way she provokes this move is to examine family life for Latinx children using new media as part of an after-school program (Gutiérrez, 2016b). Beyond a focus on how the program supports the school's work, Gutiérrez observes "everyday ingenuity" in ways that reshaped educations beyond schooling. The nonformal educations and family life that Gutiérrez encountered offer distinct worlds and reveal "alternative social realities" (Gutiérrez, 2018) in which Latinx youth are agentive, historically situated learners. These examples offer some of the countless educational worlds at work beyond the co-constructed schooling worlds that aim to "solve" the "problem" of educating immigrant-origin students. Where thinking like a school shows many worlds as a matter of expedience (and occasionally acquiescence to community demands), these worlds show "a world where many worlds" fit (Escobar, 2020, p. 9), and educational worlds full of alternative possibilities.

CONCLUSION: CHALLENGING THE ONE BEST SYSTEM

From the perspective of those engaged in struggles for rights, these histories pose dynamic and relentless challenges in terms of who and what counts in schools and a broader challenge in terms of what counts as America in the United States. Across these histories, scholars have shown conflicts (Ravitch, 1974), exclusions (Valenzuela, 1999), and fights for more equitable conditions (Santiago, 1986) for immigrant and emergent bilingual students in schools (see also Conchas, 2001). For schools, though, such histories have also represented opportunities to reassert a liberal melting pot both as a narrative and as a direct purpose of schooling. Different systems and answers used in schools, even when they challenge the logics of the one best system, may be subsumed into that very system. The nature of the one best system sees dual language not as a competing world but as a new route to inclusion. Ideas, practices, and the very logics of these answers may veer from the one best system. But they operate in a world where schools set the rules of the game, making it quite difficult to generate and sustain other educational worlds. That is not to say that places like newcomer schools simply conform. Classrooms and schools are full of powerful organizing work that challenges oppressive systems, moving against the interests of a system bound to whiteness and nationalist interests. Even in English-only classrooms or highly standardized settings, students and teachers engage in subversive pedagogical practices (Bondy, 2016; Fine et al., 2007). The argument here is simply that at the level of a one best system, these worlds must navigate a system only seeking to sustain itself within the U.S. landscape.

Moreover, any worlds created—any work happening—within these institutional borders must reckon with the weight of a system with clear boundaries for what counts as school and rigid measures for what school does. Success here becomes linked to racial, linguistic, national, and cultural norms. There are countless examples of when best answers do not emerge, when subtractive schooling continues, and when "schools themselves perpetuate inequality" (Valenzuela, 1999, p. 16). When something like documentation status or perceived "language ability" stand in conflict with this system, schooling success stands in conflict with one's identity (Chang, 2016).

Yet, thinking like a school is a deeply limited and partial perspective for schools. Other perspectives fundamentally challenge the one best system. Tyack (1974) points to community groups resisting the one best system in the 1960s, suggesting that families "rejected 'equality' if that meant Anglo-conformity, sameness, and familiar failure in the 'one best system'" (p. 284). As long as there have been institutional forms of inclusion, there have been dynamic forms of resistance. The one best system occasionally welcomes these answers but strives to incorporate them into its singularity. In thinking about the possibility of a pluriverse, Escobar (2020) suggests that we "stop thinking about our worlds with the dominant categories that created these crises" (p. 6). This pluriversal possibility is not the many best answers that schools have institutionalized within the confines of categorical thinking but a contestation of the normative measures of linguistic, academic, and other schooling categories.

The possibility of pluriverse is the possibility of schools becoming open to differences. The pluriverse reveals many different practices floating through educational ecosystems. More importantly, it offers different ways of thinking about education and different possibilities for configuring schooling. A pluriverse provokes educational worlds in which youth are not included in a one best system but make their own equal worlds. Even as the one best system weighs on those participating in this project, it is these other kinds of worlds that dominate their educational lives. Before wading into these worlds, the following chapter spends a bit more time within the institutional perspective, seeing how schools make sense of and aim to produce immigrant-origin youth as categories of people with certain desirable (for schools) qualities and dispositions.

CHAPTER 3

The Birth of the Newcomer as an Educable Subject

Mary Antin's (1912) book, *At School in the Promised Land*, talks about experiences at school as a recently immigrated child. Growing up in Polotzk, Russia, the image of America stirred a new educational life for Antin as it became "the center of all my dreams and speculations" (p. 7). She thought of and longed for a life in the United States, waiting for her father to ask the rest of the family to join him in Boston. In 1894, Antin emigrated to the United States and enrolled in Boston public schools. She writes that "the apex of my civic pride and personal contentment were reached . . . when I entered the public school" (p. 40). On that first day, she bounded to school with her sibling, their father leaving them with Miss Nixon, Antin's new teacher. Antin describes the feelings swirling among them. "I think she [Miss Nixon] divined that by the simple act of delivering our school certificates to her he [Antin's father] took possession of America" (p. 44). It was in school that Antin and her family could belong and even become American.

At first, she joined a "special class," where Miss Nixon taught her English. The class included scant affirmations as "the teacher knew just when to let us help each other out with a word in our own tongue" (p. 45). Throughout her school days, she describes moments of accommodation, responsiveness to her linguistic needs. There is a clear joy in participating in the school. "I was going to learn out-of-the-way things," she writes, "that had nothing to do with ordinary life—things to *know*" (p. 51). Yet, she is clear on her schooling experiences and the purpose of school, writing that "the public school . . . has made us into good Americans" (p. 52).

Antin's story does not stand in for a general experience of immigrant-origin youth in U.S. schools. It even contrasts some of the harsher depictions of schooling experiences at the time (McGinity, 1998). Yet responses to the book expose a broad discourse around schooling and immigrant youth. In the book's foreword, the publishers quote New York City superintendent in the 1910s, William Maxwell. "Education and social influence," Maxwell describes, "may triumph over the obstacles of heredity and the circumstances of environment" (cited in Antin, 1912, p. iii). The publishers are clear on the book's audience, intending it for teachers and anyone who might become a "truer American." These sentiments, when placed against the more explicit anti-immigrant rhetorical coursing through the United States, aim toward assimilationist affirmation. Yet they also reveal the discursive makings of immigrant-origin youth and schooling. Their educability was bound not to their identity, interests, or anything else, but to their emerging Americanness.

* * *

On a typical day during the 2018–2019 school year at WISH, Leo walked through the halls seeing flyers in multiple languages. One announced a rally for immigrant rights. It encouraged teachers and students to attend. A friend stopped him before class, striking up a conversation in Spanish. A teacher joined in, still in Spanish, the three of them chatting about nothing in particular. His morning included an advanced placement (AP) Spanish literature class. What he shared, about Rulfo one day or Martí's *Nuestra América* another day, linked his personal experiences to the class. During lunch, he participated in a task force that sought his ideas and opinions on how to make school more welcoming and supportive for the school's immigrant identity. His day often ended with a U.S. history class. The teacher, Nick, often asked students to bring in personal connections about immigration as part of the class discussion. Leo's educational experience at WISH served many purposes. There was a clear, inextricable link between his immigrant identity and his schooling life.

As described in the previous chapter, U.S. public schools have responded to and considered the schooling of immigrant-origin students in fractured ways since the dawn of the common school movement. Mary Antin and Leo share the position of "newcomer," a word, a status, that deeply influenced their schooling experiences. Yet, something fundamental to how schools make sense of and educate immigrant students changed between the late 19th century of Mary Antin's schooling and Leo's schooling in the early 21st century. Rather than schools remaking newcomers, assimilating them, and including them, it had become, as journalist Mary Jordan (1993) suggested in a piece in the *Washington Post*, "newcomers remaking schools."

This chapter traces the birth of newcomers as educable subjects in the 1980s. *Educability* refers to the ways discourses produced immigrant-origin youth into a specific category called "newcomer" and how institutions approached their schooling directly through understandings of this category. Where I use various terms to describe people on the move throughout the book, *newcomer* is a specific category of immigrant-origin youth that is central to the educational structures of WISH and similar schools. I explore how discourses have produced newcomer youth as a recognizable populational category whose schooling is positively entangled with their cultural, linguistic, and political identities. In the early 1980s, emerging from community struggles and discursive shifts, policymakers and educators came to make sense of immigrant-origin youth and their schooling in new ways. Whether or not youth occupied these positions, and regardless of how schools actually met these perceived needs, discourses from the late 1970s and early 1980s birthed a new political subject—the newcomer—as a subject with a range of identities and educational needs, all legible to schools and educational policies.

Using policy and curricular documents, media artifacts, legal decisions, and other archival tracings from sources, including the New York City Board of Education and the New York State Education Department of Bilingual Education, among others from the mid-1970s to the early 1990s, I genealogically trace how this subject emerged and became a recognizable and even desirable type of student from the perspective of schools. The archive I've assembled tells who these perceived subjects are and details their educational needs, specifically distinguishing them from previous immigrant groups. The process of educating newcomers, just like interventions described in Chapter 2, are driven by notions of populational reasoning. "Populational reasoning is not only about assigning children to groups. It individualizes the general attributes of populations to particular children in school through a hierarchy that ascribes a 'nature' to students" (Popkewitz, 1998, p. 46). To figure out how to best educate newcomers, schools and systems had to produce a recognizable figure called "newcomer" that had particular traits and needs.

Of course, I do not suggest that these categories exist as scientific facts or that they describe the best practices for educating immigrant-origin students. Rather, seeing how the 1980s birthed a new subject helps resist the making and use of categories. This genealogy "problematizes the very terms and concepts through which we know and understand a topic" (Talburt & Lesko, 2012, p. 11). Consequently, such inquiries open different possibilities about the educational lives of immigrant-origin youth, ones explored in the second half of this book. Ultimately, though, newcomer is a subjectivity that interlocutors in this project have constantly negotiated.

SCHOOLS RECKON WITH AND RESPOND TO "NEW" IMMIGRATION

The term *newcomer* has long been used to refer to immigrant populations in the United States. Edward T. Devine, a professor and philanthropist during the Americanization movement, asks "are the permanent race traits of the *newcomers* equal in quality to those of the present stock? We must remember that, as Professor Commons says, 'race and heredity form the raw material, *education* and environment form the tools to fashion social institutions'" (Devine, 1920, p. 373; emphasis added). This understanding of newcomers to be molded and shaped through educational institutions remained for decades, but a collection of community work, legal decisions, policy shifts, and increases in migration established the terrain that would, almost a century later, make possible newcomer subjects.

As with other scholars and activists (Reyes, 2006; Santiago, 1986), García (1999) highlights the 1974 Aspira Consent Decree as a moment in which affirmative educational opportunities arose for Puerto Rican and Latinx students in New York City. Beyond increasing school access, Aspira gave New York City's immigrant-origin students a right to include their language and culture in schools (De Jesús & Pérez, 2009). Schools were thus forced to respond to and make sense of the linguistic identities and perceived needs of multilingual youth. New educational institutions also formed to meet these needs. The year 1976 marked the creation of the New York State Association for Bilingual Education (NYSABE), which aims "to address the educational needs of English language learners (ELLs)/bilingual learners" (NYSABE, 2022). Although learning English remained a goal, with these expansions in the mid-1970s, home languages become a legitimated and legible part of students' educational lives.

Beyond linguistic identity, in 1978 in New York City, and in 1982 nationally, all immigrant-origin students, regardless of documentation status, gained a legal right to schooling. Throughout the 1970s, increasing numbers of undocumented youth attended schools across New York City. But, families often avoided registering children or, depending on their district, had to pay school fees (Blum, 1979). Responding to the change, the Board of Education "reasoned that school officials should not act as immigration authorities making immigrant status checks" (Flores, 1984, p. 512). Similarly, the Supreme Court determined that "the undocumented status of these children *vel non* [meaning "or not"] does not establish a sufficient rational basis for denying them benefits that the State affords other residents" (*Plyler v. Doe*, 1982). These legal decisions contributed to the untethering of educability and citizenship status. A legal guarantee may not have directly altered the way culture, language, or identity are considered in schools, but it fundamentally changed the "problems" of who attended schools.

Entwined with these changes, the previously mentioned population shifts of the early 1980s contributed to "overcrowding" in New York City schools (Purnick, 1984). As more newcomer youth arrived in the early 1980s, school was also taking on a more central role in the United States. While schools always cared about graduation rates and overall outcomes, high school graduation and dropouts had become a "social problem" by the late 1960s, with schooling outcomes linked to societal and individual well-being (Beck & Muia, 1980; Cremin, 1990; Fine, 1985). Research, policy, and schools came to specifically focus on educational outcomes for this emerging population of "new" immigrant (National Research Council, 2001; Steinberg et al., 1984).

Additionally, in the 1980s, "many jurisdictions responded to the arrival of waves of immigrants by making it more difficult for families to avoid enrolling their children in school, arguing that public schools were the best vehicle for assimilating" (National Research Council, 2001, p. 11). Schools thus took on a greater role in social life and the general world outside of schools. Newcomer schools, additional programming, and mechanisms such as the Bilingual Education Technical Assistance Center (which opened in 1982) came forth to educate newcomers (Friedman, 1988). Other programs maintained a focus on ESL but folded into their work an emphasis on vocational skills and "appreciation of native culture" as a way to reduce dropout rates (New York City Board of Education, 1986). School systems dominantly continued a broad assimilationist goal, but hard-won rights, expanding immigrant student populations, the identification of a "problem" for a specific population (dropping out and persistent exclusion), and schools' recognition of "the existential fact of more diverse student bodies with more diverse needs, interests, abilities, and styles of learning" (Cremin, 1990, p. 1) met to forge a new educable subject.

Though I mark the events and shifts of the 1970s and 1980s as a point of emergence for the newcomer as an educable subject, it is worth pointing to related moments coursing through the U.S. political and educational landscape in the 1960s. Anything from the Bilingual Act of 1968 to the opening of the first newcomer program in San Francisco in 1969 all contributed to the makings of newcomer subjects. An important point of distinction here is the permanency that came with International High School and related policies. Newcomer schools (rather than the temporary services of newcomer programs) were permanent places of education—ones specifically concerned with responding to the "dropout crisis" of newcomer youth (E. Nadelstern, May 10, 2017; personal communication). Writing about temporary newcomer programs, Rivera-Batiz (1996) suggests that in New York City, "students [in these schools] will be best served if the schools closely follow the mainstream curriculum and work toward moving them into regular schools as quickly as possible" (pp. 5–6). Meanwhile, newcomer schools became places where school activities responded to concerns of dropping out and exclusion. They would ultimately become a key site to produce and address the "problem" of newcomer students.

The late 1970s and early 1980s brimmed with schools and policies grappling with and responding to these kinds of educational "problems." As Lieberman (1989) points out, New York City schools acutely dealt with questions of how to respond to large percentages of linguistically minoritized students, high dropout rates, and new questions about how to include and educate a "new" population of immigrant students. The State Education Department's 1985 Diversity Report further suggests that immigrant students "represent a high risk population due to their limited English proficiency, cultural isolation and low socioeconomic status" (as cited in Lieberman, 1989, p. 7). As McDonnell and Hill (1993) later concluded, "immigrant students have unmet *educational needs that are unique to their newcomer status*" (p. xiii; emphasis added). From here, the "desire to solve these problems was the motivating factor in establishing The International High School on the campus of LaGuardia Community College in Queens, New York, in 1985" (Lieberman, 1989, p. 3). This development was not just the emergence of an educational world but the birth of an educable subject.

DISCOURSES OF NEWCOMER EDUCABILITY

In *The Cultural Production of the Educated Person*, Levinson and Holland (1996) show the competing discourses that produce groups as achieving the status of "educated." They describe how schools and other educational institutions draw in individuals and groups, including them into the broad logics of schooling. It is not that educability suddenly meant that newcomers were seen as universally included or equal. U.S. society did not shift to read immigrant-origin youth as intellectual, knowledgeable people in schools and elsewhere. Educability is, rather, the lens through which populations have become visible to schools and thus treated through certain policies and pedagogies. It is a status of being an educated person and the possibility of groups of people achieving this status.

Educability as a potential and educatedness as a status for subjects are always situated and contested notions (Corson, 2022b). An increased focus on schooling asserts that it is in this liberal institution that newcomers become educated (Abu El-Haj, 2015). Everyone in schools can potentially be educated. But, students must become certain types of everyone, imagined subjects of schooling. In previous decades, newcomers were not educable until they became citizens, learned English, assimilated, and so on. Throughout, their educability moved along marginal lines. Writing about immigrant populations' education possibilities in the early 1900s, Miller (1916) details a belief that "assimilation of the immigrant, his adaptation to American customs and ways of thought, and to a marked degree his economic and social status, depend on his *ability* to read and speak the English language" (pp. 15–16; emphasis added). Compare this sentiment to a tenet the staff of International High School identified as they mapped out the school in 1985. "In an increasingly interdependent world, fluency in a language other than English must be viewed as a resource for the student, the school and the society" (E. Nadelstern, May 10, 2017; personal communication). Students' linguistic repertoires and, as INPS and other newcomer schools have demonstrated across the years, newcomer identities became part of their educability.

Educability is not simply a matter of creating strategies or developing culturally responsive approaches but also shifting toward a new understanding of identities within classrooms. Framing these identities fundamentally differs from a localized call to reconceptualize "the 'migrant experience' through migrants' own subjectivities" (Mangual Figueroa & Barrales, 2021, p. 3). There is an element of co-construction here, but educability is largely seen from the perspective of institutions. It "contribute[s] to the normalisation of some identities and, by contrast, construct[s] others as non-normative." Such production is "a process that involves both the politics of recognition and the ways in which identities and subjectivities are (re-)produced as valued or disparaged" (Phoenix, 2021, p. 50). Where Phoenix addresses classrooms as sites in which teachers and students grapple with and participate in the production of idealized types of people, it is also a question of how institutions, media, histories, cultural understandings, and much else produce newcomers as educable. With the connected events of the 1970s and 1980s, newcomers as educable subjects joined the broader project of universal education and the individuated concerns of how to educate this new population.

EDUCATING DESIRABLE NEWCOMERS

The U.S. Department of Education (2017) provided educators with a "newcomer toolkit." The document defines who newcomers are, offers resources for students and families, and shares a series of "best practices" for welcoming newcomer students and supporting their education. It is from identifying the ways to educate newcomers *as* newcomers that schools can help construct a "rich mosaic of immigrants positively impact[ing] the United States" (p. 4) in pursuit of the U.S. Department of Education's mission of promoting "student achievement and preparation for global competitiveness by fostering educational excellence and ensuring equal access" (p. vi). Or, as a report for the National Center for Research on Cultural Diversity and Second Language Learning (García, 1991) suggests, despite vulnerabilities and exclusions, newcomers "can achieve academic success, however, when provided with appropriate instruction tailored to meet their specific needs" (p. 2). Best practices demand configuring dynamic, multicultural, yet shared images of newcomer subjects.

Newcomer subjects are never framed in the singular. Excavating discourses of educability is not about distilling a unified identity. Even still, discursive makings have created broadly recognizable subjects, ones with a defined range of characteristics and needs. Newcomer youth speak other languages. They come to school looking for educational opportunities. Established multicultural identities spill across policies and school reports, but newcomers are subjects with needs that exceed what schools have done in the past. As Short (2002) describes, "Traditional English as a second language (ESL) and bilingual education programs are not designed to serve the specific needs of these newcomers, in part, because at the secondary level, the curricula and materials are predicated on the belief that students have literacy skills and are acculturated to school" (p. 174).

Although even unifying documents such as the newcomer tool kit describe newcomers dynamically, these discourses help produce idealized traits and characteristics of the newcomer subject. I now turn to trace three characteristics of newcomers that have become visible from/within discourse. Looking from policies to journalistic accounts to everyday life at WISH, this section explores publicly encountered artifacts like a *New York Times* piece on International High School. At the same time, I conclude each section with a brief reflection with an ethnographic description to show the ways in which participants negotiate these subjectivities.

Newcomer Students Plural and Becoming Identities

Shortly after International High School opened, journalists and policymakers noticed the school's work with newcomer youth. Writing in the *New York Times,* Herbert Sturz (1988) explores "what's happening at International High." He extolls the positive academic outcomes for the "at-risk" newcomer youth who populate the school and considers that student motivation "reflects the traditional immigrant belief in the importance of education to making a new life." Sturz's passing assertion unveils complex understandings of newcomer students. There is a "traditional" value system that is unique to their identities. And yet, they arrive to schools in the process of/in pursuit of becoming other people, specifically through education. There is here a simultaneous tension and shared discourse of newcomer students being educated through plural identities and becoming identities that are to be forged through schooling.

Plural identities are rooted in understandings of an already-present identity when newcomers arrive at schools. The very term *newcomer* suggests such a history. Students arrive from somewhere else. They come as people with histories, experiences, and identities. Newcomers do not arrive tabula rasa, as a population on whom U.S. schools can write identities. In a report prepared for the New York City Board of Education, Willner and Amlung (1985) lament the use of the term LEP, which fails "to recognize the skills and strengths that language-minority students possess, including, for many youngsters, a proficiency in another language." The newcomer is a subject whose history must be explored, exposed, recognized, and incorporated into school life. An early report on International High School (Lieberman, 1989) proposes that other schools educating newcomers should learn from the collaborative, student-centered approach of International High School. As newcomer schools inscribed understandings of identities into their mission and design, it became clear that (affirmative) approaches to newcomers necessitated recognition of and support for their identity as they transition into U.S. schools. Liberty High School's (2022) mission suggests, for instance, that along with English-language acquisition, its ultimate goal of a newcomer school is "celebrating [cultural and academic] student diversity." This approach affirms the identities with which newcomer students arrive at the school. Diversity is not an aspirational feature of schooling but, rather, a starting point. In short, welcoming and inculcating pluralistic schools full of students with plural identities is central to the shared success of schools and newcomer students.

The idealized newcomer subject must share a plural identity that is legible and useful for schools. It is a means by which schools can improve outcomes. "Appreciat[ing] the tremendous resource represented by students' native languages and cultures" was "central to success" (Lieberman, 1989, p. 7). Assimilation is not the goal here, but plural identities still fit within a normative framework. Through schools, as the *New York Times* article suggests (Sturz, 1988), newcomers "make a new life." Newcomer students do not forget their past. As educable subjects, they join and shift about within the image of an "American kaleidoscope," an image that "really captures the constant flux, the persistent but changing populations and cultures that make up the overall pattern of the nation" (Jacoby, 2009, p. 39). Rather than the defined endpoint of assimilation, newcomers carry plural, becoming identities as part of a liberal multicultural project of schooling. Newcomer students are emergent plurilinguals, becoming schooled youth and developing cosmopolitan subjects.

During our first interview, Ximena spoke of her plural and emergent identity and how she has negotiated this within WISH. "Art and family teach you. It's the first source of education," she described. "Here, at [WISH], they kind of see that." Her love of art, her Latina identity, and the importance of her family became important aspects of how teachers at WISH made sense of and educated Ximena. And yet, these emergent identities functioned as support to improve her position and outcomes in school. School only saw her plurality within its own rubric, something that could not, in her words, contain the fact that "there are all these parts to me to get out." She still saw the utility in this subjectivity. Ximena said, "when I came here [New York City], I didn't know anything, but I also like the fact that I was learning really fast. [WISH] helped me." She offered examples of new knowledge, a plural identity emerging through WISH as she learned new topics and built a new academic trajectory. Ximena suggested that WISH accepted her Latina identity and interest in art as useful puzzle pieces for configuring and making sense of her educational life. Yet the contours of newcomer subjectivity rely not on fully fitting into place but, rather, on liminality.

Newcomers as Liminal/Risky/Potentials for Schools

Plurality closely links newcomers as subjects in liminal positions. Menjívar (2006) proposes liminality as an unfixed legal status, floating without resolution. Menjívar points to the fact that schooling for newcomer youth, particularly those marked as undocumented, stops abruptly and with no guarantees. With the purview of *Plyler* vanishing after secondary school, newcomer youth become educable only within the limited space of K–12 schooling. Immigrant groups in the United States have long confronted liminal positions that pose material, physical, and epistemological threats to their schooling. In 1986, the U.S. passed a bill making it illegal to knowingly employ undocumented or unauthorized immigrants. Schools and districts across the country resisted. New York City Schools chancellor Nathan Quiñonez responded that "we [in schools] have to give a clear message that we are not arms of enforcing this law" (as cited in Carrera, 1989, p. 24). In this debate, supportive schools asserted a specific role of including newcomer students and recognizing the transitory precarity remaining in everyday life.

Liminality is not only a thing surrounding schools but also a specific feature of newcomer subjects' schooling experiences. The entire first class of International High was considered to be at "high risk" of dropping out (Fine et al., 2005; Sturz, 1988). New York State Board of Regents action papers and state Department of Education reports further clarify, describing linguistically minoritized students as "represent[ing] a high-risk population due to their limited English proficiency, cultural isolation, and low socioeconomic status" (cited in Lieberman, 1989, p. 3). Newcomer subjects become visible through risk and liminal positioning. Willner and Amlung's (1985) report on linguistically minoritized students suggests that schools must recognize students' positioning and help them "catch up." Otherwise, "frustrated by their academic problems, these youngsters drop out, leaving public schools that have given them scant preparation for the future" (p. 41).

Within liminality and risk, newcomers become positioned as "not quite" included or "not yet" educated. They are "risky subjects" (Rodriguez, 2018) that schools must address. Certainly, these terms return to questions of how and where liminality emerges. Who is "at risk"? Of what? Questions linger in the atmosphere as reports detail student failures or journalistic accounts refer to newcomers as "high-risk" or "at-risk" youth. Risk and liminality serve specific purposes for making and educating newcomer subjects. They feed an idea of newcomer subjects' potential. Despite liminal positions, while facing and posing risks, newcomers are imbued with potential, potential that is expressed through school.

Abu El-Haj (2015) suggests that "literature shows that new im/migrant children and youth get pulled into two different Americas: either moving up the racial hierarchy to become white or down into the racially minoritized black and brown underclass" (p. 32). Tensions of inclusion/exclusion and hierarchical inclusion have played out over and over. Yet, liminality and risk were not initially linked to schooling. Where previous decades may have determined students to be uneducable or belonging insofar as they assimilated, newcomer subjects carried the potential to change the U.S. landscape. Signs hung in WISH classrooms affirming "immigrants make America great" or the Newcomer Toolkit's series of famous newcomer "contributors" to U.S. society (U.S. Department of Education, 2017). The potential of newcomer students is not to challenge anything but to be visible, to contribute, and gradually shift in/toward this kaleidoscopic vision of U.S. society. As educable subjects, newcomers come to succeed or fail. The newcomer is either a member of U.S. society—a citizen of liberal democracy (Abu El-Haj [2015] reminds us that citizenship is much more than legal status)—or a risk to it.

Miguel enjoyed being at WISH, but he occasionally bemoaned the way people in the school treated him. He described feeling like he was often on the verge of failing and this responsibility was not just about his own success but that of his family in the Dominican Republic and the United States. "It just all becomes so many responsibilities. I can't explain what's going on." He often said that he felt visible and welcome in the school, but Miguel questioned why these aspects of his identity had to become part of so many of his classes. It was also Miguel whom teachers spoke of with equal parts concern and hope. Risk and potential shared space here. "He needs to get himself together," one teacher told me. "He has so much potential." Liminality took hold, with Miguel fearing he would never achieve such potential. He lingered among feelings of engagement in the school, fears of dropping out, of not qualifying for university, and of desires to work harder to "catch up" to where he supposedly needed to be in his classes. These discourses do not simply frame newcomers as stuck in liminality. Instead, they work toward inclusion in U.S. society.

Newcomers as DREAMers/Overcomers

Another *New York Times* article details the stubborn success of immigrant students at a school with mostly newcomers (Rimer, 1990). The article, "A School in the Bronx That Is Somehow Making It," quotes a 5th-grade student who says, "'It's scary and confusing. . . . When I go to a new school, I just take a deep breath.' Now, she is in the 5th grade, a year behind and determined to catch up." As the article suggests, newcomer subjects are exceptional. Their potential is infused with ideas of overcoming obstacles, adversities, and traumas. Journalistic accounts frame newcomers in pursuit of achievement, despite these struggles. For instance, while all students at International High had been labeled at "high risk" of dropping out, Sturz (1988) notes an over 90% attendance rate and a 3.9% dropout rate. Or, as a 1990 article in the *Christian Science Monitor* details, "these immigrant children are the dreamers of the much-hailed American dream. The question is how best to make their dreams come true." That is, when given opportunity and space such as a newcomer school, newcomer subjects will pursue educational aspirations. They possess "higher educational and occupational aspirations than indigenous groups . . . and are more determined to use education as a strategy for upward social mobility" (Gibson, as cited in McDonnell & Hill, 1993, p. 7). Despite many obstacles, newcomer subjects are driven to achieve, working toward realizing their potential.

Mangual Figueroa and Barrales (2021) describe how newcomers overcoming "adversity, resilience, or assimilation" has become a trope, but it is one that is "still dominant in the educational mainstream" (p. 5). As with other discourses swirling around newcomer students, even as newcomers and others have pushed back (e.g., Abrego & Negrón-Gonzales, 2020, avowing "we are not dreamers"), there is an image of overcoming and dreaming that grounds the newcomer subject in schools. Overcoming is thus also a comment on school systems themselves. Both the history of immigration and education and dominant practices have left newcomers to fend for themselves (as Willner and Amlung's 1985 report on school systems neglecting linguistically minoritized youth suggests, p. 114). Educability emerges at the point when new programs recognize identities and cultivate newcomers' resilient attitudes. As Friedlander (1991) writes, "Educators in all programs serving these young people are aware that whatever their background, newcomer students are very willing and eager to learn and succeed, but do need an institutional cushion to prevent them from falling through the cracks" (pp. 5–6). Schools must be places where newcomers can dream and work toward a different life.

Deficit floats through notions of "dreaming" or "overcoming." Newcomers have a desire to learn, but schools must fill in "gaps" and provide newcomers with opportunities. This discourse serves to reinforce a liberal, individualistic notion of identity and achievement. It is through newcomers' grittiness—their willingness to bring their plural identities and work through their liminal positions—that schools help them overcome. Across newspapers and policy reports, there is little mention of which structures either contribute to the exclusions and violence that newcomers may experience or why such resilience becomes desirable. Instead, the focus remains exclusively on characteristics of determination and how that can alter newcomer trajectories. In this way, the newcomer is an emerging subject in the liberal, multicultural imaginary of the United States. Though questions of citizenship often remain unsettled, through educational success, newcomers join a national melting pot/kaleidoscope, where "multiculturalism [is] transformed into an American value—a symbol of this nation that has not been achieved . . . in other nations" (Abu El-Haj, 2015, p. 115). In terms of schooling newcomer subjects, multiculturalism supports an idea that part of a newcomer's path relies on their established cultural identity blending into the United States. The newcomer school both supports language and cultural history and teaches how to be included in U.S. society. At WISH, classes on U.S. history and U.S.

government, as well as field trips to the American History Museum in Washington, D.C., partially reveal a curriculum that invites newcomers to belong to this society through schooling.

Embedded in this discourse is a hopeful future. The newcomer subject is a dreamer, working toward a different kind of life. Concluding his article about International High, Sturz (1988) chronicles the struggles of a student who risks dropping out and not making it to college. Thanks to his determination and the culturally affirmative education he receives, Sturz suggests that "not surprisingly," his teachers "think he'll make it." While newcomers are thus part of a future, this discourse dictates educational futures. Newcomer subjects are those who dream not of disrupting or challenging anything at a structural level but of belonging yet to come, arriving inclusion, and contributions soon to be made. The desirable newcomer subject ultimately exists in a future that schools build.

Leo played with these dreams. He wanted to go to college. The risks and hardships he may have encountered, and his plural identity, all arrived to WISH with ambition and future dreams. As his gritty persistence led to good grades and new educational opportunities, there were ways in which the school made Leo into a kind of embodiment of a resilient dreamer. But he also resisted and negotiated this position. Speaking of other places of education, he told me how he learned to explore "what you're going to get out of the system and not what the system is going to get out of you.... You have to play the game if you want to win, but I don't want to play the game." He suggested that he knew when and how to participate in the game as a way to get by. His goal, though, was not to dream and belong, but to use the system. He wanted to return to the Dominican Republic after college and build community there. Ultimately, Leo balanced the opportunities born of his position as a dreamer/overcomer with his emergent radical desires to challenge these structures, to be a different kind of educational subject.

CONCLUSION

Concluding his sprawling second volume of U.S. education history, Lawrence Cremin (1988) draws on Margaret Mead's ideas about the future of the United States in the world. U.S. society "was the inclusion of diverse people at every stage"; therefore, a future would "have to be made transnational." It "would have to remain ever in the making" (p. 684). As new groups of immigrants arrived to the United States, and as community activism shifted political realities, schools came to imagine just such a future, one in which newcomer subjects could become part of a liberal nation, where immigrants whose subjectivities became legible to U.S. schools had a future. Directly exclusionary and anti-immigrant policies continued and even reemerged, but the making of the newcomer as an educable subject marked a shift in the "context of reception" (Portes & Rumbaut, 2001) in New York City and elsewhere.

Once more, newcomers as educable subjects should not be conflated with ideas of equality or culturally sustaining schools. From an institutional perspective, the educability of newcomers instead welcomes them into a "'hierarchy of belonging' (Wemyss, 2009, p. 133) to the US national imaginary" (Abu El-Haj, 2015, p. 196). In 1987, families and community activists from the heavily Latinx and immigrant Community School Board 6 in Washington Heights renewed calls for community control, voicing concerns from debates in the 1960s. Similar to the work of newcomer schools, they wanted more affirmative schooling and for students to stay in school. Yet, where the discursive production of newcomers fits them into the order of things, families wanted something else. They proposed a Latinx principal and better representation on the school board, and overall, they sought autonomous self-determination for their children's education. They were less concerned with schools seeing their children's identities as educable and more with reshaping schools for children who had always been educable.

Just as newcomer schools opened and expanded in the mid-1980s, and even with a school system largely supporting newcomer educational rights, New York City pushed back. After suspending the school board, Chancellor Nathan Quiñones appointed a group to pick the new school board rather than hold elections. Though community members levied critiques against the school board and individual schools, they asserted that the city denied their right to shape and have a voice in their children's educational lives (La Unidad, 1987; Snider, 1987). In this instance and many times over, the Board of Education moved to improve schools, as well as including and educating students in District 6. Yet, it did so with a clear image of who and what counts in the institutional space of school. It relied on a specific image of newcomer educability. These forms of improvement and inclusion act as reminders of what the making of the newcomer subject renders possible and also what it constrains. They remind of an invitation of inclusion to fundamentally unequal conditions for those who occupy the position of educable newcomer youth. It is these discourses that push at the newcomer youth who participated in this project, weighing on their schooling, their senses of who they might become, and everyday life at WISH.

CHAPTER 4

Surviving, Succeeding, and Making Do at WISH Academy for Newcomer Youth

> Welcome to public schools, where you never have what you need.
>
> —Barbara Howard, *Abbott Elementary*

Within the nondescript brick exterior, after the metal detector, from climbing the often-frozen escalator up too many flights because the elevator almost certainly isn't working, past the orange soda–colored walls of the co-located charter school with its eerie symmetrical designs and sterile silence, moving up another floor and hearing the first clamors of school life, having ascended more than halfway up the seeming skyscraper-sized education complex, straining to open the heavy black and red cracked, painted doors, a crinkly tarpaulin sign is the first thing visible in the school. It invites, welcomes. "WISH Academy, Where English Language Learners Succeed (Figure 4.1)."

Indeed, WISH Academy is a school that, since its inception, has aimed to provide immigrant-origin youth with linguistic and cultural support to include students in an affirmative environment. From the curriculum to professional development sessions, this stand-alone newcomer school strives for academic success while viewing

Figure 4.1. Poster Hung in Studio Building (Photo by Author)

students' identities as assets. Despite this positive framing, history and present-day political conditions pull and push WISH, prompting ongoing adaptations as the school has tried to survive in New York City's complex educational ecology. Across its brief history, the school has changed its curriculum, location, and even the students it serves. Through these changes, the school has attempted to be a genuine public school, open to and serving all recently immigrated students who arrive at its doors.

This chapter details the story of WISH, tracing its birth and describing its many tactics for survival as its stability and even existence have been challenged. Through interviews with teachers and school leaders, reflections with participants, and analysis of school and city policy documents, the chapter explores the school's evolution within the New York City educational environment. A history of WISH offers insight into how the school attended by the youth participating in this project navigates the discourses around newcomer educability. It shows the schooling structure and curriculum routinely encountered by participants. The chapter also acts as a bridge, linking the chapters that think like a school with chapters that encounter youth's everyday educational practices and historical work with a more direct focus on ethnographic study. As this chapter's title suggests, WISH's history raises questions about how a newcomer school approaches educating newcomer youth and what it costs to maintain a commitment to schooling as part of a commons amid ongoing attacks on public schools.

TRACING THE HISTORY OF WISH IN NEW YORK CITY'S 21ST-CENTURY NEOLIBERAL CONTEXT

In 2001, when Michael Bloomberg was elected mayor of New York City, neoliberalism in the form of promoting marketization and privatization while attacking public entities such as schools, was already taking hold. Bloomberg's election, though, coincided with a distinct neoliberal moment for U.S. schools. The No Child Left Behind Act was signed into law in 2002, giving increased funding for and attention to school choice and standardized testing. This led, throughout the 2000s, to neoliberal reformers pushing schools, particularly in major cities, to become more like a marketplace. Rather than attending a neighborhood school, families would be able to "choose" the best school. The quality of schools within this marketplace would also be assessed using standardized metrics to measure both student achievement and teacher quality. Under veils of choice, equality of opportunity, and closing an "achievement gap," privatization clamped on to schools. This structure became increasingly dominant in the early 2000s and clearly favored the schools and systems that fit into or conformed to its ideology.

Under Bloomberg and his first chancellor, Joel Klein, New York City very much fit this mold. From its first years, the Bloomberg administration set about trying to fundamentally transform the city's educational system (O'Day et al., 2011). In a decade bursting with reforms and mayoral control, during which time WISH opened, the city opened nearly 600 new schools and closed dozens of "underperforming" schools (Hatch et al., 2021a). Many of these new schools were charter schools. Many others were small high schools, coopting an idea from educator and prominent figure in the small schools movement, Deborah Meier, and others who sought to create collaborative, social justice–oriented schools in New York City and elsewhere throughout the 1980s and 1990s. Entangling with small schools, the city focused on creating dozens of alternative high schools to serve "at-risk" or dropout/pushed-out youth (Fruchter, 2020). The DOE created a New Schools Initiative, aiming to open hundreds of small high schools. This initiative abandoned justice and democratic structures, keeping only the size of small schools (Fine, 2012). Simultaneously, the DOE shifted to allow students to apply to any high school in the city, effectively linking the notion of choice to small schools (Unterman & Haider, 2019).

Creating small schools often meant closing large comprehensive schools and reopening the building as several smaller schools. These shifts thrust schools into competition with each other, both for students and for space. "Backpacks full of cash"—the idea that a district spends a certain amount of money on each student and that students should be able to bring that money to whichever school they choose—transformed from a political buzzword into an everyday reality. Space has always been an issue for New York City schools. During the Bloomberg years, the problem intensified. Co-location of multiple schools in single buildings increased over 60%, during the Bloomberg administration (Wulach & Kemple, 2016).

For students identified as ELLs in particular, the location and services of these schools often left students and families with little choice. A report by the New York City Immigration Coalition (2006) details extensive logistical and curricular issues for students identified as ELLs. The report details how the city closed "failing" schools predominantly serving Black and Latinx students. Small schools replacing closed schools often lacked specific programs to support students identified as ELLs.

This period also saw private organizations thrust their ideas into schools and other sites of education. Philanthropic funds such as the Gates Foundation supported everything from the New Schools Initiative to International High's transition to a formal network. Beyond schools, billions of dollars through public–private partnerships supported nonformal education programs and links between schools and nonformal programming. Corporations such as Facebook and organizations like the Opportunity Network, both of which partnered with WISH, all came together to pursue the vision of Bloomberg, Klein, and other neoliberal reformers.

All told, in the early 2000s New York City was in the midst of transformation, morphing into a kind of neoliberal carnival. Bloomberg and Klein held all the tickets, handing them out to charter school leaders, educational technology companies, and others who shared their vision of privatization and standardized accountability. Communities, teacher unions, and many others advocating for public education resisted these relentless attacks of privatization on public education. Still others, like WISH, fought for public education while simultaneously leveraging opportunities born of this context.

MAKING WISH

The founding of WISH is very much a product of these conditions. For years, the educators who came to found WISH worked as teachers and administrators in a bilingual program within a larger high school. When the bilingual program was labeled "ineffective" and phased out, several staff members began discussing the possibility of starting a school serving emergent bilingual students who would be affected by such closures. WISH's principal and a founding group of teachers conceived of WISH as a school that could both serve newcomer youth in a holistic manner and fit a particular niche by centering the arts in their curriculum. A niche would also distinguish the school within New York City's competitive landscape. The school's proposal ultimately outlined a mission of welcoming students in a culturally and linguistically diverse arts-focused academic setting. Crucial to the school's founding, those who proposed the school sought to make it a public school. Unlike many other small schools, WISH would not be a "screened" school. As the Immigration Coalition report (2006) describes, "'screened' programs rank students based on special criteria such as the student's academic record, standardized test scores, and attendance" (pp. 38–39). WISH aimed to welcome any newcomer youth, regardless of academic or behavioral background.

Around 2010, the school opened as a new, unscreened small high school with a single class of 9th graders. The initial proposal identified a site in the neighborhood in which the majority of WISH's students lived. Yet, as the principal describes, co-location issues quickly emerged. After months of conversations with the DOE, the principal was told that the proposed site was unavailable. With limited time to prepare, WISH was forced to spend its first year in the teachers union headquarters, using offices as classrooms. In following years, the school moved multiple times and expanded to serve around 300 students in grades 9 through 12.

WISH'S CURRICULUM

WISH's curricular structure has changed over the years, but much of it looks and feels like many other schools in the city. Students take classes such as U.S. history, Earth science, and algebra. The school offers AP classes and has various clubs. Teachers create their own curriculum, using EngageNY, the edtech company Newsela, and others as supporting resources. These common features of a school are not to suggest that the school obscures its identity as a newcomer school. Support for undocumented students or pride in immigrant identities are visible through informational flyers, posters of encouragement hung throughout the school, and school events such as cultural Heritage Day. In terms of language classes, the school includes English Language Arts (ELA) classes, an AP Spanish literature class, and leveled ESL classes for students. Some students pass out of ESL classes, but the majority stay in these classes their entire time at WISH.

The unofficial curriculum includes a great deal of flexibility. The school commonly operates through what teacher-leader Erin refers to as informal understandings. Few rigid policies exist to stick curriculum in place. Linguistically, for instance, WISH follows Bartlett and García's (2011) notion of a speech community model, where WISH's "language practices follow those of the school community—those of the students, the teachers, and the school leaders—rather than being externally imposed" (p. 116). Teachers and students regularly engaged in translanguaging or used dynamic practices to support learning. I observed countless moments during which teachers in an ELA class asked students to explain an answer in Spanish, teachers welcomed Spanglish into class discussions, or students created multilingual presentations. At the same time, the official structuring of leveled ESL classes disrupted these linguistic ambitions.

In its initial design, WISH aimed to foreground the arts. The principal conceived of a curriculum with arts spilling across the day, permeating every class. During its first years, WISH included several arts classes as electives during the regular school day. By the time I started working in the school, the only directly named arts class was music. What remained were partnerships with community-based organizations (CBOs). CBOs from various parts of the city work with WISH teachers to provide arts programming through after-school groups or during special learning units in ESL classes.

WISH's formal and informal curricular design aspires to reflect other newcomer schools. Gregorio Luperón High School, the school at the center of Bartlett and Garcia's (2011) study, acted as a guiding model and sometimes a competitor. Comparisons to Luperón floated through conversations with teachers and administrators. They expressed admiration for its academic results, envied its building and location in Washington Heights, and admonished its status as a screened school. Yet, WISH is not simply a replica of Luperón or a "regular" school serving newcomers. It is, rather, a unique school with lofty ideals and a distinct evolutionary path, one framed by discourses of inclusion and success and a shifting political landscape.

SURVIVE AND ADVANCE: THE EVOLUTIONS OF WISH

Across each school year, through relentless political shifts, amid changing DOE policies, WISH has thus far managed to survive in a context in which dozens of other schools have closed and where public institutions face ongoing attacks. But this is not a story of untarnished success. Survival has required maneuvering and adapting, dealing with punitive impositions, and balancing shifting visions for what is possible for the school. WISH's history is not the linear development of evaluating and seeking ongoing self-improvement. The school's evolution has included ambitious moments of reinvention, but changes have often been about figuring out how to respond to shifting conditions.

Searching for Space and Place

After that first year in the union offices, teachers packed their materials, marked their boxes, and thought they were preparing to move to what they hoped would become WISH's permanent site. Over a decade later, and after multiple moves, the school has remained far away from where school leaders hoped to establish and grow WISH. In its second year, the school moved to a wing in a large education complex in Manhattan. As the school expanded in size, they took over a full floor. When a charter school moved into the building, the DOE moved WISH to a different floor. A year later, they lost half of their floor as the charter school gradually expanded. They eventually moved within the educational complex yet again; they currently occupy their own floor.

For teachers, it seems that almost every school year has come with either a threat of or an actual move, forcing WISH to uproot and remake its home (or at least prepare to do so). The school's principal describes it this way: "We're like nomads. When we started, we didn't even have furniture." Issues of co-location and competition left WISH with little say in the matter. Philanthropic organizations and schools favored by the Bloomberg administration were able to build their own sites. Even schools similar to WISH confronted persistent battles in finding educational homes. It took Luperón over a decade of community work and strong academic results to build a new school site. WISH did not have the favoritism, financial backing, community support, established reputation, or willingness to change its structure (to a screened school, for instance) to push for a preferred, more permanent location.

This transitory pattern left teachers and students feeling uncertain and unsettled. Chatting after his history students left, Nick casually shared a rumor floating through WISH. Frequent dramatic temperature swings in classrooms were not a result of typical issues with New York City school facilities. Instead, he explained, the co-located charter school was using its ample resources to push uncomfortable air into WISH's vents, hoping to force them out. Even though WISH had remained in its current location for a full year when I began fieldwork, many classrooms still had books piled in boxes, ready for the next relocation. Teachers repeatedly claimed uncertainty about their position and WISH's future. As WISH tried to build a space, to make a home, external forces continually encroached and disrupted.

There are additional considerations of uncertainty here for a school serving immigrant-origin youth. First, given the school's location, there is a feeling of detachment. People in New York travel all over the city, especially for school, but the distance between home and neighborhood (particularly when contrasted with a neighborhood school) created difficulties for community building and general school engagement. Almost all the youth who participated in the project had to commute over an hour to get to school. As the principal explains, "I didn't want to be [where the school is located] because it's not the community who's coming to the school. I wanted to build community."

Crucially, this impermanence of space adds a layer to an already-present sense of impermanence that many immigrant-origin youth experience. In addition to transnational migration itself, immigrant-origin communities disproportionately move within cities and too often face uncertain housing situations (Newman & Wyly, 2006). For those marked as undocumented, impermanence and uncertainty pull at everyday life (Mangual Figueroa, 2019). Furthermore, this impermanence of school has happened amid rising vilification of Latinx communities and ongoing threats of deportation (during both the Obama and Trump administrations). Even as WISH has tried to create a place that is safe and stable for everyone in the school community, these disruptions of place send reminders of precarity. One participant described the uncertainty and fear of commuting to school each morning, saying that the multiple trains and long walk made them feel exposed.

Welcoming and Supporting "Risky" Students

At its foundations, WISH is a school meant to welcome and serve newcomer youth. As mentioned in the previous chapter, the subjects addressed in WISH's curriculum are framed through risk and overcoming. Much like the first classes at International High School, the students at WISH have been marked as being on the educational margins, identified as needing specific interventions lest they drop out of school. WISH does not stray from these narratives. In its comprehensive educational plans and annual reports, the school identifies aiming to include those students who fell through the cracks of other educational settings.

Support comes in the form of language classes or counseling. Like other schools, WISH also piles labels on students in attempts to identify and support those "at-risk" students. The numbers vary across the school's annual reports, but many students are considered "over-age and under-credited," meaning that the number of credits and a student's age puts them "behind" their peers. A large percentage of students (well above the DOE average as well as the average of newcomer schools) have been labeled as ELLs and have individualized educational plans (IEPs). A small but noticeable percentage of students at WISH have also been labeled S(L)IFE students, students with limited or interrupted formal education. When I conducted research at WISH in 2018 and 2019, 100% of the students were labeled as either "ELLs" or "former ELLs," with some marked as "long-term ELLs." Even as I repeatedly contest these terms and the demographic thinking that shapes schools, it is important to note their influence on WISH. After an ESL class one day, Pablo described a simultaneous tension of feeling supported and yet stigmatized by these labels. "I love my teachers. But also, this [school] isn't all of it. My friends are my teachers. Because outside of school, it's education. . . . Outside of school, inside of school, it's all [me]."

Riskiness also entangles with the school itself. Since its first years, WISH has hovered on the edge of risk, always sensing that closure or imposed restructuring lurk around the corner. WISH's graduation rate is roughly on pace with schools like Luperón. Students at WISH regularly pursue higher education. In both school report cards and in my conversations with students, the majority feel that they are supported by teachers. Yet WISH Regents scores, 4-year graduation rates, and other metrics fall behind more prestigious newcomer schools. Although it is not viewed as a "bad" school overall, it is, quite simply, not seen as successful in the same way.

According to administrators and teachers, this status is largely a consequence of the school's mission of public education that serves recently immigrated emergent bilingual students. The principal, in a compassionate and critical voice, framed it this way:

> We're unscreened because as a public servant and as a public educator— it's public education, right? When we proposed the school, I thought okay so if we're screened then it could be a private school. It could be a parochial school. But in terms of accountability. It was not. . . . I didn't get any slack. It wasn't like, "oh [WISH], they take everybody and so we understand that they all have different skills and they might have interrupted

formal education. . . . [Y]ou know, let's change accountability measures." It wasn't like that. It was "everybody's the same." Everybody's not the same. And language acquisition is, you know, it takes time. If language acquisition takes 6–7 years, and we're getting our 9th graders with limited skills, how is it that we're going to graduate them in 4 years?

The principal suggested that the school has been punished for its publicness, but in no way were they, or the many teachers who echo this sentiment, suggesting that they are taking "bad" students or that they would be a better school without welcoming "at-risk" students. Rather, they suggested that the system, especially the standardized system during the Bloomberg years, only welcomes difference when it fits the system's needs. Attention to students' cultural and language needs are necessary in that they support test scores and attendance rates.

This status, coupled with the school's location, has led to persistent issues with enrollment. In an increasingly competitive market, WISH has pursued a number of routes to enroll more students. Many students have arrived to WISH the way Matias did. "After a few days of being here [in New York City], my uncle walked me down to the big center[1] they have. We talked to the person and they said this school is filled, this one you can't go to, but this one [WISH] will take you. So here I am." The principal has judged what families are looking for in the "marketplace." She suggests that the school has "responded to a demand for college readiness courses and courses such as the AP offerings." The entire administration also spends a significant amount of time recruiting at middle schools. Despite these efforts, WISH remains under-enrolled. Under-enrollment places the school community in a precarious situation, especially since it can lead to excessing teachers or even closure (Valencia, 2012). In a city where students carry backpacks full of cash, under-enrollment has deeply impacted WISH's stability, its standing, and its ability to make autonomous decisions about issues like curriculum.

Curricular Demands on WISH

One afternoon, speaking with Erin, we began talking about her role as an ESL teacher. She described some new pedagogies she wanted to include, but our chat quickly shifted to frustration with the overall approach to language instruction at WISH. "There's ESL, and we have transitional bilingual. But it's not liked.... There's no need for transitioning out of ESL. Just offer bilingual classes!" she said. From its first days, WISH has dreamed of a school authorized to center the translanguaging already happening every day in its hallways and classrooms. Such a dream remains distant and unrealized. During its nascent stages, those proposing the school imagined a language program similar to that of INPS. Unfortunately for WISH, the market had other needs. The principal explains that "I wanted to serve ELLs without a [transitional] bilingual program. But at the time [we] wrote the proposal—the executive director of ELLs said there's a need for a transitional bilingual program." This group tried to push for building something more comprehensive and holistic but, according to the principal, the DOE said "they [the DOE] don't want that. This is where the need is." The school ultimately opened with tiered ESL classes and, on request from families, transitional bilingual programs.

Over the years, these programs have become entrenched. Looking at the school's 2021 comprehensive plan, the focus on strengthening and improving ESL classes, with no mention of different language policies, reveals a fading dream of language instruction. Centering ESL classrooms for multilingual students lays bare the rigid, deficit-minded approach forced on WISH. A perception that ESL programs have demonstrable results, which I touched on in Chapter 2, flooded New York City during the Bloomberg administration (García et al., 2018). Furthermore, as García et al. point out, these programs came to be seen as remedial. Language programs were less about community empowerment and more about using targeted instructional time to help students "catch up." The school wanted a robust, fluid language program, one that reflected and supported the WISH community. It has come to accept a program that—even as teachers navigate and infuse affirmative pedagogies—starts from a place of remediation and normativity. Tremors of assimilation return.

Like the language program, WISH's other core curricular focus—the arts—has been difficult to realize. From its inception, WISH was supposed to welcome newcomer youth specifically by centering the arts. Arts, those designing the school believed, contributed to academic success and a sense of belonging for newcomers. In its first years, the school had an art teacher, a dance teacher, and a music program. WISH never wanted to become a performing arts school for newcomers but to have multiple arts classes offered and to infuse arts into every class.

Currently, the school has only a music teacher. Professional development (PD) sessions and curricular plans almost never address the arts. In the school's most recent comprehensive plan, scant references to the arts focus on how experiences and skills in the arts can help build language proficiency.

The gradual unraveling of arts at WISH came about as funding and the school's reputation shifted. Erin describes how, "during my first year . . . the superintendent came and said we were an arts and crafts school. . . . So, [the principal] freaked out because she thought we were going to get shut down." After this visit, the school began to actively promote academic rigor, often at the expense of arts. The school prioritized boosting test scores and graduation rates. With enrollment concerns, the school also excessed arts teachers. The principal saw these concerns as entwined. "We have some arts programming. Not as much as we did because of our funding. The funding has dropped because of our under-enrollment and—it's the funding and also because the priorities have shifted and there's more of a demand for college readiness." Though students express a desire to see arts as a key part of the school day, they have gradually faded to the background.

Much like language policy, the school has relied on nonformal structures to fill the gaps for the arts. At WISH, arts-based programs now mostly run through CBOs. A local theater company, for instance, occasionally joins an ESL class to help them put on a short play in class. Participants have loved these opportunities, as well as the clubs and after-school programs that have sprung up in place of classes during the school day. Speaking about an after-school photography club, Miguel says "it's where I feel most at home." Yet, the ideas of arts and language that teachers and administrators espouse have both been pushed to the school's margins. The arts and affirmative language practices that remain rely on unstable sources of funding and commitments from teachers without training or material support.

WISH Grappling with the Twin Binaries of Inclusion/Exclusion and Success/Failure

The school's curriculum guide describes WISH's academic program as one that "prepares ELLs for a successful future by offering unique opportunities for students to excel in Regents exams, Advanced Placement courses, early college experiences, and on-time graduation." Discourses of success and inclusion govern each facet and change of the school. Adaptations, compromises, and survival mechanisms have worked insofar as they meet external criteria for the twin binaries. Every step that the administration takes, each pedagogical intervention, all do so with success and inclusion as central aims.

At WISH, in New York City in the 2010s, in almost any educational situation, success and inclusion were not processes but a status. This is visible in attendance records, standardized tests scores, and graduation rates. Success means transitioning out of ESL classrooms in a timely manner. Inclusion is achieved through kids coming to school every day. Teachers and students did not passively accept these meanings. And yet, students walked around the school with a feeling that success or failure stuck to them. The status of tiered ESL classrooms, the marks of being overage, under-credentialed, or being a student of concern for teachers, these things were known and felt throughout the school. Students sensed a rubric of inclusion always enveloping them. Matias noticed when, as we walked the halls between classes, the principal, school counselor, and a former teacher all stopped to check in on him. He described a feeling of care here, but said he knew they checked in because he "wasn't doing good with school."

Beyond individual students or teachers, WISH itself lives with the imprint of these binaries. As a stand-alone newcomer school, there is often a sense of exclusion from a broader community of public schools. Consequently, policies of increased rigor or college readiness are placed upon WISH as a way to reshape the school around institutional ideas of success and inclusion. Other schools might have the flexibility to challenge or create dynamic, internal understandings of these terms. Schools in the New York Performance Standards Consortium, a group of schools that receive waivers from the Regents, are allowed to design portfolio-based non-standardized forms of assessment, creating different notions of success; these schools are largely seen as successful (Fine & Pryiomka, 2020). Beginning during an era of heightened standardization, as a stand-alone school, and with a commitment to publicness, WISH has not been able to challenge these categories or its own status, at least on a broader scale.

Internally and informally, WISH teachers have created other ways of seeing success and inclusion. At times, these ideas veer from what the DOE and other institutional bodies might consider success. Erin described how the school supported her students' success as a matter of joy and communal learning. She identified one of the most successful moments of the school year as when her AP ELA class read James Baldwin, went to see *If Beale Street Could Talk*, and then debated the film and book at a nearby café. The intellectual conversations at the café reflect a different kind of college readiness. Students spent a day simply debating and engaging with each other. Of course, such a trip was reserved for an AP ELA class. Erin readily admitted that she carries a status of a successful teacher in the school, something that opens space for flexibility. Success might also be found in moments. Nick sincerely cheered on Miguel for arriving to school on time one Tuesday morning. Elena, a beloved science teacher, similarly championed her students coming to afterschool labs. Completing the labs was important, but she treated their very presence as a success. These practices are not meant to overidealize WISH. Amid its commitment to affirmative public schooling, WISH has struggled to attend to the linguistic needs of students who speak indigenous languages such as Nahuatl.

With dominant discourses shaping the meaning of success, everyday practices are kinds of micro navigations, successes that are not as legible during a superintendent visit or available as measurable data. Competitive and fluid notions of success melt into a centrally defined understanding. Success as moments shared among teachers and students often faded to the background as Regents scores or attendance data rushed forth. Teachers still pushed, finding moments to create different understandings of success and inclusion. When Felipe suddenly popped up after a month-long absence from school, he still felt included in the school community. As we walked the halls together after his first day back, he radiated excitement. I asked him how it felt to be back at WISH. "Good," he said. "Happy to see everyone. It's good to be here. And the teachers say I can still graduate." For Felipe, WISH created an inclusive place where he could succeed, though his success operated under a rigid and stable definition of success.

WISH VS. EVERYBODY

Schools in New York City have a number of approaches to building community and support among themselves as schools. Some, like many charter schools, are part of large networks. Here, a central office can provide PD and curricular support (as well as ensure compliance of all schools to the network's way of doing things). Others, like the Consortium schools or the "affinity groups" created under Mayor de Blasio bring together schools with shared values and identities. Still other schools generate solidarity within neighborhoods (Warren, 2005). WISH remains outside of each of these groupings. It is a single

Surviving, Succeeding, and Making Do at WISH Academy for Newcomer Youth

school, far from the neighborhoods where students and teachers live, and has no network support.[2] At WISH, there was a constant sense that the school was alone, alienated, set adrift, left to survive without support, and set against other schools. It is a school geographically and ideologically untethered, and one that has built its identity and work through insular collective action.

In one sense, such isolation generated feelings of instability. Teachers and students were not sure what WISH would look like or if it would be around the following year. If it remained, they were not sure if they would be in the same place as in previous years. The school has retained its initial administration and several teachers from those first years, but many others have left or been excessed. Students also leave WISH, transferring to other schools or dropping out of school, at a higher rate than the DOE or INPS average. In another sense, WISH has created an identity through opposition, where those in the school care for each other. They see themselves as black sheep, banded together to make their school work against the odds.

The most common way that this sentiment appears is in seeing WISH framed against narratives of public schools that do not meet the needs of newcomers. Before coming to WISH, some students arrive in New York City and spend a few months to a full school year in public schools with limited attention of any kind paid to language or culture. WISH certainly stood in contrast to these experiences. Signs around the building, such as that shown in Figure 4.2, reminded students that

Figure 4.2. Student Artwork Hangs Around the Building

they belong at WISH and that it is a school meant to meet their needs. Deficit approaches to language that students may have experienced in other schools are explicitly cast out of WISH. One teacher told me that "we're not the kind of school that would ever go around saying 'English-only!' That's just not us. We're the kind of school that is language affirming."

Teachers and administrators go a step further, embracing and explaining this stark contrast. It is a place where, according to the principal, teachers have to shift their perspective away from "traditional schools." Speaking about new teachers adjusting to WISH, she said, "you can't see yourself as a content teacher. With every lesson and every class, you have to make a lesson culturally relevant, to connect to the kids and pull them into the learning." Teachers and administrators also drew on personal experience to talk about WISH as a distinct place. Around 50% of the staff are first- or second-generation born in the United States or were identified as ELL students. Multiple teachers spoke about how they desired a place like WISH when they were students or when their parents were students. This positioning also casts teachers and students together, collectively building affirmative education set against other public schools, saying that, at WISH, they will take care of each other.

WISH also contrasted itself with other newcomer schools. Administrators in particular actively compared WISH's graduation rate to Luperón and reiterated the school's unique qualities as an unscreened newcomer school with no broader support network. I heard many times a mixture of resentment and pride as they explained how WISH never received the same recognition as other newcomer schools but still managed to build a school with unwavering commitments to newcomer youth. WISH initially pursued joining INPS but, as the principal articulated, "They only hire Internationals principals. They keep things internal." A sentiment echoes across these comparisons that "WISH is here because it is not elsewhere."

This idea is not about accolades or feelings of rejection. The school has been in constant pursuit of building networks and connections with other schools and CBOs. Ultimately, though, these points of contrast are matters of community making. As the principal described the school's publicness, she brought in a theme that popped up throughout research. WISH is a school made up of underdogs, a community banding together to make a school. "Our curriculum is different because our population is different," she explained. "They [certain other newcomer schools] want to take the cream of the crop students, but we know how to work with ours. When you have a population that's different—when you have students at different literacy levels, you have to differentiate more. We just have a different lens."

In one of our focus groups, Leo described how he was accepted at another newcomer school but his sister was not. "This is the kind of place where we could both be—where they'd take both of us." Matias then echoed this idea. "We are all friends here. Like, it's not like other schools—the point is the teachers, they want you to feel at home." The conversation then turned to an additional point of contrast. Many participants share that coming to New York City had been an isolating experience. Even when they reconnected with family or lived in a Dominican neighborhood, most participants did not feel a sense of community until they came to WISH.

Attempts to improve the school are likewise grounded in a "we take care of us" notion of community building. One of the central projects for the school year was the equity task force. For months, a group of students, and teachers, joined occasionally by the principal, met during Wednesday lunches to identify problems in the school and make the school a more inclusive space. At the end of the year, the task force presented recommendations of hiring more teachers of color and more Spanish-speaking teachers. Again, though, this is not a simple success story. Leo pointed out how rather than hire new teachers, two Latina teachers had been excessed at the end of the school year. Additionally, community building still conformed to dominant notions of inclusion and success. Mateo thought of WISH as a haven. Rather than the stress of work, WISH offered a place of care. And yet, WISH pushed and sometimes demanded stronger outcomes. One day, after history class, I heard Nick give Mateo a stern motivational conversation about working harder. I quickly mentioned that he had been working extra hours recently. "I know he has a lot going on, but work is no excuse. He still has to perform," Nick said. Here and elsewhere, community is shaped around and served the purpose of academic success.

THE COST OF PUBLIC SCHOOL

The idea of what makes a public is a contentious issue. Adding school to the mix only intensifies the conversation. From Habermas's commonly used broad conception that publics are "'private persons' assembled to discuss matters of 'public concern' or 'common interest,'" (as cited in Fraser, 1990, p. 58), many schools might call themselves public schools. Those fighting for public schools in New York City in the 2000s and 2010s have argued that the publicness of school links to local control, answerability to communities, and democratic structuring where the people making up a school have a say in budgets, curriculum, and much else (Hantzopoulos & Tyner-Mullings, 2012; Wilson, 2016). Even still, what counts as a public, and what public school even is, remain contested questions.

Newcomer schools have faced their own attacks, with critics framing them as anti-public schools that segregate and favor particular groups (Gross, 2017). Responding to these concerns, Jaffe-Walter and Miranda (2020) draw on Nancy Fraser's work to suggest that newcomer schools are examples of a counterpublic, "communities that offer the potential for individuals from marginalized groups to develop identities and critiques that are not easily forged in the wider public sphere" (p. 104). Fraser (1990) explains a rationale for counterpublics, saying that "subordinated groups usually lack equal access to the material means of equal participation" (pp. 64–65). Where broader public schools might silence or marginalize immigrant-origin youth's voices, it is within newcomer schools that such a public becomes possible. An immigrant counterpublic here becomes a place of affinity and belonging, where translanguaging reigns and Immigration and Customs Enforcement (ICE) agents or teachers shouting "English-only" have been pushed out.

Critically engaging the positioning of other newcomer schools, WISH also presents itself as a particular kind of counterpublic. Screened schools and schools relying on the support of large foundations create counterpublics, but many at WISH see these schools as counterpublics stamped with large asterisks. Screening closes off the public, even the "subpublic" of newcomers (to use Warner's term, 2005), reconfiguring who is part of the school and layering qualifications for the public-making endeavor of schooling. From another reading, though, making a screened school or pursuing funding from large foundations may simply be different forms of negotiation in the competitive, neoliberal wonderland of New York City's education system.

Regardless, WISH has aspired to a specific kind of public, one that has required ongoing reinventions. It is a school that remains a pluralistic public, struggling and always in the making. Warner's (2005) explorations of publics is relevant here. Warner suggests that a public is "poetic," thinking about the world it seeks to create and "projecting for that world a concrete and livable shape, and attempting to realize that world through address" (p. 81). The making of such publics requires people to "engage in struggles . . . over the conditions that bring them together as a public" (p. 12). The making of a school as a particular kind of public thus entails ongoing work. The kind of public WISH has made is a kind of unconditional counterpublic. Of course, there is the qualification of immigrant-origin identity, which is central to the production of this counterpublic. Beyond this forming, teachers and administrators proudly claim to welcome and support anyone arriving at their doors. These pursuits have come at great cost. Keeping the school alive has meant accepting contested spaces, altering curricular structures, and remaking its identity. At the core of WISH's particular public has been newcomer youth. And yet, even this core feature of WISH's public has been remade.

In the late spring of 2019, everyone filed into the auditorium for a final whole-school assembly. Even with solid attendance, more than half the seats remained empty. Leo read his beautiful poem about race, identity, and belonging. A few others performed. Announcements were shared. The principal offered congratulations on finishing the year. She then turned to announcements about the summer and the next year. Her last point explained that in the fall, for the first time, WISH would welcome "heritage speakers"[3] among the new 9th-grade class. Many of the 9th graders arriving to WISH the next fall would have learned English as children and grew up in the United States. As the principal announced this shift, she offered a recommitment to the school's ideals. She said that, though they would welcome some students who have a different background, they were still committed to WISH's mission of welcoming and supporting newcomers and students with an immigrant background.

From the first discussions about creating the school, the subjects of pedagogical address within WISH's public were exclusively newcomers. Now, the school pivoted to welcome and educate a new population alongside newcomers. I do not mean to critique welcoming heritage speakers or to suggest that they do not share educational identities. I share this vignette as another example of how WISH has navigated and remade itself over and over, often at great cost.

The reality of welcoming heritage speakers was that WISH's enrollment numbers kept dropping. The administration made a creative, welcoming move to remake its public, but it was a matter of survival. WISH's public remains a precarious kind of poetic invention. The school is not valueless or apolitical, but in the course of its existence, political realities have thrust survival to the center. In finding routes to survive, WISH has struggled to educate newcomer subjects in the way its founders imagined, but it has evolved to continue including newcomers and promoting their academic success.

These different maneuvers to stay open are ongoing acts of what Edwin Mayorga (2017; 2021) calls "sobrevivencia." Sobrevivencia builds on Vizenor's (2008) theories of survival as active, present, continuations of stories for indigenous peoples. For Mayorga, sobrevivencia is "an articulation of individual and collective work that is neither about survival nor transformative justice alone, but is in fact both" (2017, p. 108). It is the active work of Latinx communities to resist systems of oppression. Sobrevivencia acts as one of many reminders to bodies like school systems that Latinx communities remain present, building worlds, constructing futures otherwise. At WISH, sobrevivencia is about the individual and collective work of sobrevivencia but it is also about the enduring actions of a public surviving.

CONCLUSION

Sobrevivencia makes something. It creates new material conditions. WISH has faced serious, existential threats over the years, but it is not some zombified school, empty and dragging itself from closure. After half a dozen moves and threats of closure, during the spring semester, a number of students and teachers organized a small project. They worked during lunch and free periods. They stayed after school. The work lasted over a month, but when they were finished, the lockers lining the hallways had been painted. Generic solid reds and blues became murals, images, creations of/by/for the students and teachers of WISH. Far from their neighborhood, with funding concerns looming, they had built a place with some permanence, where they belonged. It was not offered, not authorized, but the WISH community claimed it.

Hantzopoulos (2015) suggests that "democratic schools are neither sites of transformation nor sites of despair, but rather sites where agency is negotiated, contested, and remade, often in unexpected, unassuming, and contradictory ways" (p. 345). The story of WISH is doubtlessly a story of struggle. Beyond superintendents or broad neoliberal forces, the school has many internal issues and tensions among students, staff, and administration, ones that many schools face. The public WISH negotiates is, once more, a plural thing full of dissensus.

But the story of WISH is ongoing—a small school striving to build a public grounded in affirming immigrant-origin youth and remaking itself again and again. A place that wants to be in the future and wants its students there too. WISH is, through these many negotiations and contradictions, perhaps a promissory note. That perhaps, schools can belong to the people.

CHAPTER 5

Educations in Place and on the Move

Leo: [Education] shouldn't just be about a tunnel, like just going through the tunnel and racing out.

Jordan: For me, instead of go through the tunnel, let's listen to people trying to remake them, let's try to find different tunnels.

Leo: It's like, you get out of the tunnel and then you don't know because you've never been in that position. It's about learning to be independent.

They move from class to class, bounding, sulking, sauntering through the hallways, talking and checking in. They learn science and English and U.S. history. Monday 1st period starts with music class. The last class on Friday is ESL. Stories of immigrants in the United States find their way into word problems in math class. They develop understandings of reading passages. A short book, *A Long Walk to Water*, takes months to read, but they keep on. Sometimes, in class, they freestyle rap together. In government class, they study the importance of citizens educating themselves in a democracy. During science, discussions of volcanic activity inspire connections, generating a new art project. Other classes drone on. Hands shoot up. Heads slink toward desks. In lectures, there are confused stares, active nods. Teachers hold them after the bell to offer pep talks or remind them of upcoming deadlines. Spanish literature starts and the teacher scolds tardy students not only for being late but for letting down communities by not taking schooling seriously. They play the same damn song in music class, over and over, on violins.

Conversations wind through hallways, learning, listening, creating new ways of understanding from and with each other. Plurilingual conversations. Multimodal learning. Excitement punctures the hallway as they run from class to share a video, explaining it to friends.

They greet teachers, joke with them, skirt by on the way to their next class with a promise of completing outstanding assignments. In the cafeteria, the free lunch teaches them that their nutritional health is not a matter for the school day. Sometimes they skip it just to wander the hallways together. They play fight and sneak upstairs to the gym. They test the school's limits. They see friends from other grades and different classes. They hold hands and ride the escalator all the way down. The security guards say it's the middle of the school day. They're not allowed to leave. When they arrive late, security gives them a hard time. The school maintains its borders. Outside of normal times, they cannot cross through the metal detectors without a teacher or adult family member to vouch for them and to sign and document their tardy arrival. With double periods, they take prolonged bathroom breaks. During breaks, the principal stops them, asks about how they are doing, and ushers them back to class.

The school spills into the city. They go to City College for campus tours and visit tourist sites on field trips. Buses take them to see other cities. Museums welcome them, ask them to sit in circles and guide them along the route of a tour. Guides look uncertain as they converse in Spanish. People explain things to them. After finishing a book in ELA class, they take a trip to see the film adaptation. Afterward, they debate in a café: bohemians huddled together.

School ends but WISH keeps going. After-school programs give them a place to be, extend their learning, and offer different opportunities. When the bell rings, they go to clubs and community meetings. They start a Gender and Sexuality Alliance and join a media club that meets at the school or ventures to the offices of Facebook. A college prep program teaches the basic grammar of living a specific kind of university and professional-bound life. They travel across the city to attend preparatory clubs run by the NYPD. Cops teach discipline in the afternoons. Students forge identities as studious or artsy people. They go to jobs, working afternoon and night shifts, and at times with family members. New skills emerge. They utilize different energies and knowledges from the school day as they get by.

There are other times. Learning with less structure, outside the organization of a job or club or program. Say, playing video games. Watching Netflix with English subtitles. Caring for siblings. Raising a child. Creating found art projects. Applying to university. Experimenting with lyrics, making music, and producing it. Messing with a camera and creating portraits and city landscapes. Exploring the city. Remembering the Dominican Republic. They ask each other

Educations in Place and on the Move 95

to compare it to New York City. These are more self-directed educations and, while not ungoverned, educations that move in ways distinct from the official school curriculum.

And dreams, too. Thinking about being an actor, imagining being famous, wondering what comes next. Worrying about right now. They intellectualize on the power of connecting with other cultures during a walk through the park or the possibility of fighting racism across the United States and the Dominican Republic. Using the subway requires deep questions and ongoing theorization about why it is the way it is. Questions of how people on the subway look at them with their dark skin and *voces dominicanas*. Hoping to be seen otherwise. Dreaming of millions of otherwises.

These are the educational practices of nine youth participants living in New York City and attending WISH. Their educational stories are partially visible here. Nine incomplete, entangled narratives of playfulness, curiosity, grief, struggle, joy, confusion, and education writ large. This chapter explores youths' educational practices across different spaces, looking to how educations form, move, and relate across time and space. These educations begin to creep from the shadow of the twin binaries. It has taken a while to get here. I introduced the youth who opened their educational lives to this project back in the Introduction, but I offer a more thorough presentation of each person in this chapter, starting with co-constructed biographical sketches. The bulk of the chapter playfully studies educational practices in three distinct spaces: school, structured nonformal educational spaces, and unstructured out-of-school time (OST). Looking at distinct spaces interrogates the relationship among educational practices as well as the relationship between spaces and educational practices themselves. Rather than scientifically mapping educational life, the chapter moves through affective surges, sensing and feeling practices bubbling to life, listening to where participants wanted to go, moving together, and seeing how ideas pulled at places and wedged into distinct spaces. Building on the many worlds referenced in Chapter 2, this chapter sees educational worlds made and negotiated as part of ongoing spatial flows. Educations move and reconfigure. Learning and unlearning, becoming and unbecoming are always at work and on the move.

After reintroducing my interlocutors, I trace dynamic educational practices in distinct spaces, creating temporary boundaries between places and modes of education. From there, I move to consider the educational constraints and possibilities that emerge in place. The chapter concludes by exploring the interrelationships of these educational practices, seeing how they move, stick, and appear again in different places, ultimately creating a kind of borderless curriculum of everyday educational practice.

NEWCOMER YOUTH PARTICIPANTS

The complex educational practices that participants undertake and demonstrate, reveal different ways of understanding education, seeing what it does, how it moves, and what new possibilities emerge from such practices. Encounters with these educational practices show how education beyond institutional boundaries reveals meaningful, pleasurable, and free forms of living. With that in mind, I now reintroduce each person who participated in this project.

Miguel. Miguel describes himself as a photographer and a disciplined, serious person. I first noticed Miguel while sitting at the back of a classroom. His upright, still posture caught my eye. He often wore clothes with camo patterns or NYPD logos, reflecting his desire to join the army and then the NYPD. In the Dominican Republic, he worked with a family member on the cinematography of a documentary. The experience inspired him to learn as much as possible about photography. Even though he describes an affinity for discipline, from his own account, Miguel struggles with focus and organization in school. Miguel and I often strategized over our shared struggles with timeliness. In a most extreme example, when the majority of my participants and I went on WISH's annual field trip to Washington, D.C., Miguel arrived, sweating, sprinting, and an hour late, just as the bus pulled away without him.

Throughout our time together, Miguel thoughtfully and intentionally responded to questions. He bleeds a quiet intensity. We spent many afternoons in prolonged silence as he considered the framing of a photograph. He spoke deliberately, calculating each word. I also saw him trying to break out of this persona. At a community event in his neighborhood one weekend, he acted as the photographer. Throughout the event, Miguel moved from group to group, asking in playful tones to take photographs of groups and moments. Outside of school, Miguel's main commitments were an NYPD after-school program and WISH's photography club. He describes himself as a somewhat solitary person, but at school or on the subway, I often encountered Miguel spending time with a couple of friends, including Sofia.

Mateo. Mateo asked to join the project to explore his ideas, desires, and ongoing responsibilities. In addition to school and periodic after-school programs, Mateo worked an almost-full-time job at McDonald's. Halfway through the year, he tried to quit work to focus on school. As he talks about it, though, his family needed him to keep working. After about a month away, he returned to the job. When I asked how he felt about returning to the job, he simply shrugged it off. He said he could balance everything. He enjoyed learning how to work as part of a team and developed a diverse set of skills at his job. Mateo loves video games, sharing nuanced understandings and an intimate knowledge that led us to an ongoing debate over the best video games. His interest in manga pushed him toward learning Japanese. Even though we developed a playful relationship, and even when we talked about incredibly informal topics, Mateo insisted on calling me "mister." He loves hanging out with friends and playing basketball and video games, but there is no denying that the hefty amount of responsibility he takes on has an impact on his everyday life. Torpor drips from him as Mateo walks, but he keeps joking and playing with friends. He rarely misses a day of school, regardless of how he feels.

In our first interview, he shared a representative story of how he balances his responsibilities. After a full day of school, he worked until 11 pm. At the end of his shift, his manager asked him to work an extra hour. He said, "That's not a problem. You give me all the hours that you want. They say okay you stay here till 6 a.m. And I just stay here and work all day. So, for example, let's say, this day is Monday, right? I take my schedule to 11. And then I continue to 6 am. To come here [WISH] at 7. Then, to go to work this same day."

Jordan: So, basically you don't sleep?
Mateo: Basically, I'm not going home. I go to the home of one friend close to school. And wash everything, put my uniform on. That's the most difficult day for me.

His grades and attendance wavered, but his curiosity always hung around. Mateo loved asking me questions as well as describing the research project to others.

Sofia. Sofia joined the project when she barged in on my first interview with Mateo. Saying she was Mateo's girlfriend, she asked a question and barely waited for an answer before requesting to join the project. Interacting with friends or in class, she actively stood up for herself. But Sofia described herself as a shy student. Teachers who know her are often surprised to learn she wants to be an actor. She spoke at great length about wanting to study and pursue acting. If not an actor, or in addition to acting, she thought about being in fashion design. She additionally described herself as academically focused.

Despite initial shyness, Sofia increasingly shared her desires, especially with regard to careers. She never fully articulated why she wanted to act but talked about it constantly. As we grew closer, she began asking more and more questions about college life—about how to apply, fund, and navigate it. She also brought up a plethora of questions about acting, especially after she found out that I majored in theater in college. Beyond acting, she had a limited interest in school. Her favorite educational activities always revolved around learning new games on her phone and spending time with her family.

Leo. In my first weeks at WISH, while I was still familiarizing myself with the school, Leo sprinted up to me and asked to join the project. He explained that he wanted to be a psychologist and wanted to support immigrant communities. At first, I felt that Leo might not be a match for the study. He described his educational life as almost entirely focused on what happened in school or in service of school. Yet, in our initial chats, Leo espoused a complex educational world that spanned nonformal programs, home life, and jobs as well as creating and forming relationships with cultures and nature. Leo often takes an autodidactic approach to learning, whether it be related to a school subject or a personal interest. Throughout the year, both through his participation in school activist groups and in his life outside of school, Leo increasingly explored his racial identity and Dominican heritage. He maintained many intellectual and activist commitments. Though he is now attending university in the United States, Leo often discussed plans to eventually return to the Dominican Republic and create systematic change in the areas of mental health and education.

Matias. While I developed intimate relationships with all participants in the study, and welcomed emotional connections, I always resisted being closer to one participant than others. Undoubtedly, though, I spent the most time with Matias. We walked through various neighborhoods together. He invited me to watch him play basketball. I helped him apply for jobs. He disclosed his struggles and desires, talking openly about his life in school and at home. At various times, Matias wanted to be a basketball player or a rapper. Whenever he recorded a new song, he would excitedly open YouTube on my phone and show me what he had created. He also constantly showed an impulse to care for others. This part of his identity emerged whether he searched for me in the halls, just to ask, "Jordan, how are you doing today?" or when he talked about caring for his younger brother. In classrooms, Matias expressed a desire to focus and show respect to teachers, but he often found himself wandering elsewhere.

Matias's relationship with his mother and stepfather has faced many ups and downs. He was kicked out of his mother's apartment several times. He described being outside of the house as even more difficult than fighting at home, as his neighborhood has, in his own words, "lots of bad influences" for him. Matias also expressed himself constantly, especially when he wrapped me in totally unexpected hugs. At the end of the 2018–2019 school year, Matias left WISH without graduating and began working at McDonald's. He eventually took another job as a barber, maintaining an interest in returning to WISH.

Ximena. Since she was a kid, Ximena has loved making found art. She feels that art "gives me the opportunity to say things I don't say out loud." Ximena spent her childhood in a South American country before coming to the United States. As she has navigated life in the United States, she has fostered an identity of care and responsibility. This role has included acting as an interpreter for her mother for everything from bills to picking up prescriptions at the pharmacy, which she says fundamentally changed her relationship with her family. It has made her feel more adult. School is sometimes a struggle. Ximena says she "is not a student who gets a 100 in every class." At the same time, she finds artistic inspiration everywhere. When she talks about different projects, her enthusiasm is infectious. She didn't understand everything in a science class, but discussing volcanoes birthed new connections for an art project. Ximena also spends time with friends, talking about, among other things, racism, xenophobia, how people are scared of immigrants, and how "education is a way to fight back . . . a way to stop being ignorant." Among her group of friends, Ximena often finds herself playing the role of facilitator or peacemaker, making sure everyone feels included and welcome in the group.

Felipe. Felipe prefers to listen. He finds that talking and sharing his voice can sometimes be difficult, not because of an issue with English or Spanish but because the words are often not there. He loves hanging out with a friend who teaches him how to play every new video game he can find. He also loves baseball and played on WISH's team until he stopped showing up to school (and took a hiatus from this research project). Felipe prefers to "do his own thing," both spending time on his own and making his own choices. Many times, but especially during group work times, I often noticed Felipe on his own, staring toward a distant place. When I occasionally checked in, he would tell me, "I'm just thinking."

In the middle of his hiatus, he came back to WISH for a few days, joining his ESL classes as they rehearsed a theater workshop with a New York City theater company. When he tried to ask a question, the theater teacher told him to "quiet down and hold on." Felipe became increasingly upset that the teacher wasn't listening to him. He walked out of the classroom and did not return to school for a few weeks. In the spring, after months of sparse attendance, Felipe returned to school, promptly came up to me, and with little explanation, asked if he could still be part of the project. Working together, we explored his passion for baseball and, inspired by friends at WISH and in his neighborhood, making rap music. Hoping to refocus his education on schooling and trying to graduate, Felipe continued at WISH in the fall.

Luna. I had finished recruiting participants, had spent time with everyone in school, in spaces between classes, and had begun moving to nonformal educational spaces. One day, sitting with Ximena in an after-school group, Luna approached me and asked what I was doing. After sharing an overview of the project, she instantly told me she "had" to join. The moment she introduced herself perfectly encapsulates Luna. She stands up for herself, fearlessly presents herself, and wants to share so much of who she is. In her own words, Luna is "I don't know, just [Luna]. I'm fabulous." When students and teachers struggled to welcome Luna in the classroom as a transgender girl, she took out a bag of makeup, applied the makeup, and raised her hand to answer a question. That is not to say Luna entirely ignored the impact of bullying or other issues. One of the great lessons she has learned—according to her, an important piece of her education—is how to be a kind person, a "person who helps people." She said that she initially learned these values in school. But, even greater lessons took place outside of school.

> In the past I got bullied because I was fat. Then outside school, when I come out gay,[1] they told me like "I'm gonna come out clean, like I don't want to be your friend." I was like "Why" and they was like "I don't want

to be the friend of a gay person because they gonna say that I'm gay too." And I'm like "Oh, okay, don't talk with me anymore." Just follow what you think.

At WISH, though, Luna found a vibrant, welcoming community. She was always surrounded by a group of friends. Luna started a GSA for students at WISH and led a group from WISH at 2019 Pride. She participated in the media after-school program and took on active roles in a number of clubs and organizations.

Pablo. The second I finished reading my recruitment script for the first time in an ESL class, Pablo's hand shot up. He asked, "Why do you want to work with *us*?" and did not stop asking questions for over a year. A musician, fashionisto, dad, and caretaker of everyone he meets, Pablo's education spreads in many directions. Class lectures and tests often left him feeling restless, but Pablo often took on an active role, trying to make teachers feel supported. Walking the hallways, riding the subway, or standing on the street, Pablo exudes confidence. In the middle of our conversations, he shouted jokes to a passing friend or started singing at full volume in the middle of the street. It was never rude. Pablo just wanted to connect with people. He frequently left school early or did not go at all. He spent time visiting his son or exploring the city. Other times, he enjoyed staying at home and playing video games rather than going to school. Music is Pablo's passion. Almost every time we discussed his music, Pablo struggled to articulate his feelings, turning to vehement hand gestures and energetic head nods.

EDUCATION AND SPACE/PLACE

Thinking about education in spatial terms is nothing new. It is not just that education happens in many places but that, as Gulson and Symes (2007) say, "to what extent education is *education* any longer" (p. 98, emphasis in original). Gulson and Symes are largely concerned with the contours of the field of educational research, but this framing provokes questions of where, when, how, in what conditions, and with what purposes education happens. A key argument of this book is, once more, that education is happening everywhere all the time. Omnipresence does not mean that participants and I simply wandered about, allowing whatever was already happening to happen (though we often ambled through the city, finding surprising educational life). To borrow from Keith Basso's (1996) exploration of the situatedness of knowledge and place, "education sits in places." Considering space as places imbricated with, influenced by, and infused with history, culture, and meaning, interlocutors in this project engaged in educational work both in and outside of school.

But also, Gulson and Symes remind that "the concept of space is no longer 'fixed,' it is also true of the populations that occupy them: they are on the move" (p. 106). Educational practices emerge from specific places and travel. As Leander et al. (2010) ask, "How are the dynamically moving elements of social systems and distributions, including people themselves, and all manner of resources for learning as well, configured and reconfigured across space and time to create opportunities to learn" (p. 331)? The neighborhood generates a certain kind of play. Facebook's offices influence the terms of a conversation. A classroom's architecture shifts the modes of learning. The educations that take place in these different places are also always on the move. I do not want to suggest a false dichotomy here. It is not as though education outside of school is an unfettered, ungovernable activity of radical autonomy, while school offers draconian lessons of compliance. There is a complex and often asymmetrical relationship as education flows and shifts. For all kinds of reasons, what happens in the classroom appears elsewhere. Everyday learning floods classroom life. Educational practices bleed across boundaries and wander and spill across time and place. In doing so, knowledge shifts, and learning becomes something different.

To help think through education and place, I created a heuristic for us to use (see Figure 5.1). We divided a piece of paper into three simple sections representing the three educational spaces (and included spaces for past/future/memory/speculation). We discussed different educational practices happening in these spaces. A living document, we added to, revised, drew connections, and moved away from the paper throughout the year. The participants sometimes crossed things off or redirected where and what educations occurred. It acted as a simple grounding feature to see where and how we might explore different kinds of educational practice. Sometimes, in stuck moments, I prompted with questions about where they felt joy in learning or in which places they felt like their knowledge counted. The practices they valued or saw as useful always guided the project. In interviews or participant observation, I also asked them to show or describe the educational practices they had identified.

Educations in Place and on the Move

Figure 5.1. Example of Leo's Partially Completed Educational Map

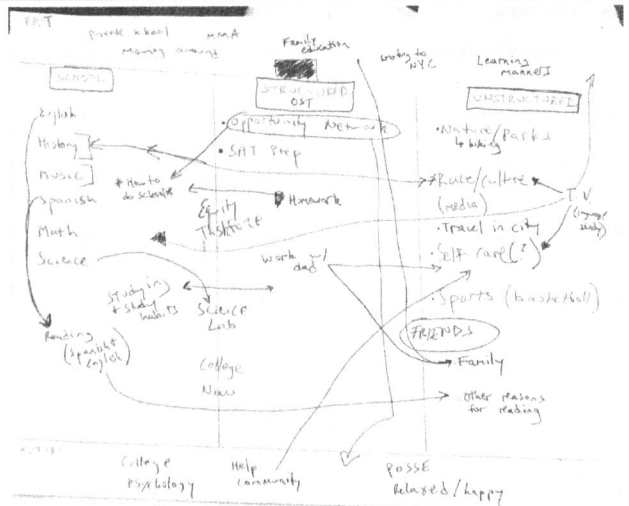

The project moved in a linear, semi-bounded way that did not represent how educations move. We started in school. I spent time in classrooms, hanging out in the cafeteria, moving through days with each participant. As relationships developed, they began inviting me to after-school activities, jobs, and eventually everyday activities like riding the subway or wandering the city. We also moved through places together. Leaving school and heading to the bus. We took field trips together or walked to school in the morning. Encountering these places and moving with interlocutors opened sensations of how different places felt, how bodies and ideas shifted as we moved about, how our ways of speaking moved.

Navigating WISH's Structure

WISH's curriculum often appears similar to that of hundreds of high schools in New York City. Its architecture varies little from other school buildings, though teachers personalize their spaces. Roaming the linoleum-tiled hallways, posters advertise upcoming events or display inclusive slogans. The school's loose, informal structuring welcomes pedagogy and curriculum that largely come down to personality and style. Every participant took a science class with Elena that used a lecture format. Mateo was enthralled by her passionate explanations of scientific principles. Matias appreciated her care and attention to him as a person but found it difficult to follow along during lectures. The music teacher often deployed an approach of demonstrating what to do and then having students play along based on his demonstration. For instance, he would play a scale on the violin. Students then used violins (the school had purchased about a dozen violins) to play along with a recording of the scale.

Six participants took either history or government classes with Nick, the well-liked "no-nonsense" teacher. This teacher routinized his class with daily PowerPoints and end-of-unit presentations or tests. Daily activities also asked students to work in groups to answer specific questions or debate a topic. Erin's class involved more open discussion. With Spanish–English dictionaries stacked on each table group, lists of English vocab on the back wall, and books stacked in random places, the class moved through conversations, writing activities, and shared reading. She maintained a loose, inviting pedagogy across her classes. Erin's "low-level" ESL class took on a very similar structure to her AP English class. Whether asking students to construct sentences that served as a baseline for identifying and debating character feelings in ESL or asking thematic questions about James Baldwin's books, Erin set up a kind of overarching structure and then facilitated dialogic work.

Though far from unified, themes of immigration filled the school day. Teachers selected texts that centered immigrant stories. History lessons connected the treatment of immigrants in the 19th century to present-day United States. Teachers spoke of their own immigration stories and asked students to draw connections. Different classes and teachers took different approaches to how they understood immigrants. One teacher spoke with students about immigration as a racialized category. She studied with students, looking at long histories of exclusion and hierarchical forms of inclusion. Another teacher provided what they called an affirmative approach but considered immigration any time people moved across borders, with no mention of the uneven violence and complex histories of those borders. With no shared vision and no guiding direction, the school simply focused on the idea that immigration is a topic for all classes.

Within this overarching dynamic structure, students learned and responded to teachers and lessons in divergent ways. Participants were enamored with a lesson and bored out of their minds or loved one subject Monday morning, only to despise it as they walked into the class on Tuesday. Our early conversations identified their favorite classes, but even these changed with great frequency. Leo relished going to school. He rarely missed a class. Early on, he asked me to come to music class. Throughout the class, he engaged with the activities, testing out a new song the teacher asked them to practice together. He seemed his regular, active self. Walking out of the class together, I asked why he wanted me to come to this particular class. "I wanted you to see how boring it is," he told me. When I asked him to elaborate, Leo said, "I don't know. It's just pointless. I just take this class because it's there."

I found myself in similar, definitely familiar feelings of boredom. Around my third month of participant observation in the school, I began to recall the rhythms of schooling, not as a teacher or researcher but as a student. I waited for bells and trudged through the cycle of a school day. I often sat, bored not by any fault of a teacher's pedagogy but by the sheer mundanity of hours on hours spent at desks, day after day. Once, Pablo asked me to hang out with him during a math class that turned out to be during a test. Seeing that the teacher was about to hand out a test, I got up to leave, but the teacher encouraged me to stay. So for the next hour I sat at a desk, silent, watching for any twitch of movement, thirsting for a sense of energy rippling into the classroom. Looking through my fieldnotes, I described the movement of pencils, the hunch of Pablo's shoulders. I observed the lack of ventilation.

> It's still only 2:15 and my back is starting to hurt. It's hard to tell how far Pablo has made it on the test. If he'll finish on time. He gets up, asks for an eraser. What's the color and shape of the eraser? Is it one of those pink rhombus ones? He seems restless, but he keeps working on the test. This is one of the rooms with no windows. Do the kids mind? Everyone seems more or less focused on the test. Eyes don't move around much. Bodies stay in seats. Is there really not anything more useful, after all my coursework on ethnographic research, that I can glean? Something more productive?

I am reminded here of a moment from *Ordinary Affects* (Stewart, 2007). "When something happens, we swarm toward it, gaze at it, sniff it, absorb its force, pour over its details, make fun of it, hide from it, spit it out, or develop a taste for it" (p. 70). This sentiment reveals so much of educational life in classrooms of WISH. Much of the school fit into the grammar of schooling. And yet, each day found little ruptures, where pleasure and learning moved together, where chaotic energy overtook quotidian practice. Students and teachers pursued and welcomed little moments to break the boundaries of classroom life. Within the common routine of the school year, students vibrated with enthusiasm. Sounds of joy exploded outside a classroom, reeling in passersby. Students buzzed during a gallery walk in Nick's history class and gasped at thoughtful video demonstrations in Elena's science class.

Beautiful interruptions pushed the day along, infusing meaning and care into the school day. In history class one day, Luna thrust her love of makeup into the center of the class. We had spent the previous period together. She slogged through the class, silent and rolling her eyes. As we reached history class, she suddenly pulled a makeup kit from her bag. Applying lipstick, she answered questions about the impact of European imperialism on India. Glancing at her progress in a compact, she began a history debate with students in the class. She spent the entire period doing her makeup and vigorously engaging in a class discussion. Perhaps it was her passion for the topic, her love of makeup, or simply the time of day, but between periods 5 and 6 Luna's energy swelled, making of the class something other than the worksheets I often observed them working on.

In a rather formal way, nonformal educations also ended up in classrooms. Theater workshops, for instance, took the form of short, project-based learning units in ESL classes. Students read the book *A Long Walk to Water* and adapted it as a short play. Dominantly, these CBO partnerships lasted a couple of weeks and fit neatly into the structure of the school day. Even with the presence of a teaching artist, students still followed their everyday routines. Slight variations popped up, such as when a class moved to the auditorium to perform. Yet these small interruptions still had to find ways to fit into the school's established routines.

So, of course, school is much more than the formal teachings in the containers of classrooms (as Leander et al., 2010 put it). School educations are also the spaces where students gleefully caught up in the hallway between 8th and 9th period. It is where they clamored their desks together for a group project while figuring out plans for the weekend. Students found escape from boredom in a stroll through the hallways. The language of instruction in the hallways was dominantly Spanish or Spanglish, but I heard English and Arabic also, as friends taught and translated. Connections formed in the cafeteria. Plans were made in the stairwell. Much learning was done in those hidden places that escape authoritative gazes.

That is not to say that school was boring, forcing students to magically steal energy in classrooms or find it in liminal spaces. It is also not to say that school was a thrilling, endlessly joyful place. Many times, I joined Ximena, Leo, and Mateo for their last two periods of the day. From Spanish literature to U.S. history, they cycled through feelings, attitudes, and different ways of engaging with the classes. Some days, Mateo barely lifted his head off the desk in U.S. History, even though he identified it as one of his favorite classes. On certain days, Sofia's hand shot up as soon as the Spanish teacher asked a question. She fought through a raucous, buzzing classroom and her own shyness. As with other examples, there were days of absences, days of exhaustion, and days bursting with playful translanguaging. Suffice it to say that throughout the school year, participants encountered a spectrum of ideas, feelings, movements, and educations. All of this is not to make bland, generic observations about schooling but to hint at the diverse, shifting formal schooling experiences that participants encountered.

School is both a welcoming place that stirs a sense of genuine belonging and a place where many participants felt a sense of "unsettled belonging" (to use Abu El-Haj's [2015] term). Luna said she felt like she belonged because of her friends, many teachers, and learning opportunities. She also said that some people did not make her feel welcome and that she often felt unsure and insecure in school. In our first weeks working together, as we walked the halls together, it was difficult to finish a sentence without running into one of her friends. This layer of acceptance lulled me into seeing her belonging as more complete.[2] Then, in science class one day, the teacher noticed Luna was running late. "Well," he said. "We can't wait for him, or her, or whatever [Luna's dead name] wants to be called now." Luna returned to this dichotomy a number of times, feeling pulled toward belonging in the school and then pushed and shamed for her existence. A different kind of unsettled belonging tug rope pulled at Felipe, inviting him in and then chastising him for behavior. He felt welcomed and then excluded. He loved school until he did something the school didn't like.

For all the space I have devoted to showing fractured responses and experiences in school, some common themes poked through. Education in school is highly structured. It operates through an institutionalized routine. The diverse learning, different projects, hidden curriculums, and much else all occur within the physical and temporal space of WISH. Access to the building and routine attendance within the school are necessary conditions for educational practices in the school. WISH's educations were not totalizing, but the school's structure guided formal educations. Bells interrupted bubbling interactions.

Tests dictated how far teachers could stray in a given lesson. Teachers and students pushed back, but the twin binaries and grammar of schooling persisted. Education in school chipped away at the notion of a container, but school as an intellectually and physically defined place remained.

Nonformal Education Work

Nonformal education often occurred in distinct places and made other kinds of education possible, but the logics of schooling seeped into nonformal education. Nonformal education was frequently slotted into a role subservient to schooling's structure. In framing nonformal education, I build on La Belle (1981), who poses nonformal education as "organized, systematic teaching carried on outside of the formal, usually chronologically graded and hierarchically structured, school system that is intended to provide particular types of learning to specific populations" (p. 315). I also position nonformal education as something that is deeply entangled with, and often follows, formal schooling. It may not be as grounded in routine and credentialing, but nonformal education adheres to similar logics.

After the last bell, WISH operates a series of clubs and nonformal programs. Other opportunities also extend into the evening. WISH's only semi-mandatory program after school was a weekly science lab. Here, students gather in small groups to work on a self-guided lab project. The lab is essentially a continuation of and added support for the regular school day. WISH's formal partnerships include the Facebook group, which Ximena and Luna both joined. Ximena described her participation as something social and a vague attempt at finding art classes through WISH. "The Facebook program—people get selected to be in it, but really it's not not art—music is our only real art here." Once a week, a group of about a dozen students gathered in a WISH classroom to discuss the technical and artistic aspects of advertising with a teaching artist not associated with WISH. In the sessions I joined, the teacher created a relaxed environment with time to collaborate on mini-projects and chat with friends. Each week had a similar structure of introducing an idea, offering a few examples, and then giving the students time to work in groups. Every other week, the group also traveled together to the offices of Facebook to hear from members of their media team. The program culminated in a year-end project in which students created public service commercials about a topic they selected.

In addition to these partnerships, several WISH teachers sponsor after-school activities and clubs. These nonformal programs emerge at the discretion of teachers, students, and administrators. Within such programs, teachers commonly reify the power dynamics of the school day. Throughout the year, I spent a great deal of time with Miguel in photography club. The teacher supported students as they learned about composition, lighting, and general rules of photography. Meeting twice a week, the club included lectures and direct instruction. There was also a flexibility and openness to the class that was less present during the school day. Miguel talked about this directly, saying he felt more comfortable during photography club, both at school and during their trips. The students spent one or two Wednesdays every month wandering the city, taking photos. The teacher went with them, encouraging experimentation and discovery. On these trips, I sensed a bit more breathing, additional flexibility while they practiced photography. In many ways, these spaces created different forms of educational community. They provided networks of support and engagement in ways that the school day did not. As Love (2019) suggests about nonformal educational programming, "these organizations were critical to our sense of community and survival," and "it was more authentic because it was our choice to enter these spaces" (p. 58). Indeed, the way Ximena spoke about the Facebook group or how Miguel described photography club made it sound like a respite, a site of joy amid school's difficulty. At the same time, in many of these spaces, the pedagogical relationships from the school day remained intact. One day, the photography teacher chastised Miguel for wanting to skip. "You made a commitment to come. This is your responsibility, *like school*," the teacher explained.

Other nonformal educational events related to WISH included field trips, optional weekend test prep, and political activities at the school. Joining these activities required a commitment and a signed form and often included prerequisites of teachers accepting students. One teacher told me that, though one of my participants had returned a permission slip, they would not be invited to join an upcoming field trip due to their lack of focus in class. The school day was, at least on the surface, unconditionally guaranteed for all WISH students. Nonformal education was commonly something accessed and authorized.

The link between sports and school meant that attendance and grades determined eligibility to participate in school sports. During Felipe's absence from school, I ran into the baseball coach. When I asked him if he had heard from Felipe recently, the coach explained that he had not and consequently needed to kick Felipe off the team. This theme of schooling's supremacy and centrality ran through many nonformal programs. Whether Felipe's grades dictated his eligibility to play baseball or the Facebook group's application and selective criteria, nonformal education functioned less as something autonomous and distinct and more as a supplement that supported and bolstered the logics of schooling.

Participation in nonformal educational programs was also selective in other, informal ways. Leo learned about the Opportunity Network from a teacher. It offered him academic grammars that went beyond the regular school day, educating toward academic and professional life. None of the other participants knew about the program, at least until Leo mentioned it to them. Some programs, like the NYPD Explorers, conversely aimed to use educations happening outside of school to, in their eyes, extend equalizing opportunities that filled gaps in the school system. These programs and their asymmetrical distribution of opportunity reflect developments started during the Bloomberg administration, both an increased institutional focus on nonformal education programs as sites of alternative opportunity and a renewed focus on creating programs with measurable results (Hatch et al., 2021b). Where these different programs and clubs stretched pedagogies and created different curricular engagements, they also continued the tracking, inequities, and general conventions of formal schooling.

Beyond WISH and its partnerships, participants and their families sought nonformal educational opportunities that worked in conjunction with schools. Miguel and Sofia spent one day a week participating in the aforementioned NYPD Explorers, a program dedicated to youth learning "teamwork and leadership skills" (NYPD Youth Programs, 2019). Miguel described activities such as marching, which was intended to increase discipline and focus. It was interesting to move between conversations with Miguel about how the NYPD Explorers worked to prepare him to become a cop or join the military and chats with Leo about how a place like the Opportunity Network prepared him for pursuing higher education. Placing their reflections on these nonformal education programs next to each other, it almost seems like a hidden curriculum (Anyon, 1980) laid across nonformal spaces. A youth marked as "promising" received a nonformal opportunity to push toward higher education, while another youth was taught to march and follow directions. Yet even as these tracked forms of nonformal education occurred, the pedagogy bore strange similarities. Leo described rote, direct instruction used to teach skills like writing a professional email or completing a job application. Miguel offered similar details of direct instruction as leaders of the NYPD Explorers explained how to march and salute.

They never quite fit within the heuristic we created, but participants mostly placed jobs as part of nonformal education. They articulated jobs as structured experiences with specific purposes. Mateo related many of the skills he learned at his job to the knowledge he needed in school. "If my boss tells me to count something or to use some equation, you know, this makes things easy in math class," he said. Other participants reported how jobs taught skills like time management, self-reliance, teamwork, and opportunities to practice English.

As with school, nothing specifically unified nonformal education spaces. An NYPD precinct's fluorescent lighting and collared shirt uniforms are far from the open-concept architecture and endless snack bar of the Facebook offices. I initially brought some critiques of these places into our conversations, asking about the role of Facebook or the NYPD in educational life. Participants pushed back, espousing their appreciation for their respective programs. As my own educations moved, we never resolved these conversations. What right did I have to critique Miguel's involvement in the NYPD program? What right did I have to say nothing? Even with focus on discipline and policing, it was in the voluntary and temporary space of NYPD Explorers that Miguel smiled and joked with other youth participating in the program.

Going to the Facebook headquarters created a sense of wonder and excitement. On the first day I joined them, I dropped into a squishy couch as Luna and Ximena crowded a wall-mounted selfie camera. They made themselves comfortable on the couches before bounding to the snack bar. Settling in, they swiveled in high-backed office chairs. As the session started, however, a Facebook employee offered procedural instructions on the next step of the process of creating an advertisement. The organization and ideas of nonformal education were commonly rendered school-like, even as these spaces diverged from schooling.

Many of these programs also generated culminating events, as if the nonformal programs built toward some ultimate end. The NYPD Explorers hosted a community event early in June, with Miguel feverishly walking around taking photos. At a swanky Manhattan venue, the Facebook group's public service ads were screened along with those of other schools participating in similar nonformal programs.

When I asked participants about how these events compared to other end-of-year events, be they Regents or big projects, many of them suggested that they were just different. To paraphrase something Leo pointed out, nobody liked tests, but nonformal programs offered opportunities to share their work, their different forms of study, in ways that school did not allow.

Unstructured Time Outside of School

Education in everyday life is not only what is left over after institutionalized learning concludes. It is not just the stuff sitting outside of school or nonformal programs. Like Harney and Moten (2013) suggest, "intellectual life is already at work around us" (p. 112). Educational practices valued and used in everyday life operated in ways as rigorous and academic as those of school or nonformal educations. Participants' everyday educational practices wound along diverging, intersecting, and parallel paths as they negotiated and played with these practices in the biggest sense of how education can be understood. These practices were scattered, incomplete, underexplored, and they filled days and spaces across the city and memories.

After months of hanging out in school and nonformal programs, I began to ask participants about other kinds and places of educational practice. I did not aim to create comprehensive maps or to catalogue educational practices into cohesive narratives (though I am temporarily doing so here). Centering care and protection and continuing a method of thin description, I simply asked a series of questions that could be discussed, demonstrated, or experienced together. "Any other places where you learn things you care about?" I asked. "What are you studying that bring you joy? Places where you feel successful?" Or, I posed, "What kinds of education[3] do you take up that are different from school?" With little prompting, participants shared learning processes, figuring out responsibilities, the development of skills, dreams, values, and philosophies.

These educational practices laid bare becoming identities and different ways of being, things not seen in other educational spaces. Some practices were recognizable as common learning activities. Sofia loved learning games on her phone. Ximena instructed friends on getting along with each other. Every person participating in the project talked about figuring out the subway. A major theme of unstructured educational practices was simply learning how to live everyday life in a new place. Leo described how, when he first moved from the

Dominican Republic, he was accustomed to greeting everyone on the bus with a smile and a "good day" or "how are you?" His first time riding the subway in New York City offered a cruel lesson as silent glares and confused murmurs taught him to keep to himself. All participants similarly discussed the process of learning and practicing language. It was neither simply a matter of applying what was learned in ESL class nor a binary of learning English and Spanish. Everyone was constantly practicing, figuring out, and testing new kinds of language. Like many unstructured educational practices, these educations were often subtle or accidental.

One afternoon, Miguel asked me to join him as he took photos in a park. En route, I tried to leave him alone as he chatted with a friend on the subway. Yet I couldn't help but notice a fluid conversation full of translanguaging. Moreover, I heard Miguel and his friend debating and explaining language, communicating the subtleties of words. For a few stops, they explored the complex meaning of a word that, depending on the language, the place, the speaker, etc. can be used as a homophobic slur, emasculating slang or take on multiple other meanings. As we exited the subway, I asked Miguel about the conversation and what he thought about the language practices he discussed with his friend. "I don't know," he said, "we just talk. I don't really think about it."

Rooted in interests and responsibilities, other educational practices were more specific to individuals or groups. Luna often spoke of how she studied and learned from people in the LGBTQ+ community. Through online learning, facilitating the GSA at WISH, and moving through everyday life, Luna was, she explained, learning how to be herself. At times, something like language learning moved into formal practiced hobbies beyond English and Spanish. Mateo emphasized an interest in taking up Japanese. "I learn it by watching. I see another person do it [a friend or on TV]. That's one of my strategies. Or, I ask questions. With my friends who are Japanese, when we watch anime I'm saying 'Bro, give me a sentence.'"

> *Jordan:* I imagine that's scary. Jumping into a new language like that.
> *Mateo:* I'm not scared. If I'm not knowing anything I just ask questions.

As seen in Mateo's description, these more specific endeavors entailed exploration and risk. They generated their own curriculum, driven by a desire to study in new directions. They entered tasks with no guarantees and guided only by uncertain pedagogies and companionship. Felipe offered a similar example. "I wanted to learn how to play Fortnite on PS4. I just learn with my best friend. I didn't know the movement of the characters, how to control them, anything. But I was learning every day. . . . He told me things like 'press the X to jump . . . throw this.' I was learning just like that." Felipe positioned himself as a learner, accepting and even asking for a kind of direct instruction. He spent days asking questions and figuring out the basics before he tried Fortnite himself.

For participants, education in everyday life was also often something quite practical. They described learning the subway as an incidental educational process of living life in New York City. As these examples indicate, though, the unstructured time and space of education in everyday life blends practical concerns with deep passions. Pablo and Matias loved making music, learning about new artists, sharing ideas with each other, co-learning, and posting freestyles or videos to YouTube. Sofia looked for every possible avenue toward acting. Even as she said that she felt too scared to join a formal program like a youth theater, she read about and thought about acting constantly.

Mateo's historical knowledge and critical lens of video games offered another example of intellectual rigor coursing through unstructured time. He spoke with great fluency on video game systems released before he was born. He analyzed and offered detailed critiques of my favorite games in ways that made me reconsider my own encounters with these games. The over-the-shoulder perspective in *Resident Evil*, he explained, goes beyond simply changing the way such games are played. It creates added closeness, suspense, and thus tension for horror games.

These forms of education were frequently communal, shared experiences as youth learned with each other. When we met, Felipe explicitly stated that he had little interest in music. By the time we sat down for our second interview, he explained how Pablo and other friends were teaching him how to make lyrics. Similarly, Sofia joined Miguel so that he could practice photography and she could think about how to make headshots. They spent several days wandering upper Manhattan, discussing dreams of photography and acting, encouraging each other and wondering aloud together about lives and learning made through these activities.

Given the diversity of spaces and activities, there is no curriculum, no organizing pedagogy for educational practices in unstructured time. Pedagogues and curricular materials shift across space, even within the same undertaking of study. Felipe learned a video game through rote instruction. He then played it, exploring through trial and error. Leo's understanding of the subway system was experimental and entangled with emerging understandings of social life in New York City. If something was shared, it was that a curriculum of unstructured time was bound to desires without ends. Even Mateo learning a language did not move with a plan but just questions of what a scene in anime meant, words he could learn and use. Like language, education in this way was not something obtained, something that participants "got" the way people will often say they "got an education" after completing a certain level of schooling. Education was, rather, something that was done, performed, practiced, and enacted. Curriculums, guided by desires and interests, moved in open flows. Learning emerged in one place and then moved in a chaotic direction. It disappeared, reappearing in a different place and in a different form. The previous sections have traced various educational practices occurring in various spaces. Now, I turn away from trapping these practices, peering toward what they make possible, how they relate across time and space, and how they metamorphose or evolve.

ENTANGLED AND MOVING EDUCATIONAL PRACTICES

This book emphasizes educational practices in everyday life. So, of course, there is a bit of preference for the magic of what happens when formal educational structures fade into the background. I do not want to hide the romantic feelings that boiled as I watched educational life, so often obscured from schooling, enacted without restraints. Educational life winds through different spaces and roars awake at any moment. Educational spaces are not stagnant, bordered hierarchies. Throughout the project, everyday life felt more welcoming of open and joyous educational practices. But felicitous wonder occurred in every classroom at WISH. Experimentation and pleasure filled nonformal spaces. Governance also snuck into every crevice, including unstructured, playful moments of study.

School and Outside Are Related, but They're Distinct Educational Spaces

If school can operate as a kind of container for educational practices, it stands in contrast to that which occurs in everyday life. In many ways, this contrast revealed itself in the energy shifts every time I walked out of the school or sensed changes in demeanor and comfort when spending time with interlocutors in their everyday lives. I noticed this distinction in full force the first time I accompanied participants on a field trip to a New York City museum.

> We walk to [the museum]. As the kids exit the school, their shoulders relax, their voices rise. . . . As we cross the threshold between the school and the sidewalk, the change is immediate. They suddenly jump on each other's backs. Laughing, play fighting. With joy, they shout to each other across the street. [Ximena] and [Leo] wrap their arms around each other. [Mateo] pops on some headphones and starts singing along to a song on his phone. It is as though everyone walked through a kind of portal that shed metaphorical weights from their bodies. The things organizing and tidying their day stay behind as they wander the neighborhood.

Encountering education in this way—as we moved from one space to another—suggests that the outside of school was freer, awash in openness and exploration. The outside of school carried fewer expected educational outcomes. During this field trip and during many other moments, I asked participants what they wanted to get out of educational events happening outside of school or what they expected from it. They often told me that they were unsure or, as Mateo responded on the walk to the museum, "We'll see." It was not only that a specific educational activity operated in this way, but that open space and time allowed for centering the unexpected.

The same was true not just of transitioning between spaces but during nonformal educational events, such as described in the following vignette:

> I join Miguel for the NYPD Explorers end-of-year event. We spend most of the day together. His usual militaristic demeanor has vanished. He is goofy, playing with his camera. Usually, he carefully frames landscape images but now he's sneaking quick, candid photos of me and smiling about catching me off guard. Other people at the event speak various languages. Miguel suggests we speak Spanish together, something we rarely do. He is patient with me, but his stoicism dissolves into a kind of exuberance. His face lifts and a grin spreads the moment he sees me. Even his posture is more relaxed. We've had a strong, friendly rapport for months, and he thanks me profusely for coming to the event, but it's such a difference between photography club in the classroom a few days ago or even chatting between classes yesterday afternoon.

The distinction between spaces was even more overt when walking through the city during unstructured times. Matias and I spent a number of afternoons wandering through different neighborhoods, especially near his favorite basketball court. The city's energy broke into WISH. Noises spilled into classrooms; the business of the streets echoed upward to WISH's floor. The vibrancy that whispered into WISH surrounded Matias and I as we walked. Walking uphill on a particularly sweaty day, Matias spoke of how walking, alone or with others, helped him think through or think up lyrics. He mentioned this a number of times, and it was often followed by Matias jumping into freestyling.

The many spaces of everyday life pulsed with charges always stirring different forms of exploration and interaction. Spatially, moving outside of WISH generated more openness. Intellectually, I observed participants moving among communities, exploring different ways of learning and types of doing. Most importantly, it was in these outside spaces that I encountered educational lives framed through risk and failure coming to life, suddenly vibrating, confident, and brimming with possibility. This distinction was not just a matter of space, and it is something explored further in the following chapter, but the subway, the park, and stoop—these were spaces where participants who had largely remained quiet and reserved, rarely answering questions and doing so with uncertainty in their voices, became confident intellectuals, expressing their educational lives without hesitation.

Outside space may be freeing, but it is not free. Control, danger, and educational governance moved outside to affirm social orders. The protections of school transformed into risks of ICE showing up and detaining those youth participants marked as undocumented. Open, exuberant learning also carried ghostly trails of concern. When participants spoke about immigration status—either theirs or that of friends and family members—it was sometimes central, sometimes background, but always a relentless concern. Learning in everyday life reckoned with this concern, like carrying a stone in one's pocket, sometimes irksome, other times forgotten, but always there. At times, participants learned sports with little worry. They also described many instances of worry taking hold, making focusing on responsibilities or other activities almost impossible, something that was more present and visceral outside of school but were felt throughout the day.

The container of schooling, even when it appeared, was not always a negative, repressive space. WISH and other schools may form around predetermined logics and goals. Classrooms and hallways, cops and doors, and bells and schedules may govern bodies. Curriculum may be largely planned and working toward a specific goal of academic outcomes. The event of schooling can, though, act as freeing in ways distinct from outside time and space. Matias described schooling as a place of refuge, apart from the world outside. He said WISH protected against many things and gave him a space apart from influences he tried to avoid in his life outside of school. Ximena also described WISH as her first community. After moving to different apartments and cities, and after transferring through multiple schools in the United States, WISH acted as a place of stability, a social place where Ximena's interests in arts and friendships blossomed. In this way, much like Masschelein and Simons (2013) argue, the school came to carry the potential to be a place separated from education in everyday life. It is a distinct space where education can operate suspended from the demands, subjectivities, and controls running through the world beyond its walls. Likewise, it can be a place removed from the riskiness of everyday life, allowing people at WISH to take up different kinds of educational adventures. This is not to make school seem like a utopia. Internal politics, asymmetrical power relations, and all kinds of borders constrict possibilities. But even in the porous container that school can be, there is a freeing potential.

School and outside were thus separated and distinct but not stable—contrasting binaries. The freeing potential of schooling was not only a spatial construct but also something that poked through the formal curriculum, where there were liberatory practices happening inside the school. And there were governing practices in everyday life, with kids instructing each other on how to be, teaching themselves what to do in normative ways. There was also a clear sense that beyond any specific practice, a broad understanding lurked, that school was where real education happens. And nonformal spaces could form to resemble this "real" education.

Assembling Schooling in Nonformal Spaces

School appeared everywhere. It went outside, crossed streets, rode subways, and reformed in nonformal spaces. In casual moments or informal chats, we were suddenly doing schooling. It clung to places that were specifically intended to be outside of school. And nobody seemed to flinch. During the museum field trip, the rhythms circulating through WISH found their way into the museum. After the vibrant, raucous exploration of the walk to the museum, a docent found our group and started a tour. She asked us to sit in a small circle and listen as she explained a topic. After a few minutes of lecture, she asked the group a review question about who knew what. She gently reminded that anyone who wanted to speak, at least youth, should raise their hands. She told students who was right and who was wrong. We then moved to the next section of the museum, with students playing and chatting with each other during the transition. The same pattern of lecture and quiz repeated as we moved through the museum. It was not an exact replica, simply making and doing school in a different space, but many of the same active, raised hands that spoke up in classes were those engaged and participatory in the museum.

The museum trip relates to my fieldnotes from my first weeks in WISH.

> Around 8th period, I realize I am reaccustomed to the old rhythms of school, moving through the hallways, knowing when students should raise hands, when and how to listen, what students can get away with (and with whom). The tone and texture of teachers' voices asks for something. The way they speak to me in one way and students in another way. I am now reacquainted with this strange ecology of a school. Sitting at the back of [teacher's] room, I recall my own boredom and desire to participate, my own engagement or lack thereof as a student. It is once more a familiar way of doing education. . . . This is what counts as *real education*.

Despite its difference in energy or the openness of experience and the semi-autonomy to explore, the museum and other structured learning spaces reified the rhythms and rote form of knowledge production seen throughout the school day. The relationship between school education and (speaking broadly) structured nonformal education was one of subservience. That is not a critique of any individual educator or any specific approaches to education. Rather, the manner of doing school hegemonically popped up in many places. Participants organized themselves in formations sitting in a circle or in rows and learned through procedures of question and answer to test knowledge.

Similarly, the mechanisms and legitimation of school took shape in different places. For weeks, Ximena excitedly told me about the culminating event with the Facebook group. All of the schools participating in the program sent students to present videos they had made that shared some kind of public service message. At the event, the program coordinator played the video. She then read each person's name and gave them a certificate of completion. They shook hands and walked across the front of the room as the audience clapped. After the event, as Ximena, Luna, and I spoke, I asked if I could look at the certificate they received. It was a simple note indicating that they had completed the program. They were both indifferent to the certificate, but its presence shifted the focus, as if their research and work in this after-school program were not serious until they received a credential. This event, which I thought would be a showcase of their work, celebrating hours spent learning and tinkering with editing and scripting, ultimately centered a formalized "graduation" moment.

I repeatedly caught myself using schooling logics as a reference point for education. In a class trip to Washington, D.C., as Ximena, Leo, Mateo, and Sofia gathered for selfies with a replica of the Batmobile, I wondered what they would get out of this time and why the focus was not on the more serious (i.e., school-like) aspects of the museum. Why, I couldn't help questioning, did they not focus on a section talking about democracy, U.S. elections, and so much else from Nick's history class? Once teachers gathered and explained the day's schedule, everyone started walking through different areas. They set up museum tours with specific objectives and gave students worksheets to complete. The museum itself presented direct instruction, both hegemonic lessons on Americanness and a general lesson that there were specific objects of knowledge, skills to be developed, things with outcomes to be had. Visitors should learn this or that about a Model T from the 1920s. They should know the date of the introduction of the first gramophone. Encountering the museum was not enough. Leo and I discussed these while walking around the Mall afterward.

> I ask what he thought of it. He tells me it was fine. Thinking about this Americanness and schoolness, I ask him "Wasn't it all a bit rah-rah go U.S.A.?" He looks confused, pauses, and says "Yeah, that's the point, right?" I suggest that it was kind of like a history textbook [something Leo and I had critiqued in previous conversations]. I mention the tiny exhibit on the Know Nothing Party[4] and how even that seemed to fit a narrative, like it's a museum that makes it seem like the United States has a pro-immigration history that students should learn. "I think that would be a different museum," Leo tells me.

The museum held certain expected learning outcomes. To problematize U.S. history itself would make it an entirely different learning experience, perhaps one less school-like. At the same time, returning to the idea of distinct spaces, the energy and formations of schooling emerged in ways that were looser, leaving more space to move away from schooling assemblages, allowing participants to encounter displays or ignore them.

And yet, the dominant logics of school had moved to this place. Categorized, demonstrable forms of knowledge took over the processes and practices of places outside of school. Dynamic intelligences and knowledges of all kinds of expressions were asked, in these circumstances, to fit into the codifying, certifying ways that schooling can approach education. Perhaps school is just the common template, a shared reference point. Walking through neighborhoods, participants decided what and where, and often how, to learn. Like when Pablo learned how to play dominoes, with shouts and constant interruptions, flows of information, and a different way of studying together, there was a boisterousness that felt impossible in a classroom. Yet the same game took shape around instructive positions. Pablo stood on the outside, and whispered a question, "Who knows what happens if I do this?" to someone. There was still a clear order, a knower, in possession of knowledge, and a learner. As Rancière (1991) suggests, this is the machinery of schooling. "To teach was to transmit learning and form minds simultaneously, by leading those minds according to an ordered progression, from the most simple to the most complex" (p. 3). Teaching and learning appeared in many places, but it was school that so often shaped the form of such teaching and learning.

Depaepe and Smeyers (2008) suggest that modern/izing states engage in an "educationalization" of all aspects of society. Educationalization includes both the rendering of all social problems as schooling matters and turning any event in social life into a pedagogical concern (e.g., traffic stops being framed through learning questions such as "Do you know why I pulled you over?"). Extending this idea, common sense understandings of schooling take over how the educationalization of society occurs. That is, the way of doing education, in whatever place or for whatever form, moves to a constant reference point of schooling. Whether a museum or a game of dominoes, school informs how learning should take place, how bodies should be organized, or how knowledge can be assessed. School here is not some monstrous blob, moving ever outward to consume and normalize all types of education. But the grammar of schooling, the common-sense understandings of how education can and should look, has a heavy pull that influences everyday educational activities. Even still, other kinds of education find ways to move and connect.

BORDERLESS CONSTELLATIONS OF LEARNING

Places of learning mark themselves with distinction—some open and expressive, others asking for calm reflection. Participants listened to and resisted what places asked. Education is never static. It refuses to be bordered, bound up, named, and held to space or time. These spaces of learning can include the school, the street, the museum, home, the park, the subway, la cancha, and the recording studio. These are not isolated or unrelated spaces but, rather, pulsing networks, entangled worlds influencing and influenced by ongoing educational practices. Education travels across time and space over and over. It follows or chases. At times, it lays dormant, hidden until a surprising moment. What is practiced in one place takes on a new shape. It continues elsewhere. It travels, teleports, forms, metamorphosizes, reforms.

Knowledge was on the move. Leo learned English from his first days at WISH. He went home and put on Netflix, which also taught him English, in a different way, with different methods. He stepped foot on the subway, not knowing the cultural codes of public transit in New York City and started speaking the kind of English he learned from Netflix (specifically, the show *Wild 'N Out*). It was only strange looks that indicated something was off. The lessons of the subway offered new kinds of language education. Leo practiced English with friends, in the hallways, back on the subway, and in class. These educational practices melded with social lessons of space. The subway is where you keep your head down, not needing to talk to people. Mind your own business. The English of school, he learned, was different from the English practiced with friends or what was used on TV shows. And yet, he kept studying. So it changed again, moved with him. He shaped learning just as it shaped him. He started using language much closer to what he learned at home in playful essays in ELA classes. He infused Spanglish into comments he made in formal school council meetings.

Manners of study like craftwork also move. To bear down on a thing, study it, try to know it. And then, quite suddenly, somewhere else and at some other time, without warning or preparation, a new way of thinking about it comes forth. A new technique reveals itself. Someone offers a passing comment and a skill is unlearned. What was supposedly grasped is reconfigured. Craftwork and learning push onward. Something is lost, certainly. The clear path becomes murky. But now routes have become visible and more educations unfold all around. Mateo learned teamwork at school, working on history projects. It taught him to compromise, play to his strengths—as he said, "to work things out." This knowledge paid off when his boss reminded him that teamwork was essential to his job. He learned when and how to move around the grill and how to listen to other employees in the kitchen. Even in moments when he spaced out and burned his hand on the fryer, he came to understand how these lessons related, fitting into a larger educational project of a skill about working with others. It ultimately made the job more enjoyable and the shifts easier. Mateo figured out how to support new employees or confront colleagues about spending too much time at the register without helping prep food in the back. Teamwork skills bled together as he prepared history slides for a presentation, working with his classmates. He realized it wasn't divided, like working an individual station and rotating, but, rather, everyone taking their own role and supporting others. "I finished my slide for the presentation, but let me see how your slide looks," he said. He related this back to shifting understandings of his role with other workers at McDonald's. During one of our interviews, he suddenly paused, and said he was not sure how he missed it, but teamwork was also essential to playing basketball.

School subjects unexpectedly popped up with force and connection to everyday life. Felipe engaged in very little of his history class beyond a love of watching videos and being able to hang out with a friend at the back of the room. One day, while playing Fortnite with a different friend, he saw "a whole something of pyramids in the game." He did not know why, he could not explain it, but he connected to it. Something struck him and stuck with him. This small moment playing Fortnite led to discoveries and a deeper engagement with history assignments that also mentioned pyramids, to more focus in the next history unit, even as the class moved into focusing on the Age of Revolution and other topics with little relation to the pyramids. But Felipe also returned to the pyramids on his own. He took up his own routes of study. As we spoke in our first interview, he shared facts and ideas about them and offered details about their uses in different civilizations. I asked where this inquiry might lead; he wasn't sure. It was just a pure inquiry that moved from game to independent study to history class and elsewhere. The movement of educations from place to place is both nonlinear and nonhierarchical. Though Felipe's interest in pyramids spurred school and unstructured learning, such endeavors do not prop up school as the legitimate or superior site of education. There was ultimately no place or purpose for Felipe's study beyond interest. Eventually, he told me that while he still played Fortnite, his interest in pyramids had trailed off.

Ximena was desperate for formal art classes at WISH. The school hadn't had an art teacher for years. Yet, she found and made art in school and outside of school. In school, she took small inspiration from looking at computer models of volcanoes in science class and then used these for art projects on her own. She used critiques of a manifest destiny painting depicting westward expansion to think through her own artwork. This idea from school sparked an art project at home. She worked on it for months. Conversations with family at home reshaped the project. The project was the project. It never moved to school and was not meant to be used in some other way. Even still, ideas from the project then appeared when she raised her hand in an ELA class to talk about how found things can have different uses, going on and on about reinvention and appropriating for different purposes.

This is a simple, beautiful idea: Education is something relentless and moving. Across subjects, times, places, groups, tasks, ideas, it is all connected, a shifting knotted mess of joy and struggle. Education is always there, carried inside people and things, flowing among so much, moving and making possible something new. Policymakers and researchers might try to carve it up, divide it and contain it, but education resists. The everyday life of educational practice opens new ways of living, beyond school, against labels, and in search of freer ways of being.

This way of exploring education—as something moving, in the making, and decentralized—evokes rhizomes, the image of thought of nonhierarchical, nonlinear knowledge filled with entries and pathways making up multiplicities (Deleuze & Guattari, 1987). The educational practices participants and I explored reflect a rhizomatics of education. Even the heuristic we made for charting educational practice (see Figure 5.1) looked like the tangled roots of a rhizome, with practices curving through mazes of place, entangling with different knowledges, bursting forth in participatory moments of expression, or fizzling out as new avenues of thought or new types of learning arose. Thinking through the many educational practices of which participants spoke or which they enacted, I found myself stuck within this image, not staring down at a tangled knot of education work, but still bound up in these movements. At times, there was a spark, something to map and make sense of it all. A pyramid stirs learning that can be discussed, observed, and explored in conversation in multiple places at different times. Though a complex assemblage of practices, connections were possible. Pyramids linked Felipe's different forms of study. Or language education occurred through Netflix and ESL class.

Pedagogies and places shifted, and a curriculum was not established, but linkages were discernible. Other times, though, educational practices seemed less like borderless flows and more like the movement of electrons, jumping unpredictably. Educational practices teleported like the magical novel *Exit West* (Hamid, 2017), where closet doors in Greece open onto a courtyard in London. Where Hamid's novel finds people on the move jumping from place to place, education itself travels, moves with bodies and moves them. Ideas, practices, connections burst to life and transport through the making and doing of education.

Matias had moved on from practicing English with me. He initially asked me if we could try it out together. He appreciated learning in class or practicing elsewhere, but often asked specifically to chat with me as a form of practice. For weeks, though, we had spoken only Spanglish. Most of our conversations turned practical. He was thinking about leaving school and searching for a job, some way to make it on his own. Walking together one spring day, we spoke of responsibility and his relationship with family. The exuberance that characterized many of our walks through a neighborhood or to a basketball court was replaced with weighted steps. In the middle of the walk, he suddenly broke out in a plurilingual rap that had nothing to do with our conversation. He asked about the meaning of words and folded them into his freestyle. He tested out phrases. The walk turned into a mixed practice of language and music-making. The walk became an educational event. When I asked where all that came from, he barely missed a beat, smiling as a form of reply and jumping right back into trying out different lyrics.

There were also educational practices that both fit into a messy trajectory and escaped from it. Miguel's interest in photography emerged, he said, from spending time with his uncle on a documentary shoot in the Dominican Republic. Studying with a friend, learning in after-school programs, and practicing on his own, he developed the craft. Learning photography was nonlinear, but it followed the paths of Miguel's interests. Developing his craft at strange times during the school day, he unlearned one thing or added a new idea, say switching to black-and-white photography. Through conversation and analysis, Miguel and I might have further mapped where these interests came from and how they evolved. Using his photographs, we could have created a narrative of this ongoing educational journey through photography. It was also possible (and maybe even preferable) to let movement take hold, welcoming the wonderous ramblings of education across everyday life.

These practices moved across time and space, offering the possibility that education can be something productively chaotic, borderless, and without definite form or direction. To trace Miguel's learning trajectory with photography would be like creating a curriculum of ooze. It always drips from the hands that try to contain it. The point here is that pieces of knowledge, academic interests, skills, and intellectual passions emerge in different places and translate, journey, and jump from place to place, idea to idea, sticking and spilling. Rather than a progression from school to less formal spaces to independent learning, all acting to solidify institutional ideas about education, education moves anarchically. It starts anywhere; say, Matias walking with a friend up Amsterdam Avenue. Then it pops up in school, as he sneaks up to the gym to learn a new move. The crossover he learned at school pops up as he plays back on the first court. But then, he is back in ESL class, pantomiming a foul shot. He rehearses it in front of the building after school. Basketball mixes with music as he sings along with Pablo while taking invisible jump shots. Then Pablo is suddenly focused on the violin in music class. After messing around in the back of the room all week, he focuses in on specific rhythms, listening to them, attempting to replicate and remake them. And then he is with Felipe at the back of ESL class, doing a worksheet together and humming something similar to what he played in music class. And Felipe is humming a song in the hallway when he bumps into a teacher who reminds him that he loved Felipe's poem from the previous schoolyear. And, as the phrasing goes, and . . . and . . . and. . . .

CONCLUSION

These educations serve no (school)master beyond desire. When I asked what they wanted to get out of certain pursuits, participants shrugged their shoulders or responded with uncertainty. These were not answers of indifference but of living with/in educational practices. They were not about moving toward graduation or the mastery of a specific skill. Of course, Luna wanted to improve her skills with makeup. Ximena undertook art with dedicated passion. The frenzy of educational life that I am offering here does not negate the possibility of sustained study, of specific outcomes. Rather, it gestures toward other possibilities for education. Toward living lives where education is not about "catching up" or "overcoming" but of freely practicing what one wants and who someone wants to become. The most common refrain from participants was just to be in it, to do it, to see where it leads. To be in acts of studying alone or with others.

Such provocations also do not suggest that "anything is possible!" in or through education. Racism, xenophobia, transphobia, and classist forms of exclusion heavily influenced participants' educational practices. What moving educational practices do suggest is that, beyond any institutional intervention or category, youth engage in fulfilling, joyous, useful, immersive, and escapist possibilities throughout everyday life. These practices seep like heavy fog through everything they did, sticking like grains of sand, disturbing the skin and sometimes impossible to shake off. They are always there, on the move. Education is possible as a place, a borderless land of desire and creativity. But that does not mean that educational institutions welcome or recognize educational life on these terms.

CHAPTER 6

Undocumented Educations

> When I came to this country, I started from zero. I learned about new things. . . . I adapted to the school system. And I was doing better. But when you come to the United States as an immigrant, your life changes. It's all change. You feel like you learn in your maternal country. But then you think that you are wasting time. That the thing you learn is, like, that you don't need it. You come and it's like you don't know nothing and you have to catch up.
>
> —Miguel

There is a short movie about immigration and education that I used to play in my teacher education classes (Levien et al., 2009). The movie opens with a child named Moises and his parents eating breakfast. At 5 a.m., he is already studying at the kitchen table. Moises and his father get ready and head to school, where his father works as a janitor. During the school day, Moises is ready for a big standardized test that will be administered later that afternoon. He knows the math, but he struggles with English-language word problems. As the class goes through the motions of final test prep, his teacher struggles to understand or support him. She asks the principal for support and the opportunity to translate some of the problems into Spanish. The principal suggests that she focus on kids with a likelihood of passing. At lunch, Moises chats with another child who suggests that the principal wants "kids that don't speak English" to skip the test. Moises considers joining this classmate in ducking out of school and skipping the test. The film then flashes back to Moises and his mother crossing the border. As Moises recalls this moment, he decides to stay and take the test. He returns to his classroom, struggling through the test. The word problems still do not make much sense. His teacher still cannot help. A classmate continues taunting him. But Moises pushes on. Moises looks up from his test in frustration and sees his father washing the classroom window and encouraging Moises. The final shot is of Moises, seen from the father's perspective, blurred by soapy water, taking the test.

In choosing this short film for my class, I wanted students to consider two things. First, I center the obvious concerns about subtractive schooling. There are some policy issues that emerge when the teacher is not allowed to offer the test in Spanish. Critiques about how the principal treats students like statistics become visible. These moments in the film depict issues teachers might encounter and offer preservice teachers examples to explore how linguistic and cultural affirmation can unlock already-present knowledge. From this first consideration, the movie provides a generative discussion for teachers to think through how to build culturally responsive classrooms and make linguistically affirmative pedagogies part of their curriculum and teaching. It is a clear, if oversimplified, activity that illuminates experiences of and pedagogical support with immigrant-origin students.

Second, I asked students to think with the movie's final image. Students asked questions about why the movie stopped here. How come the point of view shot from the father's perspective, watching Moises behind the film of soap falling across the window, ends the film? Why not close with Moises succeeding on the test? Conversations veered toward what happens next. The final shot is full of ambiguity, and people speculate on Moises's future. It is a matter of how it is read, but there is something else here. One's future is framed through sitting in school and sticking with the test. Moises's future stands as open and uncertain, but there is much outside (literally, in the case of his father) that does nothing more than look in. I have watched this movie dozens of times and I am always left wondering about both what knowledge and futures are opened at this moment and what knowledge and futures are foreclosed. The movie depicts some aspects of the vibrancy of Moises's life, but his father's knowledge and ways of being are left as background support. His father looks from behind a barrier toward Moises's possible schooling success (and by extension, success in the new land of the United States).

I think this movie offers a clear example of a strange contradiction in some forms of culturally and linguistically affirmative schooling. Knowledge is already present, yes, but it is a school concern. Inclusion and success in school are simply matters of translation. Something like mathematical knowledge is already there, waiting to be proven, written down, legible to the teacher, the school, and the state test. Of course, individual teachers nurture linguistically and culturally affirmative classrooms. Rather, there are overarching demands in how schooling has been made and used in the United States that create tensions and constraints for teachers. Consequently, educational practices fall outside of legitimated institutions and sites, or appear in marginalized, liminal ways—what I term "undocumented educations." Through resisting, conflicting with, or simply not fitting into the grammar of school, they do not fully "count" as education. In places like newcomer schools, such educations may become legitimated only insofar as they converge with the logics and aims of schooling.

These tensions frame this chapter. Where the previous chapter explored worlds of education bubbling to life with liberatory potential, appearing in different places and moving, this chapter looks at how educational life becomes formalized and legible within school and how these educations open new opportunities. The chapter also explores what happens to other types of education, those that participants regularly practiced beyond the boundaries of inclusion or success in schools. I show how the desire and joy of everyday educational practices find their way into schools but exist in the shadow of the twin binaries. Before turning to the final chapter, I conclude with some provocations of what happens to educational practices that are not made legible within formal educational spaces.

A REFLECTION ON AUTHORING AND DOCUMENTING

Before turning to the heart of this chapter, I would like to offer some caveats concerning the chapter's title and contents. The chapter title, "Undocumented Educations," came up as participants and I discussed how some of their educational practices in everyday life were possible in school but they were always marginalized and precarious. This way of talking about educational practices closely mirrored how some of those participating in the project spoke of their or a family member's documentation status. But I have long held discomfort with the term. In this book, I do not share who disclosed their (or family members') documentation status or how many did so. Even as all of the youth participating in this project encountered and expressed feelings of precarity, regardless of documentation status, the aims of thin description helped push these ethnographic moments beyond the scope of this book.

And yet, the way everyday educational practices mirrored these moments kept popping up. I thus cautiously returned to the idea of undocumented educations. Crucially, the link between immigration status and the legibility of educational practices remains loose. The point of referring to educational practices as "undocumented" is not to seek their documentation and, thus, inclusion in formal education. Much like immigration status, undocumented educations arise from the racist, capitalist production of borders rather than individual pedagogies.

Finally, I want to note the ways in which I left much undocumented myself. There were plenty of moments in this work when my position as a white U.S. citizen or limitations as a researcher created silence or liminality. Where participants identified certain educational practices as central to their lives, from appropriateness or unease, I occasionally pushed these practices aside. I never wanted to be the arbiter of legitimacy, but ultimately, the project left many provocative educational practices underexplored. This limited scope was, in some ways, intentional. Methodologically, I worked throughout this project to explore tensions between making educational practices visible in institutional spaces such as school and how that opens them up to forms of governance (Corson, 2022a). Working with participants, I pursued ways to keep their educational practices from both marginalization and domination.

LEGITIMATE EDUCATION IS SOMETHING TO ACCESS

Teachers at WISH rarely veered toward Freire's (2018) banking concept, the idea that students are passive beings waiting for teachers to deposit knowledge and skills into their brains. Despite humanizing pedagogies, there was still an understanding that some forms of education were to be privileged and preferred, like those found in school, and that these legitimized forms of education could be attained. Legitimated educations render certain types of education as legible and privileged, part of a codification and commodification of education within institutions. These educations served the dominant society, were accessed in institutions like school, and were obtained. I heard over and over, "once I get my education," or "in the Dominican Republic, I got my education [at this school]." Of course, participants did not accept this order of things. Leo bemoaned the structuring of legitimated educations as some kind of scarcity model. "Why is school so competitive?" he asked. "I should get these things [opportunities, learning experiences, etc.] because I'm human."

Accessing education was often something quite literal. During Regents testing, Matias found me near the school entrance. He explained that he was trying to enter the school to take his test but he had arrived late. Matias said that the security guards would only allow him into the school if I signed him in. After walking with him through the metal detectors, I asked what he would have done if he did not find me. In a banal tone, he said that he probably would have just skipped the test. A few weeks earlier, I had encountered a similar incident when I bumped into Pablo on the subway in the middle of the day. When I asked what he was doing, he said he arrived late and that his teacher barred him from taking a practice test. Having spent time outside of school with Matias and Pablo, it was clear that whether playing video games or wandering the city, those times would have been full of educational work, but they were supposed to be in school, "getting" their education.

The notion of physically accessing legitimated forms of education moves beyond school. Participants commonly encountered issues accessing educational activities. Mateo talked about his love of science, mixing these expressions with frustration that he could not find or afford a place to explore his interest. He eventually found an after-school program but missed the deadline to sign up. Sofia similarly described not knowing how or where to go to learn about acting. The two of us spent some time searching for classes and scholarships, but she said she was also scared and did not have the money or time to apply. These barriers popped up everywhere. Education that thrived across everyday life became subordinate to education as a divided, finite, and stratified commodity. Other forms of education were not cast out but were pushed aside.

Mateo spent much of the year working almost full-time at McDonald's and struggling in classes like science and social studies. His job was difficult. He frequently tried to quit. Despite bosses and exploitative pay, the job was also full of generative educational practices that Mateo valued and used. These educations always fell to the side when school came into the picture. When one of his teachers stopped me in the hall and asked if I knew what was going on with Mateo, I hinted that he appeared tired and that I knew he has an after-school job. The teacher nodded and told me that he "needs to get his shit together. There is no reason why he can't be successful in here." The teacher had not ignored Mateo's situation. In fact, this teacher often listened and expressed understanding. Rather, a fundamental tension ran through the discourse of success, centering it in school. Sometime later, the teacher reprimanded Mateo when he seemed unfocused, saying, "What are you going to do if you don't get an education here? Out there, it's a whole different story." Mateo did not disagree. He saw the job as a matter of survival, something that opened access to legitimated education. He mentioned multiple times that the job created an opportunity to apply for a McDonald's-run scholarship and tuition assistance program for employees. Even other places of education bolster the legitimacy of schooling. Labor and learning at McDonald's may be worth it, according to these ads, because they can help further schooling education. This is not just a hidden curriculum of who is taught to do which kinds of education (though it does reinforce Anyon's [1980] framing) but is also a reassertion of what counts as desirable, "real" education.

Such conceptions reshape education, molding it to fit limited purposes, privileging specific ways of knowing and being. Even in the affirmative space of WISH, education served the broader structures that had produced marginalization in the first place. That is, legitimated education can alter trajectories, but it is part of an exploitative structure. The impulse of universal education is not to assume already-present educational lives or to see how education might challenge the social order but to see how to include and improve outcomes for more and more people. This cordoned-off approach governs and codifies knowledge rather than creating open-ended explorations. That does not mean that other educations vanish but that they are pushed underground, made fugitive, people practicing such forms of education "never graduate, they just ain't ready" (Harney & Moten, 2013, p. 67). Schools keep working, taming education and including new people. In a place like WISH, constructed on the foundations of student identities, these identities must pass through the school's filter.

At the same time, the borders of legitimation and legibility do not always safeguard a bounded form of education. Every day educational contestations spilled through WISH. Hallways, lunchtime, teachers challenging dominant frameworks—these liminal times and spaces refused to simply move along. Milling about in front of the school or hanging out in the gym on the top floor, participants equally prepared for a test or took up other educational practices that moved elsewhere. One day, Erin tossed aside her worksheets, asking Pablo, Matias, and others what they wanted to discuss, what was new. English continued as study, but it became something else. She asked about music and listened as some kids sang favorite songs. Pablo asked, "Ms., what about you?" and students opened a barrage of questions. Inevitably, in moments like this, the bell would ring. The borders snapped back to life. Matias and Pablo lingered to freestyle together between 8th and 9th period, but the principal called down the hallway "Let's hurry it up, there's learning to be done."

When these moments stand in contrast to legitimated forms of education, school becomes a place for serious learning—the kind of education that changes lives. I observed plenty of playful, wondrous moments between those participating in this project and teachers at WISH. Yet interactions were conditioned on access to and proper participation in the overarching project of schooling. Engaging in legitimated education was something easily taken away. When certain participants set off a stink bomb in the stairwell, they were suspended for five days. They lost their chance to continue the serious process of "getting an education." Though some of their jokes were admittedly disruptive to others in the school, "being taken seriously means missing out on the chance to be frivolous, promiscuous, and irrelevant" (Halberstam, 2011, p. 6). Unserious education burst through in moments, but it remained disruptive and precarious.

THE SUPPLEMENT OF OUT-OF-SCHOOL TIME

Legitimation organizes education. Some things become marginalized. Some are made undesirable. Scholars of nonformal education (Halpern, 2002; Heath, 1983, 2012; Nocon & Cole, 2006) critique the ways in which school takes over other kinds of education. Nocon and Cole describe the transformation of an after-school program, where "the goal of preparing children to participate fully in economic life and democratic society was to be achieved by standardizing and homogenizing the behavior of the poor and immigrant through controls" (2006, p. 116). Demands for academic outcomes, the development of specific school-based skills, or even time spent performing school activities like homework encroached on nonformal time and space. An opportunity to see what else is possible and what counts in educational research is lost behind the curtain of formalized structures.

School's supremacy moves beyond what happens in nonformal education spaces. It influences their construction and purpose. In March, I joined Luna and about 50 other WISH students for a field trip to the 9/11 Memorial and the World Trade Center. Luna and her friends seemed extra playful, basking in the early spring weather. Previous weeks had not included any kind of formal connection to this trip.

With the majority of the 10th grade wandering the observation deck atop the World Trade Center, I had no complaints, but my teacher brain had become accustomed to the need for New York City teachers to "prove" the educational value of a field trip, linking it to learning standards. There was a governing pedagogy to the observation deck. The elevator rapidly ascended to the top floor. Mystery and anticipation stirred as we stood in a dark room listening to narration about New York City. Then, amazement and wonder as curtains rose and the city appeared before us. Beyond such pedagogy, students spent the majority of the morning sitting in groups or pointing to various parts of New York and New Jersey. Teachers joined in, but it was a morning free from instruction. Then I asked a teacher why they had selected this trip. "Honestly," they told me, "they are taking tests at [WISH] today and we needed these kids out of the building." The day included exploring the city and kids learning with each other in all kinds of ways, but the trip's ultimate, official purpose was to make sure that what was happening in school was uninterrupted, expedient.

And yet educations were still there, on the move. After lunch, waiting until we could hop the subway back to WISH, I noticed how Luna was teaching another student how to do her hair in a certain way. They chatted back and forth about the process. Other students around them began to play, singing together. Even earlier, when we walked around the 9/11 Memorial, students explored in different ways. Some looked at the pools from afar. Others placed their hands on the names on the parapets. Joy, play, exploration, and meaning-making emerged beyond the dictates of empty curricular intentions. They existed in the moments and events between youth and then funneled back into or faded behind legitimated education as we arrived back to the school building and continued the second half of the school day.

Whether the Facebook group offering the credentialing measure of a certificate of completion or the NYPD Explorers saying that their program provides the discipline and structure to succeed in school, nonformal education became subordinated to the aims and processes of legitimated education. This prominent way of approaching education reflects education as a matter of strict control. As Agamben (2013) writes, "what it [here, school] wants is not to order and to impose discipline but to manage and to control" (p. 5). If education moves beyond legitimated places or forms in different ways, it must be brought into control or rendered expendable. This may require the removal of bodies (by, for instance, a field trip) that could disrupt the demonstration of legitimated education. It could mean redirecting desires toward "real education." It could also mean the very general ordering of schooling practices like grading or labeling students as "at-risk."

Regardless, legitimated education distinguishes itself as superior, authentic, and part of the maintenance of a social order rooted in control. Deleuze proposes societies of control as an extension of Foucault's disciplinary society, "in which the institutional regulation of individual and social life proceeded in ways that were continuous and unbounded" (as cited in Crary, 2014, p. 71). Legitimated education does not stop at the school doors. Its curriculum is not bound to the school day. The logics, shapes, and general manners of this kind of education reach outward. They invade nonformal spaces and everyday life. They loom over other educational practices as school assembles in spaces beyond school. There is, of course, resistance to these controlling structures. But predetermined, knowledge-controlling forms of education permeate and burrow into educational practices in everyday life.

EDUCATION, EQUALITY, AND OPPORTUNITY

The idea of legitimating certain forms of education is that these educations can help more students succeed, opening avenues for participating in and improving society. Specifically, the discourse of education and opportunity is bound up with immigrant identities moving through WISH and other places. To quote INPS (2019):

> Since the early 1600s when the first Europeans began settling New Amsterdam, there has been a continual arrival of immigrants from all continents seeking a new life and opportunity on these shores. Today, as a society, we recognize that quality public education opens the door to vast opportunities, and we place great value on educational attainment.

In our time together, participants and I often spoke of complex relationships between opportunity and legitimated education.

Both formally and in nonformal, disruptive ways, school was one educational opportunity among many. Participants affirmed the narrative that school itself was an opportunity to study, to belong, and to open and pursue new pathways. Speaking generally on her thoughts on education, Sofia suggested that "some people left their country to find a better education for their kids. So opportunities can give more opportunities." Despite his thorough critiques of the school, Leo viewed WISH as necessary on his path to college, a place that could forge and support his future. He also pointed out how WISH was part of an educational structure that helped him pursue his goals. The Opportunity Network supported and extended the work of schooling (again, supplementing) by teaching him to create a résumé or compose a professional email.

Life in New York City was also seen as an opportunity. "When people are illegal here, and they want a better life. Someone legal, they don't appreciate the opportunity," one participant explained. They continued, saying that this opportunity was entwined with education but that it did not necessarily mean an opportunity to take advantage of school. They detailed opportunities to roam the city, to learn with strangers, and to create and play all over. Mateo saw an educational opportunity in school as well as with work and friends. Work, in particular, was where he could learn a language or make money that gave his family a better life. He also understood school as a site of opportunity to pursue higher education. There, he would be able to use his work at McDonald's to support his learning materially and intellectually. Although he saw college as a future and necessary pursuit, Mateo also spoke of it as something distant and abstract, receding to the background of everyday educational demands.

Ximena thought of education and opportunity in a broad sense. "Education is an opportunity that is given to you. It gives you the opportunity of no longer being ignorant." She clarified that such opportunity happens all over in different ways, but especially at WISH. As with Mateo, she talked about school as a place brimming with opportunity. At the same time, she did not center or privilege school. "School helps," she explained, "but there are some things—it's more your own education. There are some things that school doesn't help with." Her family gave her the opportunity to "be a responsible grown-up." In learning, Ximena saw opportunity to participate in society and challenge it. She learned how to pay bills and shop, but she also saw that learning was an opportunity to become someone else, someone fearless and strong. These kinds of opportunities can also be found inside school. Luna described her work with the school counselor as a time when she had the opportunity to explore and express her gender identity in ways that home life had not yet allowed. For Luna and Ximena, there were both convergences and tensions between opportunity within the rubric of legitimated education and the opportunities for educations to lead elsewhere.

At other times, and for other people, the opportunity to be successful or included in one educational place came into more direct conflict with the opportunities of other places. When Felipe returned to WISH after weeks away, we chatted after school one day. He told me that opportunities for play and hanging out were readily available during the school day. The things he wanted to learn, though, the educational practices that made him feel happy and fulfilled, were not to be found in school. In fact, spending time in school often prevented him from pursuing such opportunities. With many absences and struggling grades, he had quickly come to associate school not with opportunity but with failure. When he came to school, teachers yelled at him and reminded him that he needed to work harder or focus his studies. Meanwhile, outside of school, Felipe took up all kinds of educations, studying video games or forging friendships in ways that never made him feel like a failure. For Felipe and others, the everyday experience of being in school was explicated as an opportunity but felt like something else. Felipe returned to school partially out of the expectation that it was his only opportunity to "further his education" and that future opportunities hinged on the credentials school could offer.

Mateo found analogous relationships between the opportunity of school and other kinds of education. He described both as opportunities, but as opportunities in competition with one another. Time spent at work or pursuing interests like anime meant time away from the serious educational work of school. This conflict moves to the heart of legitimated education. Even if someone pursues education outside of school, say, the vocational learning of a craft or the joy of an amateur hobby, it moves through formal, legitimated processes. Moreover, legitimated education operates through scarcity and utility. There is only so much time in the day, and there is only so much learning that can be accomplished—only so many spots in college and only so many competitive jobs to find. From the perspective of legitimated education, knowledge, language, all of education is achievable, possessable. If students do not find a place like WISH, they become dispossessed from these educations. At WISH, if Matias snuck upstairs to hang out in the gym, he was simply missing out, leaving undocumented his own educational pursuits.

Within this scarcity model, equality is achieved through the undertaking of legitimated education. Of course, obtaining this opportunity may be hindered by any number of social factors. The goal of schools is simply to properly carve things up, equitably distribute opportunity, and make sure it is legible and measured. A goal is, once more, to perfect the impulses of universal education. Participants and

I were lured into making use of this conception of education. Miguel often told me, "I have to have more focus" and "There is a lot of complaints that I am not using this opportunity [of school]." In our first interview, I asked everyone what education meant to them and how they understood it. They identified it as a kind of pathway to becoming more equal in the world. Participants faced racism, poverty, and persistent forms of oppression. WISH offered an opportunity for a different kind of life, one in which students could alter their trajectories and become more equal. Leo, for instance, pointed out how his sibling had graduated WISH and started college with a full scholarship.

Yet participants did not always experience school as an opportunity to become equal. Even the affirmative environments of WISH could become oppressive. Pablo described how he could drape himself in a Dominican flag for the school's Cultural Heritage Day, but he was expected to behave in a certain way, speak a certain way, one that felt quieter, reserved, "play[ing] by the rules of school," as he put it. He often defied these expectations but bemoaned the expectations floating through the school. If he "did those things too loud" he became "a problem." Similarly, Felipe stormed out of theater rehearsal, a rehearsal for a play about how immigrant youth use opportunities. The play was intended as WISH students' interpretation, a story of pursuing refuge. Felipe did not find opportunity in the performance or participation but in leaving. These contradictions do not suggest some fixable flaw in WISH. It is also not a suggestion that school should not be a site of educational opportunity. This framing of the equality offered in legitimated education points to understandings of education, opportunity, and equality welded into the very framework of modern schools.

As with legitimated education in general, this conception sees equality as something achieved, offered to those who pass through schooling to become educated subjects under a specific rubric. The educated person, as a status described in Chapter 3, is someone who comports themselves properly, who shows that they are equal through how they act (as in the Spanish, *ser bien educado*), through what they learn, and through their ongoing participation in legitimated forms of education. The educated person is one who uses the opportunity of school to become an educated person. Pursuing this form of educatedness/equality at WISH, participants had to figure out how to do school as much as they had to cultivate knowledge and skills. At times, that meant learning when to adapt to the structures of schooling, like Miguel arriving on time or Felipe not fighting with a teaching artist in ESL class. Other times, it meant balancing when or where to subvert these ways of doing education.

Legitimated educational forms moved into everyday life, teaching inequality, instructing on who was a knower, and what was needed to work toward the opportunity of equality. My conversations with Matias often veered toward what he wanted in the world. In addition to the dreams he espoused, he returned several times to simply wanting people on the subway, people he walked by in the city, to see him as a person who knows things, as a good person, and as someone full of potential. From the perspective of legitimated education, Matias would perhaps need school and related educations to work toward becoming this kind of person. Yet such a framing only thinks like a school. It centers schooling's narrow purposes while silencing other possibilities. It moves from the institutional frameworks that have produced unequal conditions in the first place. The point here is not to suggest abandoning schools but to ask what is left in the wake of such pursuits.

From another perspective, equality is not the product of leveraging opportunities found in legitimated forms of education. Equality is not handed out to the youth able and willing to take what schools can give. It is, instead, already there, not waiting for description or marking down but simply being, expressed against uneven social conditions. This perspective was, I admit, an assumption I held at the beginning of this project. Yet the more time participants and I spent together, the more I understood that educational practices challenging dominant frameworks of education were part of everyday life. Moreover, I came to see the ways in which these educational practices acted as ongoing experiments in equality. Yes, participants and their families pushed for opportunities through legitimated forms of education and a general changing of the conditions of their everyday lives. But, as Leo said, "You have to play the game if you want to win, but I don't want to play. The game's not fair."

Just after Matias reiterated his fear about being seen as uneducated on the subway, he showed me a new music video he had made. From my fieldnotes:

> He stands in the dimly lit street, lyrics pouring out, unabashed, intricate, in Spanish. He doesn't look around, just stares ahead, slightly grinning. All the things I've overheard teachers say, concerns they've shared about his schooling. His own feelings about how people see him. He defies them. There he is, fierce, engaging in intellectual activity in public.

Recorded and documented for the camera. In the video, he is emancipated from what any teacher or other person could teach him.

The lives of those who participated in this project are not interchangeable with others marked on the margins, but these ideas echo Hartman's (2019) writing in *Wayward Lives, Beautiful Experiments*, which builds on Audre Lorde. Participants' educational practices "*were never meant to survive*, and yet . . . are still here" (p. 37; emphasis in original). Even where they have not succeeded through the opportunities school aims to provide, and even when the world seems to say that they are not yet equal, they resist. Through their educational practices in everyday life, ones that move against the logics of legitimated education, they show how they are always already equal. A question remains, however, of what happens to these practices when they are not meant to survive, when they are not incorporated into, and even refuse, inclusion in these spaces.

SUBJUGATED VS. UNDOCUMENTED EDUCATION

School, particularly as it racializes immigrant-origin youth, all too often dictates the terms of learning and marginalizes all that it deems undesirable. Foucault (1980) presents this as "subjugated knowledge,"

> A whole set of knowledges that have been disqualified as inadequate to their task or insufficiently elaborated: naïve knowledges, located low down on the hierarchy, beneath the required level of cognition or scientificity . . . these unqualified, even directly disqualified knowledges . . . and which involve what I would call popular knowledge, but is on the contrary a particular, local, regional knowledge. (p. 82)

Elsewhere, Foucault (1978) continues that legitimated knowledge cast out other knowledges. "It would be driven out, denied, and reduced to silence. Not only did it not exist, it had no right to exist and would be made to disappear upon its least manifestation" (p. 4). Specific, hegemonic knowledges, or education in general, stand in direct contrast to other kinds of educational practices, especially those that go beyond or challenge the logics of schooling.

Such practices are, of course, common in schools. Schools racialize (or continue existing racialization) and dictate education for immigrant-origin students in ways that subordinate their educational experiences (Conchas, 2016). Unlike the dominant encounters of oppressive, marginalizing education (e.g., Valenzuela, 1999), participants in this project all attended a school that welcomed and encouraged students' transnational identities and translanguaging practices. Foucault's framing of subjugated knowledge provides a useful juxtaposition and reveals, to an extent, the same effect of something else. In the face of bureaucratic and institutional demands, everyday educational practices were often rendered "undocumented."

CULTURALLY RELEVANT TEACHING TO DEMANDS OF SCHOOLING

The culturally relevant teaching that aimed to build on students' "funds of knowledge" most often responded to their positions as immigrants. Text selections, details in history class, and even math word problems used immigrant narratives as ways of connecting to students' identities and knowledges. Even as these topics emerged, as teachers affirmed students, they reshaped and fit them into the logics of schooling, taught to the desirable newcomer subject. For instance, several participants read a Sandra Cisneros poem about immigration for an ESL class. After reading the poem and discussing some vocabulary, students were asked to identify the main idea of the poem and how it related to their own journeys. Their experience was filtered through an objective posted on the board and a written assessment. Mastery of schooling knowledge became central. In another class, students read a text on the "immigrant story." As soon as they finished the text, the focus turned to a series of tips for reading techniques. I later asked Matias, who was in both of these classes, what he thought. He told me that he did not really connect with the story, saying, "I didn't really get anything [out] of it at all. That stuff, it's not for me."

At WISH, cultural relevance was often treated as something stable, unproblematized, and rarely political. The figure of the newcomer and the story of the immigrant could be essentialized and broadly incorporated into any school subject. Student knowledge and identity proved useful insofar as it could serve the hierarchical demands of school's legitimated education. Every fall, WISH holds a Cultural Heritage Day. Pablo arrived wearing a Dominican flag. Sofia painted the flag's colors on her cheeks. Students moved through the halls singing bachata. In a strange contrast, the formal curriculum did not change. Between 7th and 8th period, Pablo explained how he wore the flag to inspire a "Dominican way of knowing things." He talked about how important it was to learn how to play dominoes and how he studied little facts about Dominican life in general while playing. Just as Pablo found his rhythm, describing what he meant by this, his explanation was cut off so that he could start class. Beyond students' outfits and interactions with one another, and a whole school event later in the day, it seemed like just any other day.

Leo pushed to change the curriculum. He asked that U.S. and global history classes investigate the Trujillo dictatorship. The teacher loved this idea and, Leo told me, tried to think of ways to find space for Leo to take up such an investigation. The teacher did not say "no." In fact, it seemed to be a welcome intellectual pursuit. But it would have to fit into the scope and sequence and serve the demands of schooling. He would have to prove his knowledge on the school's grid of intelligibility. If someone studies and critically engages a topic but no teacher is around with a rubric to grade it, did they really learn anything?

This structuring of education was not an issue of teaching or administration. Teachers often promoted what Bajaj and Bartlett (2017) call the "multidirectional aspiration" of immigrant-origin youth. Where Bajaj and Bartlett center transnational curricula focusing on youth's higher-education aspirations exceeding that of the United States, WISH teachers supported and were "preparing students for transnational possibilities" of many kinds (p. 32). Erin often encouraged Pablo and Matias with their music. Sometimes she folded it into a lesson, asking them to prepare something about a specific text. There were many times, though, when she simply opened space for them to work and play, to explore their musical aspirations.

But then, inevitably, a test would approach. An administrator would walk by the door. These precious moments would vanish. Ximena would doodle in the margins of her notebook and then wander back to note-taking, fearful of missing something. Where everyday educational practices allow for these moments to simply be without any further demand, legitimated education requires stability, linearity. For schools, aspirational moments like these needed to either assimilate to the logics of schooling or they became precarious, uncertain. They lingered but could, depending on the demands of the school day, be pushed out.

CONCLUSION

Scholars theorize issues of legality, legibility, and citizenship, answering a call to generate "nuanced theories about undocumented life" (Gonzales, as cited in Aguilar, 2019, p. 153). These concepts are "both material and ideological," acting through racial and linguistic discourse and practice (Negrón-Gonzales, 2013, p. 1286). Theorizing "undocumented-ness" asks for formulations of "the numerous daily practices undertaken by undocumented young people which require them to bridge the schism between belonging in a place they do not have a legal right to" (Negrón-Gonzales, 2013, p. 1286). Emerging from such theorization, I suggest that many everyday education practices that wind, wander, and create new possibilities enter schools or other educational institutions and become undocumented. Like Negrón-Gonzales suggests, they force youth to navigate a kind of schism, one between the subjugation of educational practices and their assimilation to legitimated education.

Primarily, undocumented educations took shape around authorization, excess, and conflict. When experiences, interests and identities so closely linked to the lives of WISH's students did not relate to or serve the interests of school's measurable, hierarchical, legitimated education they became, in a way, illegalized in the school. Joyous events of learning were seen as kinds of "undesirable funds of knowledge." There were often forms of knowledge expressed in classrooms that were seen as undeserving of legitimation. Where participants described these practices as rooted in their interests and identities, they became inconveniences or innocuous passing moments in school. A teacher sat silently, waiting as Ximena extolled the joys of her artwork. Then they continued the lesson. Formal curriculum moved beyond essentialized ways of including immigrant stories and experiences, but undocumented educations pushed the limits of what could count, when, and how within school.

Certainly, educations that become undocumented could leave school behind. They are not the same as documentation status more broadly, where youth or family members face perpetual, all-encompassing risks of detention and deportation. They did, however, particularly when contrasted with legitimated forms of education, generate feelings of frustration, of instability, of uneducatedness, a kind of idea that their educational lives could be destroyed or discarded without consequence. Furthermore, as pointed out in the first chapter, school carries increasing importance, pushing immigrant youth to see the centrality and necessity of legitimated forms of education.

Undocumented educations appeared in more general ways, sometimes stumbled on by chance. Late in the year, a teacher approached me about Felipe. He said that I absolutely needed to ask him about his poetry. By this point, we had worked and studied together in many settings. Although Felipe had mentioned an interest in music, he never mentioned anything about poetry. When I next saw him, Felipe explained that he had been given a writing assignment and wrote a poem; but he had not had similar opportunities since then. I asked what he thought about writing poetry. He responded that he enjoyed it, but there was no real reason to continue unless it was assigned. Whether as a passion or a skill, his relationship to poetry had been left to linger, a reverie for Felipe and the teacher. As Leo put it, speaking about his desire to see more Dominican history, "nobody disagreed or said no." In fact, these educational pursuits were encouraged. It was just that, in Leo's words, "time just runs out, like they don't have the time or the people to do it. So they just move on." Where legibility and borders reign, the open flows of moving educational practices conform to school or exist with a perpetual possibility of being left aside. Perceived needs to push immigrant youth toward institutionally defined images of success and inclusion in a system of dominant knowledge does not necessarily suppress other ways of knowing and being, but it does leave them lingering, waiting for moments when there might be time or when they might be applicable to the lesson at hand.

As I just described, undocumented educations are educations that exceed or refuse the prefigured aims and logics of schooling. They are not "model," "desirable," or "deserving" forms of education that can be incorporated into legitimated education, even in additive schools. In fact, these educational practices often challenge the curricular borders school has made. Against legitimated education, open everyday practices did not become undocumented. As education moves beyond legitimated forms, there is no border to mark what counts, no evaluation to formalize and guide the curriculum. Beyond the horizon of success and inclusion, even askew from justice or self-discovery, education becomes and does something else. An exploration of this something else sits at the core of the following chapter.

CHAPTER 7

New Possibilities and Conceptions of Education

> He preferred irreverent students much more than docile ones. His gamble was on those who were capable of recreating thought, life, and the social order.
>
> —Walter Kohan, *The Inventive Schoolmaster*

In the last weeks of fieldwork, Matias and I walked through Manhattan on a sweltering August afternoon. We reminisced about our time together. He talked of his new job at McDonald's and speculated on the future. What might life look like in a year? Where might he be? I asked a few questions about school. He had passed some Regents and failed others. Matias planned to return to WISH in the fall, finish his remaining requirements, graduate, and enroll in a nearby community college to play basketball. A coach had recently emailed him to gauge his interest. As we walked, we spoke about our summers. For the first time in months, he seemed content. When we reached the corner where I told him we would part ways, we both lingered, held by nostalgia. Sensing a need for a few more minutes, I asked if he wanted me to walk with him to the basketball court where he planned to play pickup. We agreed to say goodbye once we reached the court.

> We walk a few blocks to the court. As we arrive, he sees some kids he knows. It's time to say goodbye. I extend my hand, but he quickly slaps it away, comes in for a hug. He looks over his shoulder and waves as he walks onto the court. I see him say a few words to someone he knows. He lines up where they're shooting for teams. He waits his turn and I watch him take a shot, curious if the hype he's put around his game stands up to how he looks while playing. His form is good but the shot clangs off the rim. He gets back in line with everyone else. Some more kids arrive. It's a diverse group of teenagers arriving from all over the city. Like countless

other basketball courts, they've formed their own rules, ways of making teams, figuring out how to play together. I lose myself in these thoughts, wondering about learning relationships and self-governance. When I refocus I can't find Matias in the crowd of kids talking and waiting to join a team. I start to walk away and take one more look to the court, but I can't find him in the crowd.

As I near the end of this book, I find myself thinking with Mangual Figueroa's (2014) writing about exiting research. She poses questions about researchers' responsibilities to the people and communities with whom they work. A central responsibility I tried to hold with my participants may sound strange and contradictory. I aimed to refuse borders, the violent lines that create exclusion, that seek to name and dictate the terms of education that produce risk and marginalization. And yet, I wanted to enact specific boundaries, affirming youth's autonomy and placing strict limits on the scope of this project as a way to resist the coloniality of research. I constantly encountered and welcomed ethnographic refusals—where participants or I actively excluded educational practices or decided not to include them in the project. I see refusal and the making of a project with specific limits as part of my responsibility here. Our relationships, and their educational lives, were not bound by this project.

This day with Matias highlights a tension born of these different kinds of bordering. Matias and I explored the city, learning and conversing. We crossed neighborhoods and topics and worked through pasts and futures. He embraced me. We connected. And then he moved off on his own. His educational life continued, outside of school and beyond the borders of research. This project was never about improving schools, finding best practices, or even narrating the educational lives of immigrant youth. It is, rather, about engaging the ways that schools have made sense of immigrant-origin youth and asking what possibilities or new understandings of the role of education emerge through encounters beyond institutional, sense-making boundaries.

Living in a tension among borders, this chapter thus turns to honor a responsibility of both refusal and an ungoverned kind of legibility. It studies with possibilities born of embracing connection and community, with participants' educational practices neither fading into a crowd nor folding into the dominant discourses of education. I have spent much time provoking an idea that something else is out there; new possibilities and conceptions of education emerge through everyday educational encounters. In this chapter, I explore one possibility of what this something else can look like, a potential curriculum beyond the horizon of the twin binaries. How can such educational practices challenge dominant understandings while keeping education uncodified, anti-foundational, and on the move? Education, this chapter proposes, might act as a wild daydream, something ungovernable, emergent, and desirous. This understanding of education centers Halberstam's (2011) question, "Do we really want to shore up the ragged boundaries of our shared interests and intellectual commitments, or might we rather take this opportunity to rethink the project of learning and thinking altogether?" (p. 7). Exploring these inquiries, education's messy, playful, and open potential ultimately drives the chapter.

WILDNESS AND EDUCATION

What kinds of educational worlds become possible when educational practices do not seek legibility and refuse to wither or stagnate? One possibility is to see them as *wild*. Wildness is "a mode of mess making in a world obsessed with order" (Halberstam & Nyong'o, 2018, p. 456). Wildness "abandons the security of coherence" (p. 454). In short, wildness is that which both falls outside of the entrenched, rigid social ordering of things and resists categorization within these structures (see also, Halberstam, 2020).

Halberstam is cautious with using the term *wildness*. It is not an idea to uncritically venerate. He reminds that one conception of wildness emerges from colonial imaginings and ties directly to desires of governing. In that sense, wildness is everything that falls outside the colonial order—it is savage, in need of taming. All that is wild must be expelled or violently included. This kind of wildness is destructive (of knowledge, of bodies, of land) and sterilizing. Alternatively, but still within the grid of coloniality, wildness conjures the romantic image of wanderlust. It is the philosopher or writer roaming "unexplored" landscapes on a path of self-discovery. These entwined ideas of wildness are perfect images of modernity and whiteness. In education, colonial wildness presents knowledge as something to domesticate and control. It is where ideas are made for classifying and utilizing. Learning is about understanding and adapting. Different ways of speaking, different forms of thinking, and different practices of intelligence all share a common, hegemonic reference point. Other knowledges, different ideas may be included, but they must be tamped down and adjusted to fit into the order of things.

In school, that means organizing and disciplining bodies, ideas, anything that is part of "the wild." This kind of school becomes a place to file or organize. It is a place to harness all that can adapt to its preexisting logics. Mechanisms form to uncover who and what is "at risk" of not achieving legitimated education. From there, schools create pathways of inclusion, "best answers" to bring those outside or on the margins into the warmth of order. This colonial relationship between education and wildness is visible, for instance, in the genocide and epistemicide of American Indian residential boarding schools. These schools took on a "civilizing" project, teaching against what they considered wild and undesirable. Conversely, colonial wildness frees a select few to autodidactically explore (say, the Peter Thiel scholarship, which gives youth $100,000 "to build new things rather than sitting in a classroom"). Their perceived intellect and entrepreneurial spirit allow a privileged curiosity to wander the shores of thought, exploring and conquering unknown territories of education. Despite seeming autonomy, this education, rather than disrupt, in fact affirms the order of things. Beyond these examples, residues of colonial wildness stick to classrooms through the demands of the twin binaries, with success and inclusion flowing along institutional paths of order. Additive schooling and social justice educators are here forced to wrestle with the demands of a white, bordered, capitalist system where all must be documented and ordered.

As a final caution, Halberstam (2020) considers wildness through queer anarchies. I recognize the situated, archival work that built this conception of wildness but suggest that the everyday educational practices that participants expressed offer a different view of the wild, one that brims with risk but excavates the wild potential of education. They brought forth understandings of education that left behind the tidy frameworks of school or the explanation of education as a status. Wildness was always resistant, partial, and obscured. It was full of uncertainty as it moved and reshaped. Respecting the potential of wildness meant holding these educational practices without a thought of fitting them anywhere. "Wildness is not the lack of inscription; it is inscription that seeks not to read or be read, but to leave a mark as evidence of absence, loss, and death.... [W]ildness can give us access to the unknown and the disorderly, and we will enter there at our own risk" (Halberstam, 2020, p. 50). Living in the uncertainty of unanswering "What does this act of learning do for Mateo" or "For what purpose is Sofia studying this thing?" was part of wildness's potential. To see that educational practices might not seek legibility, might not seek ends—certainly not ends meant for researchers—showed that other educational practices already exist, flourish, and make possible both different ways of being in the world and different moves toward the future. To be sure, wildness is not synonymous with undocumented educations. Some undocumented educations seek legitimation. Also, sometimes learning a skill is simply learning a skill. But wildness is always around, a possibility of a kind of passionate undertaking that moves beyond the confines of success or inclusion.

Wildness is not just the educational practices taking place on the physical "outside" of schools. It emerges "instead as an epistemology, a terrain of alternative formulations that resist the orderly impulses of modernity" (Halberstam, 2020, p. x). It may have a spatial component, but wildness moves beyond the very logics governing educational orders. As seen throughout this book, pedagogical relationships in all kinds of places show the widespread use of education as a way of organizing and ordering thought and being. Objectives, assessments, and disciplining forms of learning (the many implicit and explicit lessons on what it means to be a good, productive citizen), all show an education that is bound to order. And, as with undocumented educations, these are educations concerned with legitimacy.

Wildness pulls away from enclosure to wander amid messy questions. Halberstam asks if wildness can "instruct us in new ways of listening, different forms of knowing, and alternative logics of embodiment, aesthetic expression, desire, history, and beauty?" (2020, p. 52). What if other kinds of education leave behind the hierarchies, pedagogies and curriculum, and the very structuring of schools? Would that challenge schooling? What, educationally, might happen instead? What if education arrives at something completely unanticipated? Uncertain? Inconclusive? What if teachers and students do not know what to do with a thing? What if such things move against the very roots of schools, of dominant histories, of borders, making demands and contestations but not striving toward specific outcomes. Perhaps, then, researchers and educators might listen to those educations all over that crane toward other worlds, bursting against the confining structures of the way things all too often are.

Wildness shares much with other theories explored in this book. Whether the intellectual forces of everyday life found in the "undercommons" (Harney & Moten, 2013) or the vibrant lives of those marked on the margins (Hartman, 2019), wildness is concerned with contesting how structures are made and maintained. Wildness deals with that which slips from and rebels against these structures. These slippages are not absences or documentation but the opening of new intellectual adventures (Rancière, 1991) that pound at the boundaries of thought, of learning, of intelligence. Rather than breaking down barriers and widening pathways, wildness challenges the very foundations of education. These provocations say that Mateo's engagement with a video game is serious intellectual work and that it need not be incorporated into existing curricular structures, instead thinking with something like Mateo's love of video games is a form of study that carries potential to rethink education's role in disrupting the social order.

POTENTIAL OF EVERYDAY EDUCATIONAL PRACTICES

Ximena made art using available objects to say what she felt could not be said in school, could not be shared elsewhere. The work did not fit into any of her formal schooling endeavors. It was not meant for a college application or a future major. "I just do my own thing," she said. "It's just what comes to mind. I don't paint—I don't do—unless a person really inspires me, or like that person said something and it got stuck in my chest and I just want to paint it all out." Maybe her art will move inside, hang in a studio or be workshopped in some class. It should! I loved the pieces she shared. But her study of art, the practice of making it, and even the works themselves, were beautiful expressions of untamed creativity. Ximena took disorganized lessons from books, from events in her life, from nobody and nothing in particular. She looked at a Monet painting in a book. She heard someone talk about found art as an approach. Ideas and inspiration poured in from all over. And then, playing with bottles and other objects, Ximena made unfinished work. The connection to Monet was not clear. The point was not in the outcome, in its success. The purpose was in the doing.

For me, the pull of order remained. I encouraged Ximena to pursue art school. From an educational perspective, I wanted to learn, to understand, to make sense of the works. But their wild potential as both works and modes of study welcomed a different kind of educative force. They stirred and expressed something for Ximena, just as they did for me as someone encountering them. Her art changed things, for her, for me as someone who encountered it. Our relationship shifted a bit after exploring her artwork. Changes were hard to name and resisted sense-making. It was subtle but jarring, like walking out of a really good movie in the middle of the day, wandering the city in a state of bewilderment.

New Possibilities and Conceptions of Education

Wild educations formed anti-instructional pedagogical relationships. In school, the hallway, walking to the subway, Pablo and Matias rapped together. They built off one another, listened, and resisted a how-to approach. But their performances taught one another. I spoke to Matias about their methods:

Matias: I practice. I like my estilo/style. But [Pablo], he give me consejos/advice. I came to value it a little better because he's got experience.
Jordan: Que tipo/What kind of advice?
Matias: Like the lyrics, what I have to do to mejorar/improve. Like, the theme.
Jordan: So, like refine? Where do you learn this?
Matias: Well, together but I got my own words, my own lyrics. But I listen to a lot of English rapping, Spanish rapping. For me, the English rapping has better lyrics . . . Lil Baby, Drake, Meek Mill. . . . My favorite is Lil Baby because he talk about his life, what he's been through. But all that. That's my passion.

As they listened to different artists, they learned together. It led to a lot of stuck moments that often remained unresolved, sensations of uncertainty in learning. And yet they kept playing, messing around, making disorderly music. Some days they huddled at the back of a classroom and repeated the same bars over and over, trying to work something out. Other times, they communicated their friendship through lyrics, walking the halls and laughing as they essayed new lyrics, bouncing together with unbound language. Where school had tried to order and incorporate anything they had, here were these small moments of unrestrained intellectual practice. Pedagogies built off rapping, found ways to bring it into classroom activities, to work toward mastery. Pablo and Matias had little interest in this, not waiting for school to authorize their education, practicing on their own terms, and taking or abandoning their own routes. In such moments, listening to them was to understand that educational life moved elsewhere, that school had not missed something; it was simply not possible in schools, at least not in the way schools dominantly function in the United States. These were moments of learning and figuring out that did not ask to be trained, categorized, and ordered.

Luna, again, with her makeup kit, playing around during class. Teachers sometimes affirmed, sometimes ignored her using it, or asked her to put it away. She did not want to be disciplined or miss the opportunity to (learn to) use it, but she did not ask for permission, never sought input from teachers. Matias was boisterous and unabashed on the subway. Felipe, doodling on a paper, as he said, thinking his own thoughts in the back of a classroom. Unauthorized learning, unbounded routes of study, figuring out how to live against hierarchical pedagogical structures. These were flashes of wildness as an educational practice. They did not seek inclusion but flourished outside of the bordered makings of legitimated educations that pursued measurable forms of success that strove only toward completion, accreditation, and achievement.

Wildness is not opposed to craftwork or training. Art and rap demanded deep commitment to study and practice. Routine, strategy, negotiation, and much else can all partake in wild educational practice. But the purpose—the way of taking up education work, ways of being in education—these all shift. Wildness is opposed to mastery. It refuses the linearity that shapes so much of schooling. The normative reference point of both what topics are taught and learned as well as determined starting points and outcomes of learning are left behind. Wildness does not begin from assignments, from expectations, or from ambition, but, rather, from desire. Within joy. And struggle. It might begin in the middle, as one is already immersed in a text, struck by it, caught by how it pushes, and one pushes with it, toward different worlds, different ways of being in the world. Movement is unpredictable as it flows with imagination and creativity. Progress is immeasurable, uncontainable in standardized evaluation.

Miguel's photography developed over the course of the year. The technical knowledge or use of rules was not necessarily something wild. He learned about framing. Black-and-white photography caught his interest. Persistence in taking and learning photography, he suggested, helped him improve. Wildness emerged when he started questioning the rules of "good" photography. He left behind the instructions of his after-school teacher, stopped asking if things looked right. Chaotic street scenes, full of action, became a dominant focus of his work. Eventually, he stopped asking for approval, no longer wanted to know if a photograph was "good."

At the same time, order and structure defined much of Miguel's identity, spurring his interest in becoming a cop or joining the army. Police are a force bent on destroying wildness and maintaining order, but these career interests did not preclude Miguel from wild educational practices. "Let *wildness* stand here," Halberstam (2020) writes, "for the faltering efforts of incorporation, as a name for all that quietly and in insignificant acts picks away at the fabric of hegemony" (p. 49). These practices were not Miguel rebelling (at least not yet) but building his craft against the script of order.

Wildness may resist order (the order of domination), but it should not be confused with rudeness. Amid speaking of resisting WISH's curriculum, Leo interrupted us, reminding that, "for us Spanish speakers, manners goes inside of education. Educación." In its anticolonial stance, and even in its disorderly ways, wild education may welcome comportment. It is just that behavior is about emergent relationships and collective care rather than prefigured ways of learning how one is supposed to be in the world. Wildness refuses the cultivated, educated figure. It moves against the authorized, governing form of citizenship and moves toward different relations. It was visible when Pablo, despite sharing misogynistic lyrics with me only minutes earlier, joined our first focus group, wrapped his arm around Luna, kissed her on the head, and asked "¿Como estás?" Wild comportment was most obvious in Matias's values of caring for everyone around him. He never hesitated to give me a huge hug. Every time he entered a room, I observed him check in with the teacher to see if they were okay. He so often spoke of wanting to provide and care for his younger brother. I initially balked at some of Matias's affectionate behaviors. As our relationship progressed, however, I realized that his understanding of education in this way showed respect not governed by the logics of the school's code of conduct or my unease. It was learning to be in a relationship of mutual, unrestrained care.

Wildness is thus both individual and collective. It reflects an individual move of learning to become ungovernable. It is part of the ongoing navigation for immigrant-origin students to escape grids of intelligibility in favor of freedom. Yet wildness works through a mutualist form of educational care, respect (including respect for the unknown), the weird, the misunderstood. It is a personal intellectual adventure. And wild educational practices are built collectively. Engaging in wild educations can thus mean becoming ungovernable while still owing a responsibility to think and learn toward other educational possibilities.

Sometimes, wild educations occurred in orderly places and used others' knowledge. When WISH partnered with a prominent New York City theater company to adapt and perform a story that students read in ESL class, I watched the teaching artist grow increasingly frustrated with the ways that participants played with the text. At first, the performance looked like complete chaos. Pablo, Matias, and Felipe kept messing with the blocking the teacher tried to set up. As rehearsals continued and disorder mounted, I started to see a different performance, a choreography of learning and making lying beneath the surface of learning lines and movements. Even in these moments, students performed and expressed roles like actors. Such educational life is found in non-pedagogical acts, in a refusal to explain, and to translate. In the life of this classroom, despite the teacher's earnest efforts and desires to produce a play, wild educations came about as living, speaking forms of truth-telling that resisted governance, moved beyond categorization, and, to use Luna's phrasing, refused to be known as anything other than fabulous.

Just as wildness is not a state of being, it is also not a destination. Yet it forms and is enacted in places. It is the place where education should not happen—where it has not been stamped and approved. I do not mean only places marked by marginalization and exclusion, where policymakers and researchers so often do not see education. Wildness is that which exceeds the given curriculum, bursts out of the structure of the school day or the movement through everyday life. Like Rancière's (1991) conception of equality, it is verified when Mateo and a friend at work stop to talk feverishly about manga, engaging in an intellectual exchange against the productive demands of their job. Wildness seeps through when Miguel skips photography class to wander the city and take photos anyway. These moments show "a wildness that refuses and resists the order of things, a wildness that offers unpredictable and undead refusals to the regimes of representation that seek to swallow up difference altogether" (Halberstam, 2020, p. 178). As with equality, the external demands of outcomes, of the formal curriculum shape and influence the enactment of wild educations. They appear in moments, often within the formal spaces of education, at ordained times of learning. And yet wildness escapes.

Performances in this way are not those surprising moments when "at-risk" students shout out the correct answer or shock the teacher with a rare participatory hand in the air. Ability should be abolished and intelligence should be a beginning assumption. Instead, wild educations push a teacher, a researcher, a curriculum person, to stop the curriculum, to ask why the curriculum has been built in this way in the first place. In doing so, it may spur new questions, finding additional moments for the rebellious work that teachers already undertake, different kinds of curricular adventures in classrooms and beyond. Wildness breaks through the educational melting pot, the kaleidoscope, and any image of the liberal order of education that leaves hierarchical difference intact (Abu El-Haj, 2015; Levinson, 1996). In that last school assembly, Leo's poem was a shock. The principal had given a little preview, suggesting a poem about immigrant ingenuity and success. Leo instead expressed the racialized hierarchy on which his inclusion stood and shared uncertainty and critique of his position as someone seen as educationally successful. In the middle, his voice shook. He pushed through, repeating the poem's title in the last line, "I am mixed." The performance of the poem challenged everyone assembled in this space. It provoked a moment of unlearning and broke down the categories used to divide knowing from unknowing.

Even in this authorized moment, at the appropriate time, Leo expressed something against the order of things, challenging the purpose of an event meant to highlight and celebrate the orderly movements along the course (e.g., celebrating graduates and honors). Enacting cultural, linguistic, personal, and historical knowledges, Leo refused to become anonymous, incorporated into the structure of the school, or made into some kind of model, assimilated (even if assimilated through asset). And he refused to be silent and marginalized, to accept and wait for the proper, "civilized" way of doing legitimated education. His forceful poem did not end the assembly. The administration did not seem angry or even irked. As he finished and applause trickled through the auditorium, the principal cautiously ambled to the front for the next item on the agenda. But something changed in the air. As Leo explained later, it was not the response or the outcome. It was the telling that mattered.

Against the official knowledge of institutions, as opposed to the governance of informal spaces and everyday life, wild educations travel. Rather than liminality or political self-actualizations (some kind of *conscientização*/critical learning–action), knowledges expressed in wild educations were undetermined, unstuck. They emerged in nonformal settings and everyday life—in fourth, fifth, sixth spaces, and beyond. They were messy, often explained in stammering, uncertain terms. Exasperated gestures stood in for what could never be articulated. They were often ethereal, disappearing behind a rigid pathway of educational life shortly after appearing. They were ongoing, made and produced, expressed not through the mastery of a test or the demonstration of learning but as "a magical ecstatic performance" (Halberstam, 2014).

DAYDREAMS OF NEWCOMER STUDENTS

From our first days together, participants and I discussed their dreams. They imagined jobs and families and living situations, imagining futures of endless possibility. I asked questions about what their lives would look like in 5 years, in 10 years. Dreams included making new families, pursuing intellectual interests, and forging careers. Often, these dreams opened new futures, with school success leading to university and becoming different careers making different lives. Discussions and imaginings opened new possibilities and generated visions of possible, hopeful educational futures—futures toward which participants could work. But those are not the dreams of which I speak here. This first kind of dreaming intimately bundles the future and education. "One of my dreams in the future is to go around the world, to travel," Mateo told me. "And it's so important to know something about everything. So all of that [studying language] can be helpful." Mateo often spoke of his passion for learning languages like Japanese with a vision of perhaps one day traveling to and maybe even working in Japan.

These kinds of dreams, and this rendering of the future, can open educational trajectories and offer desirous visions toward which to work. As Bussey and Inayatullah (2008) write, "education is central to how any future is to be realized" (p. 1). But the future is not just an open site of educational possibility. It can also be a place of disjuncture, contested and subject to control. Jaffe-Walter and Lee (2011) show the need to create a "capital-rich" setting for immigrant-origin youth as a way of supporting them in pursuing college. They also reveal a schism between teachers and administrators pushing (and students working toward) college and the realities of future job markets and students' socioeconomic positions. Beyond dreams and reality, researchers, policymakers, educators, and broad discourses compose and steer educational futures. Rodríguez-Gómez (2022) describes how the future acts as a technique of governmentality "that materializes in educational institutions and works to constitute and assess youth subjects within and through their educational experiences." She explores how "educators work to steer students in specific directions by making certain dispositions and behaviors more desirable than others" (p. 5). The future is here still a site of possibility, but it is one that slots into the twin binaries. Desirable aspirations guide youth toward a future that will either be realized (graduation, college, achieving personal goals) or not.

Other kinds of dreams drift from the governing moves of future thinking. Daydreams bubbled to the surface of our conversations, things with a veil of similarity to and yet radically different from the aspirational nature of future dreams. These dreams were more chaotic and fantastical, driving toward surprising, unpredictable places. During our second interview, Pablo moved into this different kind of dreamscape. In one continuous thought, he spoke of becoming a fashion designer, a rapper, wanting to go home and take a nap, being a great father as his kid grows up, a basketball player, and half a dozen other imaginings of near and distant futures. In a sense, Pablo expressed vague aspirations within capitalist structures, within systems that value measurable success. And yet, as we spoke, something else arose. I asked him about his plans for some of these things. "I don't know, I'm just talking," he said. Thinking differently with these ideas does not negate the incomparable felicity that would arise if some of these futures were realized. Yet when I asked him about fashion a few days later, Pablo's interest had waned. These continuous imaginings of different and intersecting futures were not describing his plan to become a mogul or creating a curricular map of his life. Instead, he expressed a scrapbook of ideas. Just casual daydreams.

Daydreams veer from the goal-seeking, future-oriented dreams that dominate educational discourse. Like college or the common educational question "What do you want to be when you grow up?" such dreams, enacted within schools, might become kinds of cruel optimism (Berlant, 2011), an objective with definite ends that material conditions often thwart and desire refuses to abandon. The future and daydreams need not stand in opposition. But daydreams move elsewhere. They do not look forward but underneath, to the side, into scattered, unknown, and deterritorialized terrains. They start anywhere and move everywhere. Perhaps, a daydream touches the future or moves into present conditions. The future pulls forward, like a rope. But daydreams tug, vibrating like the flicking of rope pulled taut.

As daydreams emerged, they seemed romantic, escapist, avoidant. Matias, suddenly interested in basketball, daydreamed at the back of class about becoming a professional basketball player. Daydreaming may be associated with dissociating, checking out. In a sense, these acts were "the daydream of a subject whose only antidote to structural disenfranchisement is a literal surge of vitality and mobility" (Stewart, 2007, p. 116). Stuck in the confines of a future he was told to have and one that was increasingly closed off, Matias veered toward other imaginations. At the back of a classroom, his body pantomimed with this kind of vitality. Foul shots. Euro stepping on the way to throw out a tissue. He daydreamed in thinking, feeling, acting across the day.

Daydreams are not big. They are not imaginations igniting another world in the way in which Kelley (2022) provokes the possibility of "freedom dreaming." Daydreams here are thought and acted against the productive demands of institutionalized educations. They move against the forward motion of the future, the engines driving schools, and the impulses of linear progress. They are places, acts of radical alterity. Not empty fantasies or momentary escapes from oppressive orders. Instead, the moment of a daydream conjures a portal, "a dream of possible lives into ordinary affects so real they become paths one can actually travel on" (Stewart, 2007, p. 116). Daydreams open paths of alterity, choreographing different possibilities to think and be and learn and become otherwise.

DAYDREAMS AS EDUCATIONAL ACTS FOR NEWCOMER YOUTH

In one of his final lectures, Foucault (2008) links the courage of becoming oneself through acts of truth-telling to the possibility of people being otherwise. He uses the Greek word *parrhesia* to describe a different kind of truth-telling. Parrhesia, or rather the "parrhesiast," is "someone who says everything he has in mind: he does not hide anything, but opens his heart and mind completely to other people through his discourse" (Foucault, 2008, p. 1). This concept is more than simply sharing ideas or speaking without restraint. It is not about uncovering some stable, transcendent truth. Productive risk drives parrhesia as an anti-authoritarian form of truth-telling expressed directly against the truths told in dominant discourse. Parrhesia is not the mastery of concepts or self-realization within the confines of dominant systems. It is not a schooled truth but something else entirely, "not the professor or the teacher, the expert who speaks of *tekne* in the name of tradition" (Foucault, 2008, p. 25). In this way, parrhesia is an educational act that welcomes deeply personal truths. It excavates and expresses something against the order of things.

So when school and other educational discourses speak truths of inclusion and success, they instruct toward futures of graduation and employment in a capitalist order of modernity that requires some to be left out and fail (Varenne & McDermott, 1998). Daydreams speak of an otherwise truth. They suggest a value, a worth denied in so many ways. One day, Miguel seemed to stare at a clock the entire

45 minutes of science class. Later, I asked him what he was thinking about. He said he was thinking about the experience of making movies with his uncle and about maybe doing it again. He wondered aloud what it would be like for him to go to the Dominican Republic to film a documentary. Wandering thoughts framed him as an active part of a production. Within the daydream, he moved beyond his success in the class, away from the school's curriculum. Classroom life and his future-oriented goals of becoming a cop dissolved into a different kind of image. As he sat in class, his imaginings verified a world where he acted and mattered differently. I asked for details, and Miguel passed through sensory elements of sand and sun and production noises. He shifted to talk about himself, enmeshed with everyone else in a film crew as they might figure out how to make a movie. And then he headed for another class.

Daydreams invite a world without specific limits. It was not just for others to see participants in new ways but for them to reimagine themselves. It does not matter (at least within the confines of parrhesia) if daydreams become lived realities. Of course, it does not preclude this possibility. Daydreams are simply a verification of learning, imagining, and realizing that one can always think about other ways of living. Daydreamed acts of parrhesia also knotted with authoritative truths. Leo explained,

> A daydream of mind is like, well, it's my insecurities. How can I learn about myself in a way that I can regain that confidence? For me, it's all about learning to be yourself and be independent. That's all I want. . . . It doesn't matter if I'm a firefighter. It doesn't matter how I'm serving the community. I gotta know the way I can help the most and it's gonna be healthy for me.

Leo daydreamed about worlds where he took on many different jobs, but they all included him helping his community, supporting others, and caring for them. Daydreams did not call forth future success, actualizing specific positions. As Leo daydreamed, he saw his community as cared for and equal, without the governance of what he or his community "should" become.

To dream new possibilities is a subversive, nonnormative truth, one that is also deeply educational. Parrhesia stands against the structured truths of "the professor, the technician [the teacher]. The prophet, the sage, the person who teaches" (Foucault, 2008, p. 19). In school, I saw daydreaming cut down over and over. At one point, as daydreaming had come to the fore of our studies together, Mateo and I were caught in a daydream in between classes. In an act of interpolation, I was not sure to whom the teacher spoke when they literally cut in with, "Hey, stop daydreaming!" Ambling routes of daydreams are cut off as the present and the future as a technique of governmentality (Rodríguez-Gómez, 2022) rush forth. Despite imminent interruption and refocusing, daydreams remained possible, ready to break participants from the confines of the future. Of course, this discussion leaves behind the always-present possibilities of teachers as parrhesiasts. But the education of daydreaming showed emergent knowledge, thinking and feeling in thought. Foucault points out that this is a form of wisdom, but daydreams also show an education of telling truths through imagination. As Pablo suggested amid his ongoing list of careers and actions, "music, it's another life . . . there's all different things, but it's all just me." Not the stable, unitary subject of Pablo thinking about what job he might do or what place he might take in the world, but of performing countless possibilities of different educational lives, "glimpsed unsteadily in the light of the present like the flickering of a candle" (Stewart, 2007, p. 59). The interview ended. The teacher refocused the student. Grades and college applications and jobs and bills reminded of the kinds of futures discourse produced. Daydreams, though, moved elsewhere, lingered and hummed, waiting to be conjured once more.

DAYDREAMING IMPRACTICAL EDUCATIONS

"When you come to the U.S. as an immigrant, your life changes, it's all change," Miguel said. He felt a sense of education as a race, one in which immigrant-origin youth start far behind. Demands of this nature are a dominant presence in schools. Yet, as Miguel shared, there is an increased urgency for immigrant-origin students. They need to catch up linguistically. They need to make up ground academically. They have to move faster to graduate on time. As previously discussed, educational research centers this idea, placing "ELL" and "SLIFE" populations outside the norm, off course from competitive academic success. (e.g., Suárez-Orozco et al., 2010). Consequently, every educational moment counts, everything must be productive, useful, working toward these ends. Immigrant students must push toward the desirable futures that include them where they were once excluded. Teachers and students at WISH often teased the rules and regulations of the charter school with whom they shared space. At the same time, there was a palpable urgency, with teachers and students sensing a need to spend school time "catching up." One of the biggest impediments to exploring everyday education practices was always that students felt a crush of time, an overly packed schedule filling their days. We so often walked to the subway together as they told me about pressure moving in on them from jobs and other commitments.

There were times when it seemed that scheduling occupied every moment of participants' lives. Sofia's visible exhaustion or Leo's missing of meals showed a crushing demand on their educational lives. Again, this is a demand that many youth face, but one that takes a distinct form for immigrant-origin youth. Even still, participants made time for other things, where they were not educationally working toward future goals. Catching up may have floated through the ether, but participants spent time daydreaming as an educational practice that served little use in schools or catching up in general. In fact, daydreams were educational acts that were specifically unproductive and impractical for the aims and logics of schooling.

In *24/7*, Crary (2014) suggests that capitalism's outward thrust has intruded on every aspect of life, leaving a singular escape. Going to sleep moves away from the relentless demands of being productive and participating in capitalism's seeming omniscience. In a similar way, the permanent demands of educational productivity toward a governed future appear in the logics of schooling. There is no time to challenge or think about the prefigured purposes of education when one must race to the finish line, in competition with others. Sleep is lost to prepare for the test. Work and school demand time and focus over desirous pursuits of knowledge. Play and pleasure might pop up, might be a useful tool even, but they can exist only insofar as they serve these broader aims. Maybe a balance can exist, where hanging out with friends, learning hobbies outside of school, and working toward academic achievement all function together. However, education must be productive.

But participants messed around. They stopped racing and daydreamed impractically. The first time Sofia and I spoke about her everyday educational life, I asked her about some things she like to learn. She said that she loved a particular app on her phone about fashion. I asked about what kinds of educational activities she found most useful in her everyday life. She told me a bit more about the app. When I asked about where she sensed educational success, she returned once more to the app. I posed school-like questions of what she studied and learned from the app. She said all kinds of stuff, but mostly just that she used it as a place where she could play. Ito et al. (2009) describe this kind of educational exploration in a thorough ethnographic project on youth "hanging out, messing around, and geeking out" with new media. The authors challenge the exclusivity of in-school educations and describe both a generational and school-based divide. New media, they show, offers sites of collaborative and productive exploration. At the same time, learning, mastery, and accomplishment push their framing of messing around away from daydreaming and back toward the logics of success and inclusion. Hanging out, messing around, and geeking out are all still about being educationally productive, albeit through different pedagogies, in other places, and with different materials.

Sofia played on her phone while daydreaming and resisting the productive demands of education by playing with no direction, no end in mind. One day, sitting in a classroom just after school ended, she talked to me about various daydreams while playing on her phone. "I want to be independent. I want to have my own place. My dream is to become an actress. Even though people say it's hard, I don't think that way." We kept talking as she played on her phone. Not hanging out or geeking out but just rambling. Sofia expressed dreams of the future and waded into flickering daydreams, moving back to her phone as somewhere to play.

Where the persistent demand of education "fixes" people into specific positions and governs them to always be productive, in pursuit of what they are supposed to learn, master, who they are supposed to become, daydreams make something else possible. They defy the logics of an education that races forward toward specific ends. They are an "irrelevance to the operation of the mind or the pursuit of knowledge" (Crary, 2014, p. 12). Participants lost themselves in ways that, at first, seemed to have little relevance to a study of educational practices. As we proceeded, they teased out more and more how new routes away from "the permanent daylight of reason" (Nietzsche, as cited in Crary, 2014, p. 24) passed through dreamy knowing. They thought out loud about unreasonable risks and dreamed of unknown possibilities.

CONCLUSION

Particularly considering all that has happened in the world from the start of this project to now, I wonder about the futures that have been enacted and foreclosed. During COVID and the uprisings of 2020,

I have tried to stay in touch with everyone from the project. Some folks have shared updates and expressed plans for the future. I have lost contact with many participants. Of course, much has changed. I have changed. WISH has changed. But these years offered a glimpse of what dreams and practices have come to be. Perhaps a better line of questioning would be to ask what new educational possibilities have arisen. From a genealogy of schooling transnational youth, of histories of a newcomer school, with seeing the flows and formations of everyday educational practices and how they may be undocumented, what different understandings or ways of approaching research and education work can emerge here?

There are many educational worlds beyond the horizon of success and outside the grid of inclusion. Wild daydreams are but one possibility that unsticks the movements of educational practices from legitimated educations. When wildness and daydreams act, they refuse the definitional, productive, categorizable educations that systems demand. What these educational practices do, instead, is exist, operating not as potential for something yet to come but as interminable potential in itself. The potential of immigrant-origin youth to express and experiment in their equality and enact other kinds of futures, not ones that they occupy, but ones that they make. Wild daydreams may not be exclusive to immigrant-origin youth, but these ideas emerged from their everyday educational practices. Where wild daydreams specifically relate to immigrant-origin youth is the way in which youth are so often presented as problems for which education systems must present solutions. The history of legitimated education and immigration in the United Sates is a history of finding solutions, seeking to solve the "problem" of immigrant-origin students. Wild daydreams show, in the most beautiful and unrestrained way, a need to remain a problem, to learn and make and act against solutions. To show that other kinds of futures are possible and bubbling throughout everyday life.

Epilogue

> To begin with the otherwise as a word, as concept, is to presume that whatever we have is not all that is possible. Otherwise. It is a concept of internal difference, internal multiplicity. The otherwise is the disbelief in what is current and a movement toward, and an affirmation of, imagining other modes of social organization, other ways for us to be with each other.
>
> —Ashon Crawley

I have tried to resist the deep allure of school. It is not something to oppose. Of course, I wanted everyone involved in this project to feel included in the institutional space of school. I wished nothing but unimaginable academic success for everyone at WISH. With this book, though, I hoped to center other ways of encountering and thinking about what education is, how it is done, what it does itself, and who does it in these ways. And yet, the force of schooling pulls at me. As Matias and I texted in the early months of 2020, I was thrilled to hear about him learning new skills and generally being happy. I also could not help a sinking feeling when he told me that he had dropped out. By the spring of 2021, Matias and I were no longer communicating. He had not responded to my last emails. When I texted him on WhatsApp, it appeared as though he no longer used that phone number. His last text simply said, "talk soon." In June 2021, I received a surprise text from Erin. A picture of Matias, grinning through his mask, dressed in robes, preparing to walk for graduation.

Looking at the picture, the temptation of schooling success won me over. But there was something else. The joy I felt looking at that picture reminded of the possibility of schools. This project has moved beyond the physical and intellectual boundaries of school, stretched toward new educational worlds. I find myself, here at the end, doing the exact thing I wanted to avoid—thinking about a better model of school.

INTRODUCING A SCHOOL OF OTHERWISE

Hartman (2019) presents her work *Wayward Lives, Beautiful Experiments* as "an archive of the exorbitant, a dream book for existing *otherwise*" (p. 7, emphasis added). In taking up overlooked and fugitive lives from the archives, she fabulates the possibility of another world, one lived against oppressive norms. I conclude this book with a fantastical imagining—one influenced by Hartman's speculative play but emerging from educational discourses, as well as the ideas and experiences of those who participated in this project. Beyond and against categories of "newcomer" or "at risk," used to govern and dictate educational inclusion, this epilogue wades into thinking about the possibilities of a school in an abolitionist tradition and one of unconditional embrace. A school not for improvement or reform but one made for being and thinking of an educational otherwise.

THE SCHOOL OF OTHERWISE: A SCHOOL MADE FOR BEING AND THINKING OTHERWISE

Such a school is a wild daydream. It resists governance. Its occupants do not behave, do not shuffle from class to class in an orderly fashion. Dissensus reigns. It is a daydream oriented toward wonder rather than achieving objectives. Minds drift. Imaginations run wild. The task at hand may be lost in a swirl of questions. Trying to make the school of otherwise exist out in a world, forms of governance will creep in like spies, taking notes to make sense of it all. Organizing students and teachers like pieces on a game board. Building hierarchies. But the school tears these down and reasserts the equality of everyone there. It is a school that resists all forms of governance, even its own, moving against itself in favor of always-becoming emancipation. Aspirations for the future are welcome in the school. It is simply a standpoint of resistance and freedom. In this way, a wild daydream of a school takes shape.

The school of otherwise is a place of care, refuge, planning. A sanctuary space against the outside world and yet very much within the world it helps make. Walls and rooms and materials fill the space, but the school pops up elsewhere, too. School is a place/event/idea and an ongoing engagement within and beyond the world. There is no lottery, no placement center. It is public, part of the neighborhood and the community. Space is not applied for and approved. The school of otherwise is occupied. It is not segregated but a place of affinity. In order to occupy the school of otherwise, one must come to recognize the equality of everyone in this radical space. This school is not for everyone. And yet it is. It is for everyone who is there. That means it must constantly change, malleably adapting to its occupants. That also means exclusion: no America First, no transphobes, and no English-only. In fact, only translanguaging. Anti-hierarchy forever. The school refuses gentrification and changes that would exclude the people who have made it. This is the starting point. The rest is a playground of equality, an experiment always in the making. The school emerges from the people who show up and make the school together. The school community decides, but one is not immediately banished for not yet seeing someone else's equality. You wake up and try again.

The school has an open curriculum: alive, moving, and unstuck. Demanding uncertainty, play, subversion, rebellion, and coalition. The rigorous intellectual work is completed not by philosophers and scientists for students to understand but by the school's occupants. That is not to say the school starts from zero. Students do not need to rediscover the Pythagorean theorem. The lessons of the past and the world are there. Everyone in the school teaches each other. But the knowledge is also truly of those in the school and the lives and histories they bring. In the school of otherwise, people read the canon of themselves. And read Cervantes, too, since Leo wanted to. He may be alone or share the reading with others. But there is intellectual work to be done by those within the school. Students do not bring funds of knowledge to bolster an already-present curriculum. Their lives, intelligences, and philosophies unmake and experiment on the school—this is curriculum. Questions, interests, passions—these things invite new materials and routes. There are still languages to learn, plays to be performed, political actions to take. The curriculum is bound to a question of what everyone in the school owes to each other. It is a curriculum grounded in mutualism. Yes, it is radically democratic. Felipe can throw up his hands in frustration and leave. There is no disciplining teacher to say, "Stop that, or else. . . ." Standards of all kinds have been abolished. He will miss the performance. He may not learn the thing at hand, but he will study elsewhere. The school will check in and ask him to return. Learning is not the central task of this school. When students freely join educational projects, they do so collectively, with commitments to the projects and people they join. And yet it is not a curriculum of consensus. The questions are asked at each moment: Whose knowledge is centered here? Why? How can it be otherwise?

Teachers are there. They have a craft, belong to a union, pursue a calling, and take on dynamic pedagogical positions. Teachers still know things. They are not just ignorant schoolmasters. Sometimes, Ximena wants someone to tell her an answer or explain how to solve a problem in science. And yet, there is no curriculum guide for otherwise. Perhaps teachers become beacons or igniters of intellectual adventures. Teaching otherwise, against current conditions, opposed to existing structures, drives teaching standpoints. Teachers provoke exploration without coercion; discomfort is grounded in limitless care. They might set the conditions and develop new projects for educational encounters. Yet they must pledge, and ask students to join them in this pledge, to seek out and tear down borders, to be present with one another, to be a different person from yesterday. Teachers might also simply toss someone a book and ask if they would like to read it. Or live out their own passionate educational lives as an invitation with no required response. Pedagogical relationships shift, become horizontal and enmeshed. Some educational projects may be sequential, linear, and sustained. They can occur in daily, routinized study groups. It takes time to learn cultural histories or calculus. Inquiring together or finding avenues of resources requires a commitment. Students read and study in groups for most of a morning. A reading group lasts several weeks and disbands; or they read something else, study elsewhere. Some students linger, find themselves on the periphery of a science experiment. Schedules and materials are negotiated and changed, coordinated among impermanent committees. It is a bit chaotic and things are missed, messed up, and inefficient. But it is remade and unmapped. New routes burst forth from circumstance or dreams and evaporate into memory. Achievement has not been abolished, but it fades into the background, morphs from a status into an emergent, ethereal activity. Maybe some people never want to learn English. Some folks decide on a new subject. Or spend their time relaxing. Everyone needs time to fuck around, to be unproductive, to refuse the demands of bordering regimes, to fit in, to produce, to move forward. Desire moves the curriculum.

The day is short but the school is always open. People need a place to be, to work and conspire, to accompany and organize. Some people hang out late. Others arrive late. Perhaps projects spill from the school doors out into the neighborhood. Matias and Pablo want to study elsewhere. Miguel and Sofia want to hang out in a classroom. Education flows throughout the day, a confusing, entangled understanding of inside and outside. The outside is not only a place, but also a refusal of enclosure. It is outside of confinement, spatially and intellectually.

Regardless of space, the event of schooling is, at times, "suspended" (to use Masschelein and Simon's (2013) notion of *scholē*, which describes times of study or free time) from the demands of the rest of everyday life. A car engine becomes a thing to play with rather than fix and use. One can be in the school, playing without the utilitarian demands of the world. But this can also happen on the subway. It is the undertaking of education that becomes suspended. At times, to use Matias's notion of a space of refuge, school is a place apart, protected by and for its occupants. The suspension becomes physical, guarded, and cared for by its occupants.

At other times, school is very much within the world. There is a curriculum and pedagogy born of students collectively organizing, the dreams of those students who say, "I am undocumented and unafraid." That means that the space of school must be a space used to suspend education and protect its occupants, but one that breathes with porous boundaries, allowing collective belonging. Within the school, danger or risk do not stick to bodies. Behavior management, discipline, rules, these facets live by the common refrain "We take care of us." There is no truancy officer, no cops allowed at all. If someone does not show up, that is okay. But are they okay? What do they need? How can the school support?

Joining a long abolitionist tradition, its changes are part of a changing of the fundamental conditions of social ordering. The School of Otherwise is no utopia. It is not a panacea. It is amoeba-like, with no sharp edges, but it respects its limits. Of course, people must keep it up, but they have other commitments and pursuits. Maintaining this living space, councils might form and committees might come about. In the chaos of different ideas, identities and interests might be lost. The School of Otherwise always needs time to reflect. Folks still need to take up specific roles. Yet, there is no administration. No bosses. Maybe, though, anyone in the school can lead. Abolishing hierarchy means no leadership roles in bureaucratic forms. Leaders instead emerge in moments, take on temporary roles, and contribute in specific, contextual ways. They are very much like Rancière's Jacotot, leading from ignorance, seeing a problem and posing an adventure to pursue it. They ask and advocate and support.

Policy is a strange term to consider when imagining a school grounded in daydreams. When I talk about policy, I do not mean the funding structure or programmatic aims of the school. These aspects of the school will always be contingent on who is in the school, where they are, and what it looks like. However, the budget and funding will all be seized. Pro-immigrant, pro-public rules will form. The school will plan against the educational order in favor of liberation and equality.

CONCLUSION

Looking at the current logics and structuring of schooling in the United States and elsewhere, education is something already determined. From the perspective of the system, the only role of students and teachers is to navigate, survive, and maybe push for reform. Modern bureaucratic policies of schooling have placed educational specialists into the role of dictating student's needs. Researchers and teachers need only to tweak and improve toward a dream of universality. The School of Otherwise aims to smash this entire system, building in its wake a dreamlike school of radical possibility.

The School of Otherwise is a radical daydream, but it is not unique. Activists, students, families, researchers—all kinds of people disagree and fight every day for an educational otherwise. In particular, youth on the move routinely engage in educational practices that challenge the order of things, showing that such a school is not a dream but an ever-present reality, an almost-quotidian event in all kinds of places with all kinds of people. Whether Freedom schools, schools in Rojava, Zapatista schools, or countless other examples, people all over are engaged in thinking about the role of education in enacting other worlds. In doing so, people rethink who counts and what counts in education. They do so by asking questions and contesting conditions rather than by imposing new frameworks.

An aim of this book has been to see education otherwise. Many educators and activists have tried to answer questions, enact affirmative schooling, and welcome new ways of supporting and educating immigrant youth. Approaches such as newcomer schools have made marked impacts. This kind of work pushes more and more students toward success and inclusion in schools and society. Yet the work of legitimated education remains organizing or reorganizing the filing cabinet of society. At their most benevolent, schools push students out of the "risk" folder and into one marked "success." Along the way, researchers work toward perfecting the organization of this filing cabinet rather than listening to youth's questions about it, asking how they are already unmaking it. The evidence of possibility is all around, in schools, and on the move.

Endnotes

Introduction

1. The United States does not collect data on immigrant-origin youth; using ELL as a far from perfect stand-in.

Chapter 2

1. For more specific overviews of language programs in U.S. schools, see García et al. (2008).

2. Unlike *Brown v. Board*, the case did not challenge racial segregation, arguing that Mexican American students had been segregated from other white students.

Chapter 4

1. For further description, see Sattin-Bajaj, 2009.

2. I recently learned that they have, however, just recently joined a network of schools that focus on culturally responsive education as a trial member.

3. Heritage speakers are those who grow up learning and speaking a language informally, often at home.

Chapter 5

1. Luna never explicitly came out as gay. She most often referred to herself as a trans girl, but only referred to her sexual orientation in our first interview.

2. I am including this moment with caution, respecting Luna's feeling of both belonging and being excluded without fully delving into examples of violence and transphobic rhetoric.

3. Often speaking in Spanglish, we used various terms like education/educación, learning/aprendizaje, saberes/conocimiento/knowing/knowledge.

4. A xenophobic, nativist political party from the mid-19th century.

References

Abrego, L. J., & Negrón-Gonzales, G. (Eds.). (2020). *We are not dreamers: Undocumented scholars theorize undocumented life in the United States.* Duke University Press.

Abu El-Haj, T. (2015). *Unsettled belonging: Educating Palestinian American youth after 9/11.* University of Chicago Press.

Agamben, G. (2013). From the state of control to a praxis of destituent power. [Public lecture]. Retrieved from https://theanarchistlibrary.org/library/giorgio-agamben-from-the-state-of-control-to-a-praxis-of-destituent-power

Aguilar, C. (2019). Undocumented critical theory. *Cultural Studies ↔ Critical Methodologies, 19*(3), 152–160.

Anderson, B. (2006). Becoming and being hopeful: Towards a theory of affect. *Society and Space, 24,* 733–752.

Antin, M. (1912). *At school in the promised land.* Houghton Mifflin. Accessed from https://digital.library.upenn.edu/women/antin/land/land.html

Anyon, J. (1980). Social class and the hidden curriculum of work. *Journal of Education, 162*(Winter), 67–92.

August, D., & Kaestle, C. (1997). The infrastructure for research on English language learners and bilingual education. In D. August & K. Hakuta (Eds.), *Improving Schooling for Language Minority Children.* National Research Council.

Bajaj, M., & Bartlett, L. (2017). Critical transnational curriculum for immigrant and refugee students. *Curriculum Inquiry, 47*(1), 25–35.

Barrot, J. S. (2014). A macro perspective on key issues in English as second language (ESL) pedagogy in the postmethod era: Confronting challenges through sociocognitive-transformative approach. The Asia-Pacific Education Researcher, 23, 435–449.

Bartlett, L., & García, O. (2011). *Additive schooling in subtractive times: Bilingual education and Dominican immigrant youth in the Heights.* Vanderbilt University Press.

Basso, K. (1996). *Wisdom sits in places: Landscape and language among the Western Apache.* University of New Mexico Press.

Beck, L., & Muia, J. A. (1980). A portrait of a tragedy: Research findings on the dropout. *The High School Journal, 64*(2), 65–72. http://www.jstor.org/stable/40365229

Benjamin, W. (2020). Theses on the philosophy of history. In D. M. Kellner & S. E. Bronner (Eds.), *Critical theory and society: A reader* (pp. 255–263). Routledge.

Berlant, L. G. (2011). *Cruel optimism*. Duke University Press.

Berrol, S. (1969). Immigrants at school: New York City, 1900–1910. *Urban Education, 4*(3), 220–230.

Blum, H. (1979, March 19). Unrecorded aliens cost New York City millions. *New York Times*. Retrieved from https://www.nytimes.com/1979/03/19/archives/unrecorded-aliens-cost-new-york-city-millions-illegal-aliens-elude.html

Bondy, J. M. (2016). Negotiating domination and resistance: English language learners and Foucault's care of the self in the context of English-only education. *Race Ethnicity and Education, 19*(4), 763–783.

Bussey, M., & Inayatullah, S. (2008). Pathways: Alternative educational futures. In M. Bussey, S. Inayatullah, & I. Milojević (Eds.), *Alternative educational futures* (pp. 1–9). Brill.

Bybee, E. R., Henderson, K. I., & Hinojosa, R. V. (2014). An overview of U.S. bilingual education: Historical roots, legal battles, and recent trends. *Texas Education Review, 2*(2), 138–146.

Cabrera, N. L., & Corces-Zimmerman, C. (2019). Beyond "privilege": Whiteness as the center of racial marginalization. In P. Brug, Z. S. Ritter, & K. R. Roth (Eds.), *Marginality in the urban center* (pp. 13–29). Palgrave Macmillan.

Carrasquillo, A., Rodríguez, D., & Kaplan, L. (2014). New York State Education Department policies, mandates and initiatives on the education of English language learners. *Journal of Multilingual Education Research, 5*(5), 67–91.

Carrera, J. W. (1989). Educating undocumented children: A review of practices and policies. A Trends and Issues Paper. Retrieved from https://files.eric.ed.gov/fulltext/ED319585.pdf

Cavanaugh, M. P. (1996). History of teaching English as a second language. *The English Journal, 85*(8), 40–44.

Chang, A. (2016). Undocumented intelligence: Laying low by achieving high—An "illegal alien's" co-option of school and citizenship. *Race Ethnicity and Education, 19*(6), 1164–1176.

Christian Science Monitor. (1990, November 5). American dreamers learn the lingo: Amid a battle over bilingual education, a special school in L.A. welcomes immigrant children. Retrieved from https://www.proquest.com/docview/291192327/fulltext/90F0C98662F04FBEPQ/1?accountid=29054

Clark, K. B., & Batista, J. (1977, December 13). Hispanic and unequal. *New York Times*. Retrieved from https://www.nytimes.com/1977/12/13/archives/hispanic-and-unequal.html

Cochran, E., & Cotayo, A. (1983). Louis D. Brandeis High School. Demonstration Bilingual Enrichment College Preparatory Program. O.E.E.

Evaluation Report, 1981–1982. New York City Board of Education. Retrieved from https://files.eric.ed.gov/fulltext/ED231918.pdf

Conchas, G. (2001). Structuring failure and success: Understanding the variability in Latino school engagement. *Harvard Educational Review, 71*(3), 475–505.

Conchas, G. (2016). Introduction: Educational inequality and the construction of Latina/o Achievement Cases. In G. Conchas & B. Hinga (Eds.), *Cracks in the schoolyard: Confronting Latino educational inequality*. Teachers College Press.

Corson, J. (2022a). Legible and liberating: Methodologies against Governance. In C. Magno, J. Lew, & S. Rodriguez (Eds.), *(Re)mapping migration and education* (pp. 176–193). Brill.

Corson, J. (2022b). Truth-telling and education-making in a neighborhood in Mexico City. *Anthropology & Education Quarterly*. https://doi.org/10.1111/aeq.12433

Crary, J. (2014). *24/7: Late capitalism and the ends of sleep*. Verso Books.

Cremin, L. (1988). *American education: The metropolitan experience, 1876–1980*. Harper & Row.

Cremin, L. (1990). *Popular education and its discontents*. Harper & Row.

Dayton-Wood, A. (2008). Teaching English for "a better America." *Rhetoric Review, 27*(4), 397–414.

De Jesús, A. & Pérez, M. (2009). From community control to Consent Decree: Puerto Ricans organizing for education and language rights in 1960s and '70s New York City. *Centro Journal, 21*(2), 8–31. Retrieved from https://www.redalyc.org/articulo.oa?id=37720842002

de Jong, E. (2011). *Foundations for multilingualism in education: From principles to practice*. Brookes Pub.

Deleuze, G., & Guattari, F. (1987). *A thousand plateaus: Capitalism and schizophrenia* (B. Massumi, Trans.). University of Minnesota Press.

Depaepe, M., & Smeyers, P. (2008). Educationalization as an ongoing modernization process. *Educational Theory, 58*(4), 379.

Devine, E. T. (1920). The selection of immigrants. In P. Davis (Ed.), *Immigration and Americanization*. Retrieved from https://www.google.com/books/edition/Immigration_and_Americanization/-qcJAAAAIAAJ?hl=en&gbpv=1&dq=philip+davis+americanization&pg=PA3&printsec=frontcover

Dillon, S. (1994, October 20). Report faults bilingual education in New York. *New York Times*. Retrieved from https://www.nytimes.com/1994/10/20/nyregion/report-faults-bilingual-education-in-new-york.html

Duany, J. (2008). Quisqueya on the Hudson: The transnational identity of Dominicans in Washington Heights. CUNY Dominican Studies Institute.

Duarte, D. (2022, August 30). *How to undocument a narrative*. Public Books. Retrieved from https://www.publicbooks.org/undocumented-immigrants-narratives/

Duff, P. A., & Uchida, Y. (1997). The negotiation of teachers' sociocultural identities and practices in postsecondary EFL classrooms. *TESOL Quarterly, 31*(3), 451–486.

Escobar, A. (2016, June 6). Patterns of commoning: Commons in the pluriverse. P2P Foundation. https://blog.p2pfoundation.net/patterns-of-commoning-commons-in-the-pluriverse/2018/06/08

Escobar, A. (2020). *Pluriversal politics: The real and the possible.* Duke University Press.

Fairchild, H. P. (1926). *The melting-pot mistake.* Little, Brown, and Company.

Faulkner-Bond, M., Waring, S., Forte, E., Crenshaw, R. L., Tindle, K., & Belknap, B. (2012). Language Instruction Educational Programs (LIEPs): A review of the foundational literature. *Office of Planning, Evaluation and Policy Development, U.S. Department of Education.*

Feinberg, R. C. (2000). Newcomer schools: Salvation or segregated oblivion for immigrant students? *Theory Into Practice, 39*(4), 220–227.

Fernandez, N., & Inserra, A. (2013). Disproportionate classification of ESL students in U.S. special education. *Tesl-ej, 17*(2), n2.

Fine, M. (1985). Dropping out of high school: An inside look. CUNY Graduate Center. Retrieved from https://academicworks.cuny.edu/cgi/viewcontent.cgi?article=1753&context=gc_pubs

Fine, M. (2012). Foreword: Critical small schools—Windows on educational justice in a neoliberal blizzard. In M. Hantzopoulos & A. R. Tyner-Mullings (Eds.), *Critical small schools: Beyond privatization in New York City urban educational reform.* IAP.

Fine, M., Stoudt, B., & Futch, V. (2005). *The Internationals Network for Public Schools: A quantitative and qualitative cohort analysis of graduation and dropout rates; Teaching and learning in a transcultural academic environment.* CUNY Graduate Center.

Fine, M., Jaffe-Walter, R., Pedraza, P., Stoudt, B., & Futch, V. (2007). Swimming: On oxygen, resistance, and possibility for immigrant youth under siege. *Anthropology and Education Quarterly, 38,* 76–96.

Fine, M., & Pryiomka, K. (2020). Assessing college readiness through authentic student work: How the City University of New York and the New York Performance Standards Consortium are collaborating toward equity. *Learning Policy Institute.*

Fleegler, R. L. (2005). *A nation of immigrants: The rise of "contributionism" in the United States, 1924–1965.* [Dissertation]. Brown University.

Flores, E. T. (1984). Research on undocumented immigrants and public policy: A study of the Texas School Case. *The International Migration Review, 18*(3), 505–523. https://doi.org/10.2307/2545883

Flores, N., & García, O. (2017). A critical review of bilingual education in the United States: From basements and pride to boutiques and profit. *Annual Review of Applied Linguistics, 37,* 14–29.

Flores, N., & Rosa, J. (2015). Undoing appropriateness: Raciolinguistic ideologies and language diversity in education. *Harvard Educational Review, 85*(2), 149–171.

Foner, N. (2000). *From Ellis Island to JFK: New York's two great waves of immigration.* Yale University Press.

Foucault, M. (1972). *The archeology of knowledge and the discourse on language* (A. M. Sheridan Smith, Trans.). Pantheon Books.

Foucault, M. (1978). *Discipline and punish: The birth of the prison* (A. Sheridan, Trans.). Vintage.

Foucault, M. (1980). *Power/knowledge: Selected interviews & other writings 1972–1977* (C. Gordon, L. Marshall, J. Mepham, & K. Soper, Trans.). Vintage.

Foucault, M. (1988). Politics and reason. In L. D. Kritzman (Ed.), *Michel Foucault: Politics, philosophy, culture: Interviews and other writings, 1977–1984.* Routledge. (Original work published 1979).

Foucault, M. (2008). *The courage of truth: The governmentality of self and others II, lectures at the College de France, 1983–1984* (F. Gros, Ed.; G. Burchell, Trans.). Picador.

Fraser, N. (1990). Rethinking the public sphere: A contribution to the critique of actually existing democracy. *Social Text, 25/26,* 56–80.

Freire, P. (2018). *Pedagogy of the oppressed.* Bloomsbury Publishing.

Friedlander, M. (1991). The newcomer program: Helping immigrant students succeed in U.S. schools. Program Information Series Guide, No. 8.

Friedman, G. I. (1988). New York City Bilingual Education Technical Assistance Center, 1986–1987. OEA Evaluation Report. Retrieved from https://files.eric.ed.gov/fulltext/ED298787.pdf

Fries, C. C. (1945). *Teaching and learning English as a foreign language.* University of Michigan Press.

Fruchter, N. (2020, April 29). New York City's affinity district (part 2): The origins. [Blog post]. Metropolitan Center for Research on Equity and the Transformation of Schools. Retrieved from https://steinhardt.nyu.edu/news/new-york-citys-affinity-district-part-2-origins

Gándara, P. C., & Aldana, U. S. (2014). Who's segregated now? Latinos, language, and the future of integrated schools. *Educational Administration Quarterly, 50*(5), 735–748.

García, E. E. (1991). *Education of linguistically and culturally diverse students: Effective instructional practices* (Vol. 1). National Center for Research on Cultural Diversity and Second Language Learning.

García, O. (1999). Educating Latino high school students with little formal schooling. In C. Faltis & P. Wolfe (Eds.), *So much to say: Adolescents, bilingualism, and ESL in the secondary school* (pp. 61–82). Teachers College Press.

García, O. (2010). Bilingualism in education in the multilingual apple: The future of the past. *Journal of Multilingual Education Research, 1*(1), 13–34.

García, O., Kleifgen, J. A., & Falchi, L. (2008). From English Language Learners to Emergent Bilinguals. Equity Matters. Research Review No. 1. Campaign for Educational Equity, Teachers College, Columbia University.

García, O., Menken, K., Velasco, P., & Vogel, S. (2018). Dual language bilingual education in NYC: A potential unfulfilled? In M. B. Arias & M. Fee (Eds.), *Profiles of dual language education in the 21st century* (pp. 38–55). Multilingual Matters.

Ghiso, M. P. (2016). The laundromat as the transnational local: Young children's literacies of interdependence. *Teachers College Record, 118*(1), 1–46.

Gibson, M., & Bejínez, L. F. (2002). Dropout prevention: How migrant education supports Mexican youth. *Journal of Latinos and Education, 1*(3), 155–175.

Goodman, A. (2020). The deportation machine. In *The deportation machine*. Princeton University Press.

Graeber, D., & Wengrow, D. (2021). *The dawn of everything: A new history of humanity*. Farrar, Straus and Giroux.

Gross, N. (2017, July 13). The schools transforming immigrant education. *The Atlantic*. Retrieved from https://www.theatlantic.com/education/archive/2017/07/how-america-educates-immigrants/533484/

Gulson, K. N., & Symes, C. (2007). *Spatial theories of education: Policy and geography matters*. Routledge.

Gutiérrez, K. D. (2016a). 2011 AERA presidential address: Designing resilient ecologies: Social design experiments and a new social imagination. *Educational Researcher, 45*(3), 187–196.

Gutiérrez, K. D. (2016b). Proleptic and ecological approaches to design-based research. Presented at AERA: Washington, D.C., April 9, 2016.

Gutiérrez, K. D. (2018). Social design–based experiments: A proleptic approach to literacy. *Literacy Research: Theory, Method, and Practice, 67*(1), 86–108.

Halberstam, J. (2011). *The queer art of failure*. Duke University Press.

Halberstam, J. (2014). The wild: The aesthetics of queer anarchy. [Public lecture]. Conducted at Goldmiths Department of Art MA Lectures, 2013–2014. Retrieved from https://www.youtube.com/watch?v=ZDP4lcoZ9s4&t=1112s

Halberstam, J. (2020). *Wild things: The disorder of desire*. Duke University Press.

Halberstam, J., & Nyong'o, T. (2018). Introduction: Theory in the wild. *South Atlantic Quarterly, 117*(3), 453–464.

Halpern, R. (2002). A different kind of child development institution: The history of after-school programs for low-income children. *Teachers College Record, 104*(2), 178–211.

Hamid, M. (2017). *Exit west*. Riverhead Books.

Hantzopoulos, M. (2015). Sites of liberation or sites of despair?: The challenges and possibilities of democratic education in an urban public school in New York City. *Anthropology & Education Quarterly, 46*(4), 345–362.

Hantzopoulos, M., & Tyner-Mullings, A. R. (Eds.). (2012). *Critical small schools: Beyond privatization in New York City urban educational reform*. IAP.

Harney, S., and Moten, F. (2013). The undercommons: Fugitive planning and Black study. Research Collection Lee Kong Chian School of Business. Retrieved from https://ink.library.smu.edu.sg/lkcsb_research/5025

Hartman, S. (2008). Venus in two acts. *Small Axe: A Caribbean Journal of Criticism*, 12(2), 1–14.

Hartman, S. (2019). *Wayward lives, beautiful experiments: Intimate histories of social upheaval*. W.W. Norton.

Hatch, T., Corson, J., & van den Berg, S. G. (2021a). *The education we need for a future we can't predict*. Corwin.

Hatch, T., Corson, J., & Van Den Berg, S. G. (2021b). New schools in New York City: Incremental changes in transformative initiatives in the 21st century. *Teachers College Record*, 123(10), 91–116.

Heath, S. B. (1983). *Ways with words: Language, life and work in communities and classrooms*. Cambridge University Press.

Heath, S. B. (2012). Enthusiasts for learning: Leaders in creativity. *LEARNing Landscapes*, 5(2), 17–25.

Hendricks, G. (1973). La raza en Nueva York: Social pluralism and schools. *Teachers College Record*, 74(3), 379–394.

Hendricks, G. (1975). *The phenomenon of migrant illegality: The case of Dominicans in New York*. Society for Applied Anthropology (Amsterdam, Netherlands, March 19–22).

Hernández, R., Rivera-Batiz, F., & Agodini, R. (1995). Dominican New Yorkers: A socioeconomic profile, 1990. CUNY Graduate Center.

Howell, C. L. (2020). After "The One Best System." *Theory and Research in Education*, 18(2), 242–246.

Internationals Network for Public Schools (INPS). (2019). Education and opportunity. Retrieved from https://web.archive.org/web/20200824064710/http://internationalsnps.org/about-us/immigration-and-access-to-opportunity/

Ito, M., Baumer, S., Bittanti, M., Boyd, D., Cody, R., Stephenson, B. H., Horst, H. A., Lange, P., Mahendran, D., Martinez, K., Pascoe, C. J., Perkel, D., Robinson, L., Sims, C., & Tipp, L. (2009). *Hanging out, messing around, and geeking out: Kids living and learning with new media*. MIT press.

Jackson, Jr., J. L. (2013). *Thin description*. Harvard University Press.

Jacoby, T. (2009). *Reinventing the melting pot: The new immigrants and what it means to be American*. Basic Books.

Jaffe-Walter, R., & Lee, S. J. (2011). "To trust in my root and to take that to go forward": Supporting college access for immigrant youth in the global city. *Anthropology & Education Quarterly*, 42(3), 281–296.

Jaffe-Walter, R., & Miranda, C. P. (2020). Segregation or sanctuary? Examining the educational possibilities of counterpublics for immigrant English learners. *Leadership and Policy in Schools*, 19(1), 104–122.

Jenkins, M. (1971). Bilingual education in New York City. [Report]. New York City Board of Education.

Joffe-Walt, C., & Glass, I. (Hosts). (2022, March 11). School's out forever. [Audio podcast episode]. In *This American Life*. Retrieved from https://www.thisamericanlife.org/764/schools-out-forever

Johnson, L., & Pak, Y. (2019). Teaching for diversity: Intercultural and intergroup education in the public schools, 1920s to 1970s. *Review of Research in Education, 43*, 1–31.

Jordan, M. (1993, July 28). Newcomers remake schools. *Washington Post*. https://www.washingtonpost.com/archive/politics/1993/07/28/newcomers-remake-schools/c3045028-4d77-4caa-9736-d6b5bbfc3369/

Kelley, R. D. (2022). *Freedom dreams: The black radical imagination*. Beacon Press.

Krohn-Hansen, C. (2012). *Making New York Dominican*. University of Pennsylvania Press.

La Belle, T. J. (1981). An introduction to the nonformal education of children and youth. *Comparative Education Review, 25*(3), 313–329.

Lambert, W. E. (1975). Culture and language as factors in learning and education. In A. Wolfgang (Ed.). *Education of Immigrant Students*. Toronto: O.I.S.E.

Lambert, W. E., & Tucker R. G. (1972). *Bilingual education of children: The St. Lambert experiment*. Newbury House.

Lather, P., & Kitchens, J. (2017). Applied Benjamin: Educational thought, research and pedagogy. *Journal of Curriculum Theorizing, 32*(1).

La Unidad. (1987, February 16). Schools for the people. *La Unidad*. Retrieved from https://unityarchiveproject.org/wp-content/uploads/Schools-for-the-people.pdf

Leander, K., Phillips, N. C., & Taylor, K. H. (2010). The changing social spaces of learning: Mapping new mobilities. *Review of Research in Education, 34*, 329–394.

Lee, S. (2012). New talk about ELL students. *Kappan, 93*(8), 66–69.

Levien, R., Dilley, J., & Levien, Z. (2009, June 16). *Immersion* [Video]. YouTube. Retrieved October 14, 2022, from https://www.youtube.com/watch?v=I6Y0HAjLKYI

Levinson, B. (1996). School difference and school identity at a Mexican *secundaria*. In B. Levinson, D. E. Foley, & D. C. Holland (Eds.), *The cultural production of the educated person: Critical ethnographies of schooling and local practices* (pp. 211–238). SUNY Press.

Levinson, B., & Holland, D. (1996). Introduction. In B. Levinson, D. E. Foley, & D. C. Holland (Eds.), *The cultural production of the educated person: Critical ethnographies of schooling and local practices* (pp. 1–54). SUNY Press.

Lieberman, J. (1989). After three years: A status report on the International High School at LaGuardia Community College. [Report]. LaGuardia Community College.

References

Liberty High School. (2022). Our mission. [Website]. Retrieved from http://www.libertyhsnyc.com/

Lleras-Muney, A., & Shertzer, A. (2012). Did the Americanization movement succeed? An Evelution of the Effect of English-Only and Compulsory Schooling Laws on Immigrants' Education. Economics Department, University of Pittsburgh and Economics Department of UCLA.

Love, B. L. (2019). *We want to do more than survive: Abolitionist teaching and the pursuit of educational freedom*. Beacon Press.

Malakoff, M., & Hakuta, K. (1990). History of language minority education in the United States. In A. Padilla, H. Fairchild, & C. Valadez (Eds.), *Bilingual education: Issues and strategies* (pp. 27–43). Corwin Press.

Mangual Figueroa, A. (2012). "I have papers so I can go anywhere!": Everyday talk about citizenship in a mixed-status Mexican family. *Journal of Language, Identity, & Education, 11*(5), 291–311.

Mangual Figueroa, A. (2014). La carta de responsabilidad: The problem of departure. In D. Paris & M. T. Winn (Eds.), *Humanizing research: Decolonizing qualitative inquiry with youth and communities* (pp. 129–146). SAGE Publications Inc.

Mangual Figueroa, A. (2019, April). How immigration and education policy collide in a "post-truth" era. Paper presented at American Education Research Association Conference, Toronto, ON.

Mangual Figueroa, A., & Barrales, W. (2021). Testimonio and counterstorytelling by immigrant-origin children and youths: Insights that amplify immigrant subjectivities. *Societies, 11*(2), 38. https://doi.org/10.3390/soc11020038

Mann, H. (1868). *Life and works of Horace Mann* (Vol. 3). Walker, Fuller.

Masschelein, J., & Simons, M. (2013). *In defense of the school: A public issue* (J. McMartin, Trans.). Education, Culture & Society.

May, T. (2008). *The political thought of Jacques Rancière: Creating equality*. The Pennsylvania State University Press.

Mayorga, E. (2017). *Dominance & survivance: Urban Latino communities and education in racial neoliberal urbanism*. City University of New York.

Mayorga, E. (2021). Trabajando en ambos: Toward a race radical mode of study in urban Latinx educational research and politics. *Teachers College Record*, 01614681211063968.

McDonnell, L. M., & Hill, P. T. (1993). *Newcomers in American schools: Meeting the educational needs of immigrant youth*. RAND Corporation.

McGinity, K. (1998). The real Mary Antin: Woman on a mission in the promised land. *American Jewish History, 86*(3), 285–307.

McGrath, I. (2013). *Teaching materials and the roles of EFL/ESL teachers: Practice and theory*. A&C Black.

Menjívar, C. (2006). Liminal legality: Salvadoran and Guatemalan immigrants' lives in the United States. *American Journal of Sociology, 111*(4), 999–1037.

Miller, H. (1916). The school and the immigrant. The Survey Committee of the Cleveland Foundation. [Report]. Retrieved from https://books.google.com/books?id=7ellAQAACAAJ&newbks=1&newbks_redir=0&hl=en

Mirel, J. (2010). *Patriotic pluralism: Americanization education and European immigrants*. Harvard University Press.

Mirra, N., & Garcia, A. (2020). "I hesitate but I do have hope": Youth speculative civic literacies for troubled times. *Harvard Educational Review, 90*(2), 295–321.

Miyares, I. M. (2004). From exclusionary covenant to ethnic hyperdiversity in Jackson Heights, Queens. *Geographical Review, 94*(4), 462–483.

Moll, L., Amanti, C., Neff, D., & Gonzalez, N. (1992). Funds of knowledge for teaching: Using a qualitative approach to connect homes and classrooms. *Theory Into Practice, 31*(2), 132–141.

Montalto, N. V. (1977). *The forgotten dream: A history of the intercultural education movement, 1924–1941*. [Dissertation]. University of Minnesota.

Moran, R. F. (2010). Equal liberties and English language learners: The special case of structured immersion initiatives. *Howard Law Journal, 54*, 397.

Morison, S. (1990). A Spanish–English dual-language program in New York City. *Annals of the American Academy, 508*, 160–169.

Mujica, B. (1995). Findings of the New York City longitudinal study: Hard evidence on bilingual and ESL programs. *READ Perspectives, 2*, 7–34.

National Research Council. (2001). *Understanding dropouts: Statistics, strategies, and high-stakes testing*. National Academies Press.

NeCamp, S. (2014). *Adult literacy and American identity: The moonlight schools and Americanization programs*. SIU Press.

Negrón-Gonzales, G. (2013). Navigating "illegality": Undocumented youth & oppositional consciousness. *Children and Youth Services Review, 35*(8), 1284–1290.

Nero, S. J. (2005). Language, identities, and ESL pedagogy. *Language and Education, 19*(3), 194–211.

New York City Board of Education. (1986). Grover Cleveland High School Project CAUSA. [OEA Evaluation Report]. https://eric.ed.gov/?q=CAUSAS%2B&id=ED281975

New York City Department of Education. (2022). Graduation results. Retrieved from https://infohub.nyced.org/reports/academics/graduation-results

New York City Immigration Coalition. (2006). So many schools, so few options: How Mayor Bloomberg's small high school reforms deny full access to English language learners. [Report]. The New York Immigration Coalition & Advocates for Children of New York.

New York City Immigration Coalition. (2020). New data shows crisis among newcomer immigrants in NYC schools. [Press Release]. Retrieved from https://www.nyic.org/2020/02/new-data-shows-drop-out-crisis-among-newcomer-immigrants-in-nyc-schools/

New York State Association for Bilingual Education (NYSABE). (2022). Purpose and objectives. [Website]. https://www.nysabe.net/about-us/purpose-and-objectives/

Newman, K., & Wyly, E. K. (2006). The right to stay put, revisited: Gentrification and resistance to displacement in New York City. *Urban Studies*, 43(1), 23–57.

Ngai, M. M. (2004). *Impossible subjects: Illegal aliens and the making of modern America*. Princeton University Press.

Nieto, D. (2009). A brief history of bilingual education in the United States. *Perspectives on Urban Education*, 6(1), 61–72.

Nieto, S. (2015). *Why we teach now*. Teachers College Press.

Noboa, J. (2021). *Leaving Latinos out of history: Teaching U.S. history in Texas*. Routledge.

Nocon, H., & Cole, M. (2006). School's invasion of "after-school": Colonization, rationalization, or expansion of access? In Z. Bekerman, N. C. Burbules, & D. Silberman-Keller (Eds.), *Learning in places: The informal education reader* (pp. 99–122). Lang.

Noguera, P. A. (2003). "Welcome to New York, now go home!" Multiple forces within the urban environment and their impact upon recent Mexican immigrants in New York City. *Center for Migration Studies Special Issues*, 18(4), 78–89.

Nuñez, V. (2011). Writing the migration: Pedro Henríquez Ureña and early Dominican migrants to New York City. *MELUS*, 36(3), 111–135.

NYPD Youth Programs. (2019). Police explorers: Become a law enforcement explorer. [website]. Retrieved from https://www1.nyc.gov/site/nypd/services/law-enforcement/youth-programs/explorers.page

O'Day, J. A., Bitter, C. S., & Gomez, L. M. (2011). *Education reform in New York City: Ambitious change in the nation's most complex school system*. Harvard University Press.

Olneck, M. (1989). Americanization and the education of immigrants, 1900–1925: An analysis of symbolic action. *American Journal of Education*, 97(4), 398–423.

Pacheco, M. (2012). Learning in/through everyday resistance: A cultural-historical perspective on community resources and curriculum. *Educational Researcher*, 41(4), 121–132.

Padilla, A. M. (1990). *Bilingual education: Issues and strategies*. Sage Publications/Corwin Press.

Patel, L. (2013). *Youth held at the border: Immigration, education, and the politics of inclusion*. Teachers College Press.

Patel, L. (2015). Deservingness: Challenging coloniality in education and migration scholarship. *Association of Mexican American Educators Journal*, 9(3), 11–21.

Pavlenko, A. (2002). We have room for but one language here: Language and national identity in the U.S. at the turn of the 20th century. *Multilingualism*, 21(2), 163–196.

Perlmann, J. (1990). Historical legacies: 1840–1920. *Annals of the American Academy of Political and Social Science, 508,* 27–38.

Pessar, P. R. (2001). Dominicans: Transnational identities and local politics. In N. Foner (Ed.), *New Immigrants in New York* (pp. 251–274). Columbia University Press.

Phoenix, A. (2021). Subjectification, the politics of recognition and identities in (trans) national classrooms. In L. Heidrich, Y. Karakaşoğlu, P. Mecheril, & S. Shure (Eds.), *Regimes of Belonging–Schools–Migrations* (pp. 65–76). Springer VS.

Plyler v. Doe, 457 U.S. 202, 102 S. Ct. 2382. (1982). Retrieved from https://supreme.justia.com/cases/federal/us/457/202/

Popkewitz, T. (1998). *Struggling for the soul: The politics of schooling and the construction of the teacher.* Teachers College Press.

Portes, A., & Rumbaut, R. G. (2001). *Legacies: The story of the immigrant second generation.* University of California Press.

Purnick, J. (1984, October 21). Plan for crowded school district. *New York Times.* Retrieved from https://www.nytimes.com/1984/10/21/nyregion/plan-for-crowded-school-district.html

Ramirez, M. L. (2020). Beyond identity: Coming out as undocuqueer. In L. Abrego & G. Negrón-Gonzales (Eds.), *We are not dreamers: Undocumented scholars theorize undocumented life in the United States.* Duke University Press.

Rancière, J. (1991). *The ignorant schoolmaster: Five lessons in intellectual emancipation* (K. Ross, Trans.). Stanford University Press.

Rancière, J. (2001). Ten theses on politics. *Theory & Event, 5*(3), 1–33.

Ravitch, D. (1974). *The great school wars.* Basic Books.

Ray, B. (2013). ESL droids: Teacher training and the Americanization movement, 1919–1924. *Composition Studies, 41*(2), 15–39.

Rebell, M., & Block, A. (1983). *Educational policymaking and the courts: Empirical study of judicial activism.* University of Chicago Press.

Reese, W. J. (2005). *America's public schools: From the common school to "No Child Left Behind."* Johns Hopkins University Press.

Reyes, Luis. (2006). The Aspira Consent Decree: A thirtieth-anniversary retrospective of bilingual education in New York City. *Harvard Educational Review, 76*(3), 369–402.

Rimer, S. (1990, March 12). A school in the Bronx that is somehow making it. *New York Times.* Retrieved from https://www.nytimes.com/1990/03/12/nyregion/a-school-in-the-bronx-that-is-somehow-making-it.html

Rios, E. D. (2005). "The ladies are warriors": Latina pentecostalism and faith-based activism in New York City. In G. Espinosa, V. Elizondo, & J. Miranda (Eds.), *Latino religions and civic activism in the United States* (pp. 197–217). Oxford University Press.

Rivera-Batiz, F. (1996). The education of immigrant children in New York City. *ERIC Digest, 117.*

Rockwell, E. (2011). Popular education and the logics of schooling. *Pedigogica Historica, 47*(1–2), 33–48.

Rodríguez, N. N. (2018). From margins to center: Developing cultural citizenship education through the teaching of Asian American history. *Theory & Research in Social Education, 46*(4), 528–573.

Rodriguez, S. (2018). "Risky" subjects: Theorizing migration as risk and implications for newcomers in schools and societies. *European Education, 50*(1), 6–26.

Rodríguez-Gómez, D. (2022). Disputed futures: Rural entrepreneurship and migration in postsecondary trajectories on the Ecuador–Colombia Border. *Ethnography and Education*, 1–17.

Rodriguez, S., & Conchas, G. Q. (Eds.). (2022). *Race frames in education: Structuring inequality and opportunity in a changing society*. Teachers College Press.

Rosa, J., & Flores, N. (2017). Unsettling race and language: Toward a raciolinguistic perspective. *Language in Society, 46*(5), 621–647.

Rutherford, D. (2016). Affect theory and the empirical. *Annual Review of Anthropology, 45*, 285–300.

Santiago, I. S. (1986). Aspira v. Board of Education revisited. *American Journal of Education, 95*(1), 149–199.

Salomone, R. (2008). Transnational schooling and the new immigrants: Developing dual identities in the United States. *Intercultural Education, 19*(5), 383–393.

Sattin-Bajaj, C. (2009). Informing immigrant families about high school choice in New York City: Challenges and possibilities. National Center on School Choice, Vanderbilt University (NJ1).

Schmid, C. L. (2001). Educational achievement, language-minority students, and the new second generation. *Sociology of Education*, 71–87.

Short, D. J. (2002). Newcomer programs: An educational alternative for secondary immigrant students. *Education and Urban Society, 34*(2), 173–198.

Snider, W. (1987, April 1). New York City schools chancellor fires board and superintendent. *Education Week*. Retrieved from https://www.edweek.org/education/new-york-city-schools-chancellor-fires-board-and-superintendent/1987/04

Steinberg, L., Blinde, P. L., & Chan, K. S. (1984). Dropping out among language minority youth. *Review of Educational Research, 54*(1), 113–132. https://doi.org/10.3102/00346543054001113

Stephen, L. (2013). *We are the face of Oaxaca: Testimony and social movements*. Duke University Press.

Stewart, K. (2007). *Ordinary affects*. Duke University Press.

Stewner-Manzanares, G. (1988). The Bilingual Education Act: Twenty years later. *New Focus*, Occasional Papers in Bilingual Education, No. 6.

Stromquist, N. (2012). The educational experience of Hispanic immigrants in the United States: Integration through marginalization. *Race Ethnicity and Education, 15*(2), 195–221. https://doi.org/10.1080/13613324.2011.578125

Sturz, H. (1988, July 4). The editorial notebook; What's happening at International High? *The New York Times.* Retrieved from https://www.nytimes.com/1988/07/04/opinion/the-editorial-notebook-what-s-happening-at-international-high.html?searchResultPosition=1

Suárez-Orozco, C., & Suárez-Orozco, M. M. (2014). Structuring opportunity for immigration origin children. *Bread and Brain, Education and Poverty, 125,* 1–38.

Suárez-Orozco, C., Suárez-Orozco, M. M., & Todorova, I. (2010). *Learning a new land: Immigrant students in American society.* Harvard University Press.

Sylvan, C. (2008). Promoting student success through English learner diversity: The Internationals Approach. Educational Testing Service.

Talburt, S., & Lesko, N. (2012). A history of the present of youth studies. In N. Lesko & S. Talburt (Eds.), *Keywords in youth studies: Tracing affects, movements, knowledges* (pp. 11–23). Routledge.

Torres-Saillant, S., & Hernández, R. (1998). *The Dominican Americans.* Greenwood Publishing Group.

Torres-Saillant, S. (2014). New York Dominican Writers. *Review: Literature and Arts of the Americas, 47*(2), 147–154.

Tyack, D. (1974). *The one best system: A history of American urban education.* Harvard University Press.

Tyack, D. (1976). Ways of seeing: An essay on the history of compulsory schooling. *Harvard Educational Review, 46*(3), 355–389.

Tyack, D., & Cuban, L. (1995). *Tinkering toward utopia: A century of school reform.* Harvard University Press.

U.S. Department of Education. (2017). Newcomer toolkit. [Report]. Retrieved from http://www2.ed.gov/about/offices/list/oela/newcomers-toolkit/ncomertoolkit.pdf

Unterman, R., & Haider, Z. (2019). New York City's small schools of choice: A first look at effects on postsecondary persistence and labor market outcomes. [Policy Brief]. *MDRC.*

Valdez, C., & Gregoire, C. P. (1990). Development of a bilingual education plan. In A. Padilla (Ed.), *Bilingual education: Issues and strategies* (pp. 91–105). Corwin Press. Retrieved from https://files.eric.ed.gov/fulltext/ED329635.pdf

Valencia, R. R. (2012). Activist scholarship in action: The prevention of a Latino school closure. *Journal of Latinos and Education, 11*(2), 69–79.

Valenzuela, A. (1999). *Subtractive schooling: U.S.-Mexican youth and the politics of caring.* State University of New York Press.

Varenne, H. (2009). Educating ourselves about education—comprehensively. In H. Varenne & E. W. Gordon (Eds.), *Theoretical perspectives on comprehensive education: The way forward* (pp. 1–24). Edwin Mellen Press.

Varenne, H., & McDermott, R. (1998). *Successful failure: The school America builds*. Routledge.

Vélez, W. (2008). The educational experiences of Latinos in the United States. In H. Rodríguez, R. Sáenz, & C. Menjívar (Eds.), *Latinas/os in the United States: Changing the face of América* (pp. 129–148). Springer-Verlag.

Vizenor, G. (Ed.). (2008). *Survivance: Narratives of native presence*. University of Nebraska Press.

Walia, H. (2021). *Border and rule: Global migration, capitalism, and the rise of racist nationalism*. Haymarket Books.

Warner, M. (2005). *Publics and counterpublics*. Zone Books.

Warren, M. (2005). Communities and schools: A new view of urban education reform. *Harvard Educational Review, 75*(2), 133–173.

Willner, R., & Amlung, S. (1985). Ten years of neglect: The failure to serve language-minority students in the New York City public schools. [Report]. Educational Priorities Panel. Retrieved from https://files.eric.ed.gov/fulltext/ED263247.pdf

Wilson, E. K. (2016). Blurred lines: Public school reforms and the privatization of public education. *Washington University Journal of Law & Policy, 51*, 189.

Wulach, S., & Kemple, J. (2016). Trends in school co-location in NYC. [Blog post]. The Research Alliance for New York City schools. Retrieved from https://steinhardt.nyu.edu/research-alliance/research/spotlight-nyc-schools/trends-school-co-locations-nyc

Zentella, A. C. (2010). Spanish in New York. In Claudio Iván Remeseira (Ed.), *Hispanic New York: A Sourcebook* (pp. 321–354). Columbia University Press.

Zimmerman, A., & Disare, M. (2017, February 10). New York City's graduation rate continues climb, but a larger share of English language learners are dropping out. Retrieved from https://chalkbeat.org/posts/ny/2017/02/10/new-york-citys-graduation-rate-continues-climb-but-a-larger-share-of-english-learners-are-dropping-out/

Index

Abrego, L. J., 4, 66
Abu El-Haj, T., 4, 27, 59, 64, 66, 68, 107, 157
Accessing education, 132–135
Agamben, G., 136
Agodini, R., 46
Aguilar, C., 144
Aldana, U. S., 38, 40
Amanti, C., 5
Americanization, 49
  early history for immigrant youth, 34–37
  as historiographic gap, 37–39
Amlung, S., 61, 64, 66
Anderson, B., 15
Angel of history, 7
Antin, M., 53–54
Anyon, J., 110, 134
Aspira Consent Decree of 1974, 39–40, 43, 56
Aspira v. Board of Education of the City of New York, 43–44
Assimilation, 62
Assimilationist instructional models, 36
At School in the Promised Land (Antin), 53
August, D., 35, 40

Bajaj, M., 144
Barrales, W., 59
Barrot, J. S., 41
Bartlett, L., 15, 25, 47, 75, 76, 144
Basso, K., 102
Batista, J., 44
Baumer, S., 164
Beck, L., 57
Bejínez, L. F., 24

Belknap, B., 32
Benjamin, W., 7, 18
Berlant, L. G., 159
Berrol, S., 35
Bilingual education, 39–48
  emergence as national concern, 43–45
  forms of, 44
Bilingual Education Act of 1968, 39, 40
Bittanti, M., 164
Bitter, C. S., 73
Blinde, P. L., 57
Block, A., 43
Bloomberg, M., 72–74
Blum, H., 57
Bondy, J. M., 50
Borderless constellations of learning, 122–126
Boyd, D., 164
Bussey, M., 158
Bybee, E. R., 35, 38

Cabrera, N. L., 23
Carrasquillo, A., 40
Carrera, J. W., 63
Cavanaugh, M. P., 35
Chan, K. S., 57
Chang, A., 23, 50
Chapter 720 bilingual program, 44
Clark, K. B., 44
Cochran, E., 44
Cody, R., 164
Cole, M., 135
Colonial wildness, 149, 150
Community-based organization (CBO), 76
Community spaces, 5

193

Conchas, G., 25, 50, 143
Corces-Zimmerman, C., 23
Corson, J., 16, 73, 110, 132
Cost of public schools, 87–90
Cotayo, A., 44
Crary, J., 137, 163, 164
Creativity, of education, 7
Cremin, L., 6, 49, 57, 58, 67
Crenshaw, R. L., 32
Cuban, L., 27
Cultural life of youth, 5
Culturally relevant teaching, 143–144
The Cultural Production of the Educated Person (Levinson & Holland), 59–60
Curriculum, 118
  WISH Academy, 75–76, 78

Daydreams, of newcomers, 158–160
  as educational acts for newcomer youth, 160–162
  impractical educations, 162–164
Dayton-Wood, A., 36, 49
Deficit language, 40, 86
De Jesús, A., 56
de Jong, E., 44
Deleuze, G., 124, 137
Depaepe, M., 121
Department of Education (DOE)
  New Schools Initiative, 73
Deportation, 38–39
Developmental bilingual education, 44
Devine, E. T., 56
Dilley, J., 129
Dillon, S., 43
Disare, M., 3
Discourses of newcomer educability, 59–60
Dreamers, newcomers as, 65–67
Dropout crisis, 25
Dual-language programs, 44, 45
Duarte, D., 17
Duff, P. A., 42

Educability, newcomer, 55, 59–60
Education
  accessing, 132–135
  bilingual, 39–48
  defined, 6

  equality in, 10–11
  everyday practices, 152–157
  exploring, 4–7
  immigration and, 2–4
  nonformal, 108–112
  qualities of, 6–7
  in spatial terms, 101–115
  unconditional/uncategorizable/imaginative, 10–12
  undocumented, 129–146
  wildness and, 149–152, 154–157
Educationalization, 121
Educational spaces, 101–118
  nonformal, assembling schooling in, 118–121
ELL Dropout Crisis, 3
English as a Second Language (ESL), 41–43, 61
English language learners (ELLs), 3, 73–74, 79
Equal education, 40
Equality, in education, 10–11, 137–142
Escobar, A., 6, 33, 48, 49, 51

Fairchild, H. P., 36
Falchi, L., 175
Faulkner-Bond, M., 32
Feinberg, R. C., 46
Fernandez, N., 41
Fine, M., 46, 47, 48, 50, 57, 63, 73, 83
Fleegler, R. L., 39
Flores, E. T., 57
Flores, N., 23, 24, 45
Foner, N., 39
Formation, as education quality, 6–7
Forte, E., 32
Foucault, M., 3, 18, 32, 137, 142, 143, 160, 161, 162
Fraser, N., 87, 88
Freire, P., 42, 132
Friedlander, M., 46, 66
Friedman, G. I., 57
Fries, C. C., 41, 42
Fruchter, N., 73
Futch, V., 46, 47, 48, 50, 63

Gándara, P. C., 38, 40
Garcia, A., 12

Index

García, E. E., 60
García, O., 15, 25, 42, 43, 44, 45, 47, 56, 75, 76, 81, 175
Ghiso, M. P., 5
Gibson, M., 24
Glass, I., 7
Gomez, L. M., 73
Gonzalez, N., 5
Goodman, A., 39
Governance, 12
Graduation rates, 3
Graeber, D., 8, 9
Gregoire, C. P., 41
Gross, N., 88
Guattari, F., 124, 137
Guiding theories, 10–12
Gulson, K. N., 101, 102
Gutiérrez, K. D., 5, 49

Haider, Z., 73
Hakuta, K., 37, 40
Halberstam, J., 12, 135, 149, 150, 151, 154, 156, 157
Halpern, R., 135
Hamid, M., 125
Hantzopoulos, M., 88, 90
Harney, S., 5, 8, 11, 12, 112, 134, 151
Hart-Celler Act, 1965, 39
Hartman, S., 11, 12, 142, 151, 168
Hatch, T., 73, 110
Heath, S. B., 135
Henderson, K. I., 35, 38
Hendricks, G., 49
Hernández, R., 46
Hill, P. T., 46, 58, 65
Hinojosa, R. V., 35, 38
Historiographic gap, Americanization as, 37–39
Holland, D., 59
Horst, H. A., 164
Howell, C. L., 31

Identical education, 40
Immigrant-origin youth
   cultural life of, 5
   framing of schools for, 2–3
   history, in U.S. education system, 31–51
   history of "Americanization" for, 34–37
   and marginalization in schools, 23–25
   newcomer participants, 96–101
Immigration, and education, 2–4
Inayatullah, S., 158
Individualized educational plans (IEPs), 79
Inserra, A., 41
Instructional models, 36
International High School at LaGuardia Community College, 46–47, 62
Ito, M., 164

Jackson, J. L., Jr., 17
Jacoby, T., 62
Jaffe-Walter, R., 47, 50, 88, 158
Jenkins, M., 45
Joffe-Walt, C., 7
Johnson, L., 38
Johnson-Reed Immigration Act in 1924, 37
Jordan, M., 55

Kaestle, C., 35, 40
Kaplan, L., 40
Kelley, R. D., 160
Kemple, J., 73
Kitchens, J., 18
Kleifgen, J. A., 175

La Belle, T. J., 108
Lambert, W. E., 42, 44
Lange, P., 164
Lather, P., 18
Lau v. Nichols, 39–40
Laws, schools, 35–36
Leander, K., 102, 106
Learning, 6
   borderless constellations of, 122–126
Lee, S. J., 48, 158
Lesko, N., 56
Levien, R., 129
Levien, Z., 129
Levinson, B., 59, 157
Lieberman, J., 58, 62, 64

Liminality, 63–65
Limited English Proficiency (LEP) children, 43, 61
  educational rights of, 43
Lleras-Muney, A., 35
Love, B. L., 109

Mahendran, D., 164
Malakoff, M., 37, 40
Mangual Figueroa, A., 24, 59, 66, 78, 148
Mann, H., 21
Marginalization, in schools, 21–23
  and ethnographic present, 25–28
  immigrant-origin youth and, 23–25
Martinez, K., 164
Masschelein, J., 118, 171
Maxwell, W., 54
May, T., 11
Mayorga, E., 90
McDermott, R., 24, 160
McDonnell, L. M., 46, 58, 65
McGinity, K., 53
McGrath, I., 42
Mendez v. Westminster, 38
Menjívar, C., 63
Menken, K., 44, 45, 81
Miller, H., 59
Miranda, C. P., 88
Mirel, J., 36
Mirra, N., 12
Moll, L., 5
Montalto, N. V., 38
Moran, R. F., 41
Morison, S., 45
Moten, F., 5, 8, 11, 12, 112, 134, 151
Muia, J. A., 57
Mujica, B., 45

NeCamp, S., 35, 36
Neff, D., 5
Negrón-Gonzales, G., 4, 66, 145
Nero, S. J., 42
Newcomers
  daydreams of, 158–164
  defined, 60
  desirable, educating, 60–67
  as dreamers/overcomers, 65–67
  educability, 55, 59–60
  as educable subjects, 55
  as liminal/risky/potentials for schools, 63–65
  plural identities, 61–63
  subjects, 60–61, 62
  youth participants, 96–101
Newcomer schools, 46–48
Newman, K., 78
New Schools Initiative (Department of Education), 73
New York State Association for Bilingual Education (NYSABE), 56
Ngai, M. M., 37, 38
Nieto, D., 38
Noboa, J., 24
No Child Left Behind Act, 2002, 72
Nocon, H., 135
Noguera, P. A., 31
Nonformal education, 108–112
Nonformal education programs, 5
Nonformal spaces, assembling schooling in, 118–121
Nyong'o, T., 149
NYPD Explorers, 110–112

O'Day, J. A., 73
Olneck, M., 37
The One Best System (Tyack), 31
Opportunity, educational, 137–141
Ordinary Affects (Stewart), 105
Out-of-school time, 135–137
Outside space, 117
Overcomers, newcomers as, 65–67

Pacheco, M., 5
Padilla, A. M., 40, 45
Pak, Y., 38
Parrhesia, 160–162
Pascoe, C. J., 164
Patel, L., 3, 28, 45
Pavlenko, A., 36
Pedraza, P., 47, 50
Pérez, M., 56
Perkel, D., 164
Philanthropic funds, 74
Phillips, N. C., 102, 106
Phoenix, A., 60
Place, educational, 101–115
Plural identities, newcomers, 61–63

Pluriverse, 33
Plyler v. Doe, 24
Popkewitz, T., 55
Populational reasoning, 55
Portes, A., 68
Pryiomka, K., 83
Public schools, 54–55
  cost of, 87–90
Purnick, J., 57
Pursuit, as education quality, 7

Qualities of education, 6–7

Racism, 34
Ramirez, M. L., 12
Rancière, J., 10, 11, 28, 121, 152, 156, 171
Ravitch, D., 50
Ray, B., 35, 36
Rebell, M., 43
Reese, W. J., 35, 49
Relational ontology, 6
Resistance, 7
Reyes, L., 56
Rimer, S., 65
Rios, E. D., 49
Risky subjects, 64
Rivera-Batiz, F., 46, 58
Robinson, L., 164
Rockwell, E., 17
Rodríguez, D., 40
Rodríguez, N. N., 24
Rodriguez, S., 64
Rodríguez-Gómez, D., 158, 162
Rosa, J., 23, 24
Rumbaut, R. G., 68
Rutherford, D., 16

Salomone, R., 32
Santiago, I. S., 3, 40, 42, 43, 44, 50, 56
Sattin-Bajaj, C., 175
Schmid, C. L., 36, 38, 40
School of otherwise, 168–172
  introduction of, 168
Schools
  Americanization movement in, 34–37
  as gateway of opportunity, 3
  for immigrant-origin youth, 2–3
  laws, 35–36
  as machine, 7
  marginalization in. *See* Marginalization, in schools
  newcomer, 46–48
  public. *See* Public schools
  sports, 109–110
  unstructured time outside of, 112–115
Shertzer, A., 35
Short, D. J., 60
Simons, M., 118, 171
Sims, C., 164
Smeyers, P., 121
Snider, W., 68
Sobrevivencia, 90
Space, educational, 101–118
  nonformal, assembling schooling in, 118–121
Speculation, 11–12
Sports, schools and, 109–110
Steinberg, L., 57
Stephen, L., 17
Stephenson, B. H., 164
Stewart, K., 15, 16, 105, 159, 160, 162
Stewner-Manzanares, G., 45
Stoudt, B., 46, 47, 48, 50, 63
Stromquist, N., 23
Sturz, H., 61, 62, 63, 65, 67
Suárez-Orozco, C., 3, 48, 162
Suárez-Orozco, M. M., 3, 48, 162
Subjugated education, undocumented education *vs.*, 142–143
Subtractive Schooling (Valenzuela), 25
Sylvan, C., 48
Symes, C., 101, 102

Talburt, S., 56
Taylor, K. H., 102, 106
Tindle, K., 32
Tipp, L., 164
Todorova, I., 3, 162
Transitional bilingual education, 44
Tucker R. G., 44
Tyack, D., 8, 23, 27, 31, 32, 34, 50
Tyner-Mullings, A. R., 88

Uchida, Y., 42
Undocumented educations, 129–146
  subjugated education *vs.*, 142–143

Unstructured time outside of school, 112–115
Unterman, R., 73

Valdez, C., 41
Valencia, R. R., 80
Valenzuela, A., 25, 50, 143
Van Den Berg, S. G., 73, 110
Varenne, H., 4, 24, 160
Velasco, P., 44, 45, 81
Vélez, W., 46
Vizenor, G., 90
Vogel, S., 44, 45, 81

Walia, H., 22
Waring, S., 32
Warner, M., 88
Wayward Lives, Beautiful Experiments (Hartman), 142, 168
Wengrow, D., 8, 9
Wildness, and education, 149–152, 154–157
Willner, R., 61, 64, 66
Wilson, E. K., 88

WISH (Welcome Immigrants, Succeed Here Academy) Academy, 14–15, 54, 66–67, 71–72
  cultural relevance at, 143–144
  curricular demands on, 80–82
  curriculum, 75–76, 78, 103–108
  everybody *vs.*, 84–87
  evolutions of, 76–84
  founding of, 74–75
  history of, 72–74
  and nonformal education, 108–112
  space and place, 77–78
  structure, navigating, 103–108
  welcoming and supporting "risky" students, 78–80
Wulach, S., 73
Wyly, E. K., 78

Xenophobic exclusion, 34

Youth. *See* Immigrant-origin youth

Zimmerman, A., 3

About the Author

Jordan Corson is an assistant professor in the School of Education and an affiliated faculty member of the Holocaust and Genocide Studies program at Stockton University. His scholarship is situated in the fields of curriculum studies, anthropology and education, and migration studies. Using critical ethnographic and historical methods, his work explores the liberatory possibilities of public schools and everyday educational life. Jordan lives in Philadelphia with his partner and cats.